汉语儿童与韩语儿童韵律焦点标记习得研究

The Acquisition of Prosodic Focus Marking in Mandarin Chinese- and Seoul Korean-speaking Children

杨安琪　著

天津大学出版社
TIANJIN UNIVERSITY PRESS

图书在版编目(CIP)数据

汉语儿童与韩语儿童韵律焦点标记习得研究 = The acquisition of prosodic focus marking in Mandarin Chinese- and Seoul Korean-speaking Children : 英文 / 杨安琪著. -- 天津 : 天津大学出版社, 2023.5

ISBN 978-7-5618-7464-6

Ⅰ. ①汉… Ⅱ. ①杨… Ⅲ. ①汉语－儿童语言－语言教学－研究－英文②朝鲜语－儿童语言－语言教学－研究－英文 Ⅳ. ①H193.1②H559

中国国家版本馆CIP数据核字(2023)第075451号

HANYU ERTONG YU HANYU ERTONG YUNLÜ JIAODIAN BIAOJI XIDE YANJIU

出版发行	天津大学出版社
地　　址	天津市卫津路92号天津大学内（邮编:300072）
电　　话	发行部:022-27403647
网　　址	www.tjupress.com.cn
印　　刷	北京盛通商印快线网络科技有限公司
经　　销	全国各地新华书店
开　　本	710mm×1010mm　1/16
印　　张	15.75
字　　数	425千
版　　次	2023年5月第1版
印　　次	2023年5月第1次
定　　价	63.00元

The research reported here was part of the programme "Get the focus right: a cross-linguistic study on prosodic encoding of focus in children", founded by the Netherlands Organisation for Scientific Research (NWO) under grant number 276-89-001.

CONTENTS

CHAPTER 1

Introduction

1.1 Preliminaries

In speech communication, speakers usually make information *new* to listeners more prominent in their utterances than information known to listeners. The new information is known as the *focus* of the sentence. Speakers' appropriate marking of focus can assist listeners in processing the information efficiently, and is thus helpful to speech comprehension (Birch & Clifton, 1995; Cutler, Daham, & Van Donselaar, 1997). Focus-marking is thus an important ability for children to acquire in the context of language development. This dissertation is a cross-linguistic study on how Mandarin Chinese-speaking and Seoul Korean-speaking children develop the capacity for prosodic focus marking in their speech production.

Focus can be encoded by a range of linguistic means, such as the use of particles (e.g., only, even), syntactic cues (e.g., cleft-construction, word order), and prosody. This dissertation is only concerned with the prosodic aspect of focus. Following many others, we use "prosody" to refer to both phonetic variation in pitch, duration, and intensity, and phonological properties such as stress, pitch accent, tone, and prosodic phrasing (Jun, 2005; Ladd, 1996).

The studies presented in this dissertation were carried out as a part of the research programme "Get the Focus Right: A Cross-linguistic Study on Prosodic Encoding of Focus in Children"①, founded by the Netherlands Organisation for Scientific Research (NWO). This programme investigates the acquisition of prosodic focus marking in four

① More information about this research programme (grant number 276-89-001) can be found on the programme webpage at http://focus.wp.hum.uu.nl/.

languages: Mandarin Chinese, Seoul Korean, Central Swedish and Standard Dutch (hereafter, Mandarin, Korean, Swedish, and Dutch). The overarching goal of the programme is to develop a comprehensive theory of the acquisition of prosodic encoding of focus, from a typological perspective, and with an emphasis on language-specificity and individual differences. The programme consists of three sub-projects: a PhD project on the acquisition of prosodic focus marking in Mandarin and Korean (reported in the current dissertation), another PhD project on the same topic but investigating Swedish and Dutch (Romøren, 2016), and a longitudinal study on individual differences in the development toward adult encoding of prosodic focus (A. Chen, 2014, 2016).

1.2 Motivation

Focus is prosodically marked in many (if not all) languages, but by varying means. For example, in West Germanic languages such as English, Dutch, and German (Féry, 1993; Gussenhoven, 1984; Ladd, 1996), focus can be marked via accentuation of the focal word (i.e., accenting the word with a pitch accent), while in languages such as Japanese (Nagahara, 1994; Pierrehumbert & Beckman, 1988) or Korean (Jun, 1993), focus can be marked via prosodic phrasing (i.e., prosodic grouping of words). In addition, languages also differ greatly in prosodic systems. For example, pitch is lexically contrastive in Mandarin, but not in other languages, such as West Germanic languages or Korean. The questions that arise in the context of language development are whether and, if so, how the differences in prosodic focus marking and prosodic systems between languages affect the acquisition of the language-specific focus-marking system. More specifically, what is the path to adult-like prosodic focus marking like in different languages? Does the effort involved in acquisition differ? How does the acquisition of prosodic focus relate to other aspects of the prosodic system? This dissertation aims at finding the answers to these questions.

For a long time, studies of acquisition of prosodic focus marking have been almost exclusively concerned with children acquiring a West Germanic language, making cross-linguistic comparisons inherently limited. This dissertation approaches this issue in two languages that are typologically different from each other and from West Germanic languages: Mandarin and Korean. In so doing, the studies presented in this dissertation will not only shed light on the acquisition of prosodic focus marking in Mandarin and Korean, but also enable a comparison of acquisition in these languages to acquisition in a previously studied language, such as a West Germanic language.

Mandarin and Korean differ in both prosodic systems and prosodic focus marking. Regarding their prosodic systems, they differ in the lexical contrastiveness of pitch. Mandarin is a *tone language*, in which pitch movement is lexically contrastive at word level (Chao, 1965). In this language, lexical use of pitch coexists with sentence-level use of pitch. In contrast, Korean is described as an *intonation language*. Pitch movement in Korean is not specific to a certain syllable or word, but is aligned to larger prosodic units (Jun, 2005). As for prosodic focus marking, the two languages differ in the primary prosodic cues used in focus marking. Mandarin primarily (and very likely only) uses phonetic cues to mark prosodic focus. That is to say, prosodic properties such as duration, pitch, and intensity are only increased or reduced in a gradient fashion without causing a change in the phonological category[①] (e.g., the tonal category in Mandarin) of words in focus marking. In contrast, Korean uses both phonological means, (i.e., prosodic phrasing), and phonetic means (i.e., gradient variation in duration, pitch, and intensity within one phonological category) to mark focus, but primarily uses phonological means.

Given the above mentioned differences in prosodic systems and prosodic focus marking between Mandarin and Korean, we ask the overarching research question:

> How do the differences in prosodic systems and prosodic focus marking between Mandarin and Korean shape the developmental paths to adult-like prosodic focus marking in the two languages?

The overarching research question is operationalised in two specific research questions. One taps into the lexical use of pitch in Mandarin but the lack of it in Korean, and the other taps into the relative importance of the prosodic focus-marking cues in each language:

> Research question Ⅰ: Does the lexical use of a prosodic parameter (i.e., pitch in Mandarin) influence the acquisition of the same parameter used for focus marking?

① We use "phonological category" as a general term for discrete variation in prosody. For example, in Mandarin, it is the category of lexical tones (e.g., high level, rising, low, and falling), while in Korean, it can be the category of prosodic units (e.g., accentual phrase, intonation phrase) or any other relevant classification such as the type of prosodic boundaries (e.g., accentual phrase boundary, intonation phrase boundary) and the distinction between prosodic phrasing (i.e., grouping of words) and dephrasing (i.e., deletion of a prosodic phrasal boundary between words). In West Germanic languages, it can be the division between the presence and absence of a pitch accent (i.e., accenting vs. not accenting or de-accenting a word), or the type of pitch accent (e.g., rising vs. falling).

Research question Ⅱ: Does the relative importance of prosodic focus-marking cues in a language influence the acquisition of these cues?

The effects of these factors (i.e., the lexical use of a prosodic parameter and the relative importance of a prosodic focus-marking cue) are expected to manifest in both the rate and route of the acquisition of the prosodic focus-marking cues. For the rate of acquisition, we expect to observe evidence such as the age at which children start to use a prosodic focus-marking cue, and the age by which their use of this cue is fully adult-like (or approaches adult-like form). For the route of acquisition, we expect to observe evidence like in what order children acquire the use of the prosodic focus-marking cues in a language.

To address the above research questions, we have conducted parallel studies on the acquisition of prosodic focus marking in Mandarin-speaking and Korean-speaking children. In the rest of this chapter, we provide the background literature of the studies. We first introduce the concepts of focus and focus types, and then briefly introduce prosodic encoding of focus across languages (Section 1.3). Next, we discuss the acquisition of prosodic focus marking in previous studies (Section 1.4). What follows is a review of the most relevant studies on prosodic focus marking in adult speech in Mandarin and Korean (Section 1.5). Finally, we put forward our hypotheses about the acquisition of prosodic focus marking in children acquiring the two languages (Section 1.6). Before closing this chapter, we draw the outline of the dissertation (Section 1.7).

1.3 Focus, focus types, and prosodic encoding of focus

Focus is a term used in theories of information structure or information packaging (Chafe, 1976). Information structure/packaging concerns how information is presented rather than the information itself. It reflects the speaker's assumption of what is known (i.e., given) and what is unknown (i.e., new) to the listener (Lambrecht, 1994; Vallduví & Engdahl, 1996). The given-new distinction has been discussed in two dimensions in the literature: referential givenness-newness and relational givenness-newness (Gundel & Fretheim, 2004).

Referential givenness-newness is concerned with the information status of referents, and involves the "relation between a linguistic expression and a corresponding non-linguistic entity in the speaker/hearer's mind, the discourse (model), or some real or possible world" (Gundel & Fretheim, 2004: 2). In this sense, the information status of a referent in a discourse is determined by the listener's attention state and knowledge about the entity being referred to. This entails that the speaker packages information in his/her utterance according to what is known (or given) and what is unknown (or new) to the listener. For example, the information in (1) is properly packaged, but in (2) it is not, because the second clause in (2) introduces "a rabbit" as new information which has actually been given in the first clause and thus should have been known to the listener. Moreover, referential givenness-newness is not necessarily a property of linguistic representation (Gundel & Fretheim, 2004). For example, an item that has not appeared in the conversation can have been visually presented to the listener, and thus can be referentially given. According to Chafe (1987), a referent that is in the listener's focus of consciousness is *given*, a referent that is in the listener's long term memory but is not active is *new*, and a referent that is in the listener's peripheral consciousness is *accessible*.

(1) Look! A rabbit, and the rabbit throws a book.
(2) Look! A rabbit, and a rabbit throws a book.

Relational givenness-newness, by contrast, "involves a partition of the semantic/conceptual representation of a sentence into two complementary parts, X and Y, where X is what the sentence is about... and Y is what is predicated about X... X is given in relation to Y... Y is new in relation to X" (Gundel & Fretheim, 2004: 2). For example, in (3B), "rabbit" is relationally given while "book" is relationally new. In the literature, this partition is also known as topic-focus, topic-comment, theme-rheme, etc. (Vallduví & Engdahl, 1996).

(3) A①: Look! A rabbit, and it throws something.
What does the rabbit throw?
B: The rabbit throws a [book].

Relational newness and referential newness are logically independent as pointed out by Gundel and Fretheim (2004). A referentially new item can be relationally given (or topical). For example, in (4) "gardening" can be referentially new to the listener, but it is relationally given or topical in the sentence (A. Chen, 2015). On the other hand, a relationally new word in a sentence can be referentially given or accessible, such as "book" in (5B).

① "A" refers to "Speaker A", and "B" refers to "Speaker B" in the examples.

(4) As for gardening, it is the pastime of many villagers here. (taken from A. Chen, 2015)

(5) A: The rabbit has a book and a pen, and it throws one of them. What does the rabbit throw?
B: The rabbit throws the [book].

Focus is a term that has been used to express varied concepts which are usually related to newness (Krifka & Musan, 2012). There is no agreed-upon definition for it. Based on the two dimensions of givenness-newness, Gundel and Fretheim (2004) refer to relationally new information as "information focus", for it is the information predicted about the topic. In the current study, we analyse the information structure of sentences from the perspective of relational givenness-newness. Following many others (Gundel & Fretheim, 2004; Krifka & Musan, 2012), we refer to relationally new information as *focus*. We define relationally given information as *non-focus*, which can either precede the focal constituent (*pre-focus*) or follow it (*post-focus*). Further, there are different types of focus. On the one hand, focus can differ in the size of the focal constituent (Gussenhoven, 2004, 2007), which leads to the distinction between narrow focus on a word or words, like "book" in (3B), and broad focus over a larger constituent such as a phrase or a whole sentence, like (6B). On the other hand, a focal constituent can also be contrastive. It can be an alternative to a piece of aforementioned information such as "book" in (5B), or be a direct rejection of a piece of information introduced previously, like "book" in (7B). Whereas in both conditions the focal items are regarded as being in *contrastive focus*, the latter is also referred to as *corrective focus* (Gussenhoven, 2004). Contrastive focus is typically narrow in constituent size.

(6) A: What happens?
B: [A rabbit throws a book].

(7) A: Does the rabbit throw a pen?
B: The rabbit throws a [book].

With respect to prosodic encoding of focus, generally speaking, a word is usually produced with more prosodic prominence[①] in narrow focus and contrastive focus than when not in focus or in broad focus. Contrastive focus can have additional prosodic prominence compared to (non-contrastive) narrow focus (Gussenhoven, 2004). However, as mentioned earlier, there are considerable differences between languages in how prosodic prominence is realised in production. Some languages (e.g., Mandarin and Cantonese) exclusively vary prosodic properties, such as pitch and duration, in a gradient fashion without making phonological changes to realise prosodic prominence and to mark focus (Xu, 1999). We define this way of prosodic focus marking as *phonetic focus marking*, following A. Chen (2009, 2011a, 2012). For example, in Mandarin, words are realised with the tonal identity unchanged but with a longer duration and wider pitch span in narrow focus than in non-focus and broad focus (Shih, 1988; Xu, 1999; Y. Chen & Braun, 2006). In contrast, some other languages mark prosodic focus primarily via *phonological* means; that is, via making coarse-grained changes in pitch and duration which cause changes in the perceived phonological category (See A. Chen 2012[②] for a review). For example, in English, Dutch, and German, speakers can either accent words with certain types of pitch accents (e.g., rising vs. falling) or not accent words for focus-marking purposes (A. Chen, 2009, 2011a; Baumann, et al., 2007; Baumann, Grice & Steindamm, 2006; Gussenhoven, 2004, 2007; Hanssen, Peters & Gussenhoven, 2008); in Swedish, speakers can assign or not assign a high tone to words for such purposes (Bruce, 2007; Romøren, 2016); in Korean, speakers can group or not group words into prosodic phrases for such purposes (Jun, 1993; Jun & H. J. Lee, 1998; Y. C. Lee & Y. Xu, 2010). In addition, some of these languages can also make phonetic changes within a phonological category for focus-marking purposes. For example, in Dutch, when both focused and non-focused sentence-initial words are frequently realised with a H*L pitch accent (i.e., a falling accent with the fall beginning in the stressed syllable), focused words are produced with a longer duration and lower minimum pitch than non-focused words (A. Chen, 2009). Similar situations have been reported for German and Korean (Baumann, Grice & Steindamm, 2006; Jun & H. J. Lee, 1998).

---

① We use "prominence" as a term to describe the characteristics of prosody in production in a relative sense. A word is considered as "more prominent" when it has an increased value in a certain prosodic parameter in one condition than in another condition.

② Note that some researchers take an exclusively phonetic approach in their analysis of prosodic focus marking (Eady & Cooper, 1986; Y. Xu & C. X. Xu, 2005, on English). We refer the reader to A. Chen (2012) for a discussion on possible limitations of this approach.

1.4 Past work on the acquisition of prosodic focus marking

As mentioned earlier, studies on the acquisition of prosodic focus marking have been mainly concerned with children speaking a Germanic language like English, Dutch, or German, and more recently Swedish. Before reviewing the most relevant studies on acquisition, we will first depict how adult speakers of these languages vary prosody for focus-marking purposes, because the adult-form of prosodic focus marking is the target of acquisition.

1.4.1 Prosodic focus marking in Germanic languages

In English, Dutch, and German, adult speakers primarily use phonological cues (i.e., accentuation and accent type) to mark prosodic focus. Regarding effect of narrow focus, speakers usually accent a focal word but not accent (or de-accent) a post-focal word; they often accent a pre-focal word for rhythmical reasons. (Féry, 1993; Ladd, 1996; Gussenhoven, 1984, 2004; A. Chen, 2011a). As for accent types, the falling accent H*L is preferred for both focal and pre-focal accented words (Féry, 1993; Ladd, 1996; Gussenhoven, 2004, A. Chen, under revision), though other pitch accents are also observed in these languages. Regarding the effect of focus types, Féry (1993) found no distinction between narrow focus and broad focus in the use of the H*L pitch accent in sentence initial position in German speakers' production. Baumann and colleagues (Baumann, Grice Steindamm, 2006; Baumann, et al., 2007) observed a considerable overlap of the use of pitch accents (i.e., prenuclear accent, downstepped nuclear accent (!H*), and early peak accent (H+!H*)) across focus types (i.e., broad focus, narrow focus, and contrastive focus) in German, though there are some differences in the frequency of the three types of pitch accents. There is no one-to-one mapping between focus type and accent type in these languages.

Speakers also vary duration- and pitch-related phonetic cues to mark focus when phonological cues do not suffice in these languages. Regarding the effect of narrow focus, speakers produce focal words with more prominence in pitch (e.g., a lower minimum pitch) and duration (e.g., a longer word duration, syllable duration, and vowel duration) than non-focal words (A. Chen, 2009, on Dutch). Concerning the effect of focus types, speakers produce words with more prominence in pitch (e.g., a higher maximum pitch, changed pitch peak alignment) and duration in narrow focus than in broad focus (Hanssen, et al., 2008, on Dutch; Baumann, et al., 2007, on German). They also produce words with a later peak alignment and a higher mean pitch in contrastive focus than in narrow focus in German (Baumann, et al, 2007), and produce words with a higher pitch peak in contrastive focus than in narrow focus in Dutch (Hanssen, et al., 2008).

In Swedish, a language from the North Germanic group, a different phonological cue is used to mark focus than in West Germanic languages. With respect to the effect of narrow focus, narrow focus in Swedish is realised by assigning a separate prominence-marking high tone to the end of the focal word, causing the original lexical pitch accent, either HL* (i.e., a falling accent with an early alignment of the "fall" to the stressed syllable; referred to as "accent 1") or H*L (i.e., a falling accent with a late alignment of the "fall" to the stressed syllable; referred to as "accent 2"), to change to HL*H or H*LH respectively (Bruce, 2007; Romøren, 2016). The post-focal and pre-focal words are usually produced without this final high tone (Romøren, 2016). Regarding the effect of focus types, the prominence-marking high tone occurs more frequently in narrow focus than in broad focus, and occurs with a similar frequency in narrow focus and contrastive focus (Romøren, 2016).

To sum up, in the aforementioned Germanic languages, adults use language-specific phonological cues to mark focus. Phonological cues do not always suffice for distinguishing focus from non-focus (A. Chen, 2009, on Dutch) or different types of focus (Féry, 1993, on German). Evidence from Dutch (A. Chen, 2009; Hanssen, et al., 2008) and German (Baumann, et al., 2007) showed that when phonological cues do not distinguish focus conditions, gradient cues can be used for such purposes.

1.4.2 The acquisition of phonological focus marking in Germanic languages①

In West Germanic languages, children acquire the use of the phonological focus-marking cue, accentuation, at an early age. Hornby and Hass (1970) did the earliest study on the realisation of focus in English-speaking children. In this study three- to four-year-olds were asked to describe some picture pairs in which the second pictures differed

① A similar selection of studies was reviewed in A. Chen (2015) but with a focus on children's use of prosody in reference. This sub-section is an adapted version of the review, but centres on children's use of prosody in different focus conditions, and includes the following two more recent studies: Grünloh, Lieven & Tomasello (2015) and Romøren (2016).

from the first ones in the subject, the action (verb) or the object, and the sentences were all elicited by "*what's happening?*" questions, as in (8). In each pair of sentences produced, the new item introduced in the second sentence was the target word (e.g., "dog"), and it was contrastive to its counterpart in the first sentence (e.g., "cat"). We thus treated the target words as being in contrastive focus①. It was found that the target words were very frequently accented in the children's production, indicating that English-speaking children used prosody phonologically to mark contrastive focus at the age of three to four. Using a similar picture-describing method, MacWhinney and Bates (1978) examined the production of English-speaking children aged three to five. It was found that the children used accentuation to mark contrastive focus at the age of three, and their use of accentuation still increased from three to five years old.

(8) A②: What's happening in the picture?
B: A girl pets a cat.

A: What's happening in the picture?
B: A girl pets a [dog].

Wells, Peppé and Goulandris (2004) investigated English-speaking children's intonation development from the age of five to thirteen. They examined how children used accentuation to mark contrastive focus in "adjective + noun" phrases. The child was offered a picture that was not the one he/she needed, and thus he/she had to make a correction, either on a sentence-medial colour word, as in (9a), or on a sentence-final object, as in (9b). The accent of each target word was evaluated as right, wrong, or ambiguous. It was found that the five-year-olds had more wrong and ambiguous accents than the older children in producing the sentence-medial colour words. Further, the wrong productions were mainly caused by wrongly un-accenting a colour word that should have been marked with contrastive focus, but were rarely caused by wrongly accenting a colour word that should have been non-focused. This study showed that English-speaking children's use of accentuation for focus-marking purposes in certain syntactic constructions still developed from

① In some studies reviewed in this section (Grünloh, Lieven & Tomasello, 2015; Hornby & Hass, 1970; MacWhinney & Bates, 1978; Wonnacott & Watson, 2008), the target sentences were elicited by broad focus questions (e.g., "what's happening?" or "what happened?"), which rendered the whole sentence in broad focus. However, the target word in an answer sentence may be contrastive to a counterpart in a preceding sentence. In such cases, we take the answer sentence as containing contrastive focus on the target word, following A. Chen (2015).

② In the examples in this section, "A" is the experimenter, and "B" is the participant.

the age of five to the age of thirteen.

(9) a. A: How about a green bike?
B: I want a [white] bike.

b. A: How about a black boat?
B: I want a black [bus].

A. Chen (2009, 2011a, 2011b) examined how Dutch-speaking four- to eight-year-olds used prosody to mark narrow focus as compared to adults. A picture-matching game was used to elicit the semi-spontaneous production of SVO sentences from the children. The experimenter showed the child a picture and asked a "who" or "what" question based on the picture, as in (10 A). A visual robot gave the child the answer through a headphone using a voice lacking sentence-level prosody. The child then reproduced the answer with his/her own prosody, as in (10B).

(10) A: Who protects the forest? /
What does the fox protect?
B: The fox protects the forest.

The sentence-initial words in narrow focus elicited via "who" questions were compared to the same words in pre-focus elicited via "what" questions. Similarly, the sentence-final words in narrow focus and post-focus were also compared. It was found that Dutch-speaking children frequently accented the sentence-initial and final words in narrow focus at the age of four to five, similar to adults. Different from the aforementioned studies on English, A. Chen (2011a, 2011b) further examined children's varying of accent types for focus-marking purposes in Dutch. She found that children showed adult-like preference for the H*L pitch accent for sentence-initial focus and pre-focus at the age of four to five, but only showed such preference for sentence-final focus by the age of seven to eight. The results revealed that Dutch-speaking children were adult-like in accentuation at the age of four to five, but only became fully adult-like in the choice of accent type by the age of seven to eight in the marking of narrow focus.

A more recent study on German showed an early but not fully adult-like use of accentuation and accent type for focus-marking purposes in young children. Grünloh, Lieven and Tomasello (2015) studied the prosodic marking of broad focus and contrastive focus in sentences produced by German-speaking two- and three-year-olds. In this study, the children were asked to answer broad-focus questions by describing sequences of pictures, as in (11a). The target words (e.g., "the bee" in (11a)) were thus in broad focus, though first showed up as referentially new information, and then as referentially given information. The same target word was then elicited as a correction to a wrong remark by the experimenter, as in (11b), and thus was in contrastive focus.

(11) a. ...
A: What's happening next?
B: [The bee has come].
A: What's happening next?
B: [The grasshopper hugs the bee].
...
b. ...
A: Look, X is running away!
B: No, that was the [bee].
...

It was found that the children accented the words most frequently with a high pitch accent (H*), and sometimes with a low pitch accent (L*) when the words were in broad focus and referentially new, similar to the adults. However, they accented the words more frequently with a high pitch accent and de-accented the words less frequently than the adults when the words were in broad focus but referentially given, and this tendency was stronger in the two-year-olds than in the three-year-olds, suggesting a development in the use of accentuation in marking broad focus from the age of two to three. In the contrastive focus condition, the children accented the words most frequently with a high pitch accent, and sometimes with a low pitch accent, different from the adults, who accented half of the words with a high pitch accent and the other half with a low pitch accent. Thus, by the age of three, German-speaking children are adult like in the use of accentuation and accent type in marking broad focus, but only when the focal word is referentially new; their choice of accent type in marking contrastive focus is not yet adult-like.

Similar to children speaking West Germanic languages, Swedish-speaking children use the language-specific phonological cue (i.e., the prominence-marking high tone) to mark focus at an early age (Romøren, 2016; Romøren & Chen, 2015). Romøren (2016) examined how four- to eleven-year-olds used prosody to distinguish focus from non-focus and to distinguish different types of focus in Swedish, using an adapted version of the picture-matching game from A. Chen (2009, 2011a, 2011b). In the game, the experimenter showed the participant a picture of a simple scene in which one element was missing, like the subject, the object, the action (verb), or all the elements. The experimenter asked a narrow-focus question or a broad-focus question, or made a contrastive-focus-eliciting remark about the missing information. The participant then answered the question or made a correction according to a picture in which all elements were provided, as in (12). Regarding the effect of narrow focus, it was found that the children predominantly used the prominence-marking high tone in narrow focus, and predominantly avoided this tone in pre-focus and post-focus, similar to adults. However, while the seven- to eleven-year-olds performed in line with the adults, the four- to five-year-olds showed a weaker distinction between narrow focus and post focus in sentence-medial position, different from the adults. As for the effect of focus types, children used the prominence-marking high tone more frequently in narrow focus than in broad focus, and used this cue with a similar frequency in narrow focus as in contrastive focus at the age of four to five, similar to adults. However, children used this cue in narrow focus and contrastive focus with lower frequency than adults at the age of four to five, and became adult like in terms of frequency by the age of seven to eight. Thus, in Swedish, children's use of the phonological focus-marking cue is already close to adult-like by the age of four to five, though it is still developing between the ages of five to seven or eight.

(12) A: What is the frog hiding? /
What is happening in the picture? /
I guess: The frog is PAINTING the flower.
B: The frog is hiding the flower.

From the above reviewed studies, we can see that children have started to use accentuation and accent type to mark focus in English, Dutch, and German and to use prominence-marking high tone to mark focus in Swedish at the age of three to five (A. Chen, 2011a, 2011b; Grünloh, Lieven & Tomasello, 2015; Hornby & Hass, 1970; Romøren, 2016; Wells, et al., 2004), though the use of these cues is still developing after the age of five (A. Chen, 2011a, 2011b; Wells, et al., 2004).

1.4.3 Phonetic focus marking in children

Children speaking West Germanic languages were also found to use duration- and pitch-related phonetic cues to mark focus when phonological cues do not serve the purpose well. Wonnacott and Watson (2008) studied the prosodic realisation of contrastive focus by English-speaking three- to four-year-olds. In this study, the children were asked to answer the questions "(and then) what happened?" via describing pairs of video scenes in pairs of SVO sentences, as in (13a). The target word was the subject in the second answer sentence. It was either non-contrastive to the subject in the first answer sentence, like in (13a), or contrastive to the subject in the first answer sentence and referentially given, as in (13b), or new, as in (13c). The target words analysed were all produced with a high pitch accent. It was found that the contrastive words, including those both referentially given and new, had a higher maximum pitch and intensity than the non-contrastive words, while the words in the two contrastive conditions did not differ in maximum pitch or intensity. These findings on children were similar to comparable findings on English-speaking adults (Watson, Arnold & Tanenhaus, 2005, as cited by Wonnacott & Watson, 2008). However, the children did not use duration for such distinctions, different from the adults. The results imply that English-speaking children have acquired the use of the maximum pitch and intensity, but not duration, to mark contrastive focus by the age of three to four. The referential givenness-newness of the contrastive words are not distinguished via the gradient phonetic cues in English-speaking children or adults.

(13) a. A: What happened?
B: The lion hit the giraffe.
A: And then what happened?
B: The <u>lion</u> hit the elephant.

b. A: What happened?
B: The giraffe hit the lion.
A: And then what happened?
B: The <u>lion</u> hit the elephant.

c. A: What happened?
B: The elephant hit the giraffe.

A: And then what happened?

B: The lion hit the elephant.

A. Chen (2009) examined the use of phonetic cues in focus marking in Dutch-speaking children. Having found that sentence-initial focus and pre-focus were both realised frequently with the H*L pitch accent in Dutch (A. Chen, 2011a, 2011b), A. Chen (2009) further investigated the phonetic differences between the focal and pre-focal words with the H*L pitch accent. The four- to five-year-olds did not use pitch or duration to distinguish focal from pre-focal words with the H*L pitch accent, different from the adults who used a lower minimum pitch, longer vowel duration, syllable duration and word duration for the focal words than for the pre-focal words with the H*L pitch accent. The children can vary pitch but not duration to distinguish focal from pre-focal words by the age of seven to eight. The results indicate that Dutch-speaking children's use of phonetic cues for focus-marking purposes starts after the age of five, and the use of pitch presents at the age of seven to eight, earlier than the use of duration.

Given that Dutch-speaking children at the age of four cannot use pitch to mark (non-contrastive) narrow focus (A. Chen, 2009), whereas English-speaking children at this age can use pitch to mark contrastive focus (Wonnacott & Watson, 2008), we speculate that the early use of pitch in English may be related to the expression of contrast.

Similar to English-speaking children, German-speaking children were found to exploit pitch to encode contrastive focus at an early age. In a previously mentioned study, Grünloh, Lieven & Tomasello. (2015) analysed the use of pitch span for focus-marking purposes in German-speaking two to three-year-olds. They found that the three-year-olds used a wider pitch span for the words in contrastive focus than the (referentially new) words in broad focus, different from the adults, who did not make such distinction. However, the pitch span difference observed in the three-year-olds' production might be caused by the fact that they produced a slightly higher proportion of words with high pitch accent in contrastive focus condition (about 90%) than in broad focus condition (about 85%). We thus take the findings as a weak evidence showing an early but un-adult-like use of pitch span in marking contrastive focus by German-speaking children at the age of three.

German-speaking children's use of pitch in marking contrastive focus after the age of three was studied in Müller, Höhle, Schmitz and Weissenborn (2006). The participants were four- to five-year-olds and adults. They were asked to listen to short stories based on comic strip pictures, and then answered a "what" or "who" question by re-producing an answer-sentence provided without sentence-level prosody, as in (14). The target words were the sentence-initial and sentence-final nouns in the answer sentences. The focal target words in answer to the WH-word were contrastive and the pre-focal and post-focal target words were weakly contrastive to the counterparts in the first sentence produced by the experimenter. The sentence-initial words in contrastive focus elicited via "who" questions were compared to the same words in pre-focus elicited via "what" questions. Similarly, the sentence-final words in contrastive focus and in post-focus were also compared. It was found that the four- to five-year-olds produced the words in contrastive focus with a higher mean pitch than those in pre-focus and post-focus in the same utterance position, similar to the adults, though it was not clear to us whether the differences in mean pitch were caused by the presence of accentuation in contrastive focus but its absence in the pre-focal and post-focal conditions. Thus, we take the findings as weak evidence showing that German-speaking children may vary mean pitch in a gradient fashion to mark contrastive focus at the age of four to five.

(14) A: Eva wants to bake cookies. What does Peter bake?
(OR: Eva wants to bake cookies. Who bakes a cake?)
B: Peter bakes a cake.

From the above reviewed studies, we can see that children at the age of three to five do not vary pitch in a gradient fashion to mark narrow focus in Dutch (A. Chen, 2009), but use pitch to mark contrastive focus in English when phonological cues do not suffice (Wonnacott & Watson, 2008). The weak evidence from German also suggested that children use pitch to mark contrastive focus at this age (Müller, et al., 2006), in line with the findings on English. The early use of pitch in English and German may be related to the expression of contrast. However, children are not able to vary duration for focus-marking purposes in English at this age when phonological cues do not suffice (Wonnacott & Watson, 2008), and the use of duration for such purposes is not acquired in Dutch even by the age of eight (A. Chen, 2009).

1.4.4 Summarising the acquisition of prosodic focus marking

The reviews in sections 1.4.2 and 1.4.3 show that the use of language-specific phonological focus-marking cues are largely adult-like by the age of five in Germanic languages. The use of phonetic cues for focus-marking purposes in the absence of sufficient phonological cues tends to be acquired later than the use of phonological cues in West Germanic languages. Among the phonetic focus-marking cues, the use of duration tends to be acquired later than the use of pitch for the same focus-marking purposes (A. Chen, 2009; Wonnacott & Watson, 2008).

1.5 Prosodic focus marking in Mandarin and Korean

Before we propose the hypotheses and predictions on the acquisition of prosodic focus marking in Mandarin-speaking and Korean-speaking children, we first discuss the prosodic encoding of focus in detail in Mandarin-speaking and Korean-speaking adults in this section.

1.5.1 Prosody and prosodic focus marking in Mandarin

1.5.1.1 Prosody in Mandarin

Mandarin is a tone language, in which each word in an utterance carries one of the four lexical tones[①], and the tones distinguish words (Table 1-1) (Lin, 2007). The four tones are primarily identified by pitch movements (Figure 1-1). Chao (1965) used a 5-point scale to describe pitch movements of tones, with 5 indicating the highest pitch and 1 indicating the lowest, as shown in the "pitch value" column in Table 1-1. Tone 1 is a high level tone, and its pitch stays at the highest level of 5. Tone 2 is a high rising tone, with its pitch starting at the mid-level of 3 and going upward till the highest level of 5. Tone 3 is realised as a low dipping tone when produced in isolation or in phrase final position, with the pitch starting from the half-low level of 2 and going even lower to the lowest level of 1 before rising up to the half-high level of 4. It is realised with only the low falling part before Tone 1, Tone 2 or Tone 4. When produced before another Tone 3, it is realised as a rising tone, which however, has a slightly lower overall pitch level than the canonical rising tone, Tone 2 (Peng, 2000). Tone 4 is a high falling tone, with the pitch moving from the highest level of 5 to the lowest level of 1 (Chao, 1965; Lin, 2007). In addition to pitch movements, the four tones differ marginally in other dimensions such as duration and amplitude (See details in Fu & Zeng, 2000; Xu, 1997). These properties can assist native

① In addition to the four tones, there is also a neutral tone, which is also described as a weak tone in Mandarin, and it occurs in an unstressed short syllable (Lin, 2007).

listeners in identifying tones when pitch information is not available (S. Liu & Samuel, 2004; Whalen & Xu, 1992). When produced in continuous speech, a tone influences the realisation of the following tone (known as the "carryover effect") and the preceding tone (known as the "anticipatory effect") (See detailed description of tonal effects in Xu, 1994, 1997, 2004).

Table 1-1 The four tones in Mandarin (adapted from Lin, 2007: 89)

Tone number	Pitch pattern	Pitch value	Example
Tone 1	high level	55	mā "mother" 妈
Tone 2	high rising	35	má "hemp" 麻
Tone 3	low falling (-rising)	21 (-4)	mǎ "horse" 马
Tone 4	high falling	51	mà "to scold" 骂

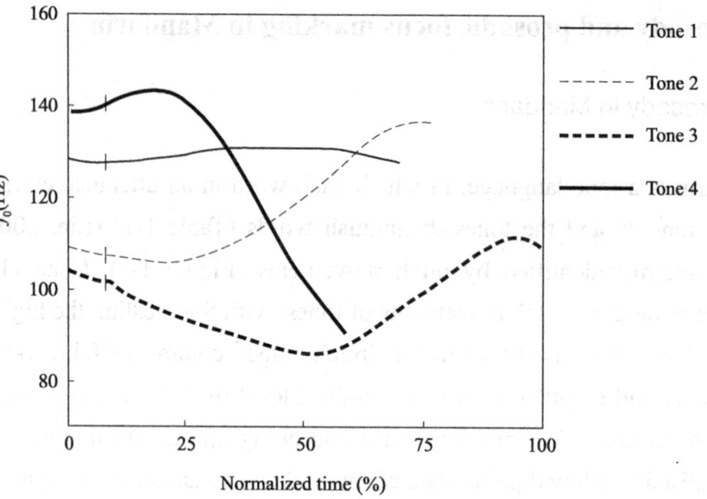

Figure 1-1 The mean f_0 contours (averaged over speakers and tokens; n=48) of four Mandarin tones in the monosyllable /mɑ/, produced in isolation (taken from Xu, 1997: 67).

1.5.1.2 Prosodic focus marking in Mandarin

Many studies have investigated the interface between prosody and information structure in Mandarin and covered a range of issues, such as the interaction of focus and tone (Xu, 1999; Y. Chen & Gussenhoven, 2008), the interaction of focus and sentence type (e.g., declaration, question, and confirmation) (F. Liu & Xu, 2005; Shih, 2004), the realization of post-focus (S. Chen, Wang & Xu, 2009; Shih, 1997; Xu, 2011; Xu, S. W. Chen &

Wang, 2012), and the prosodic distinction of information structural categories such as referential givenness-newness (Ouyang & Kaiser, 2015), theme and rheme (Y. Chen & Braun, 2006), and topic and focus (Wang & Xu, 2011). In the following, we will review the most relevant studies on the prosodic realisation of narrow focus, broad focus and contrastive focus.

The realisation of narrow focus in Mandarin was analysed in a comprehensive way in Xu (1999). In this study, the target sentences were a set of short SVO sentences with varied tones in the subject, verb and object positions. They were elicited with narrow focus on the sentence-initial subject, sentence-medial verb and sentence-final object, and with broad focus on the verb-object phrase via a set of WH-questions, as in (15). Eight native speakers read the questions and target sentences repeatedly. With regard to the realisation of narrow focus in comparison to non-focus, detailed acoustical analysis showed that the sentence-medial words① had a longer duration, a wider pitch span or a higher pitch level (for the Tone 1 words), and a higher maximum pitch in narrow focus than in pre-focus and post-focus. The minimum pitch of the Tone 2 and Tone 4 words② was lower or marginally lower in narrow focus than in pre-focus. In addition, the maximum pitch was raised to a larger degree than the minimum pitch was lowered in the focused Tone 2 and Tone 4 words, implying that the pitch span expansion in the two tones was primarily caused by the rising of the maximum pitch.

(15) A: Who touches kitty? /
What does kitty do to kitty? /
What does kitty touch? /
What does kitty do?
B: mao1③ mi1 mo1 mao1mi1
Kitty touches kitty

The effect of narrow focus in comparison to non-focus was also discussed in a subsequent study by Y. Chen and Braun (2006). The target words were twelve disyllabic names, with either a "T2T4 (i.e., Tone 2–Tone 4)" or a "T4T2" tonal combination. They were

① Xu (1999) performed detailed acoustical analysis for the words in all three sentence positions. Here we only summarise the results from the sentence-medial monosyllabic verbs (in three tones: Tone 1, Tone 2, and Tone 4) in detail, because these results are most comparable to the Mandarin data in Chapter 2 of this dissertation in which sentence-medial monosyllabic words were used as targets. The results obtained in the other two sentence positions were largely consistent with the findings obtained sentence-medially.

② Tone 1 and Tone 3 were not included in the analysis of the minimum pitch in Xu (1999).

③ The digits immediately following the *Pinyin* (i.e., romanised Chinese characters), represent tones.

elicited sentence initially as subject-nouns in pre-focus (referred to as "theme background"), as in (16a) and in narrow focus (referred to as "rheme focus"), as in (16b). Ten native speakers read the question-answer pairs repeatedly. It was found that the words had a longer duration and a wider pitch span for both syllables in narrow focus than in non-focus, consistent with previous findings based on sentence-medial monosyllabic words in Xu (1999). Thus, narrow focus is encoded with more prominence in duration and pitch than non-focus.

(16) a. A: What did Mona rent?
B: Mona rented [a car].

b. A: Who rented a car?
B: [Mona] rented a car.

The realisation of narrow focus in comparison to broad focus was investigated in an early study by Shih (1988). In this study, disyllabic target words with different tones on the first syllable (i.e., "jin1 tian1 (today)", "ming2 tian1 (tomorrow)", "mei3 tian1 (everyday)", "hou4 tian1 (the day after tomorrow)") were embedded in a sentence, as in (17). Each sentence was read repeatedly as a plain statement (i.e., arguably similar to broad focus) and then with narrow focus on the target word. It was found that the words had an expanded pitch span (with the highest pitch being higher and the lowest pitch being lower or unchanged), a longer duration and a higher intensity in narrow focus compared to broad focus. Shih's findings were supported by Xu (1999), based on acoustical and statistical analyses. In Xu (1999), words had a longer duration, a wider pitch span, and a higher maximum pitch in narrow focus than in broad focus. Subsequent studies by Xu and colleagues on Mandarin showed consistent findings on the encoding of narrow focus in comparison to broad focus when the latter was changed to a whole-sentence broad focus (S. Chen, et al., 2009; Xu, 2011; Xu, et al., 2012). Thus, focus types differing in the size of focal constituent are prosodically distinguished in Mandarin read speech.

(17)	Lao3 Wang2	TARGET	yao4	mai3	yu2
	Lao Wang	TARGET	wants	to buy	fish

As for the effect of contrastive focus, Y. Chen and Gussenhoven (2008) compared the prosodic marking of contrastive focus to non-focus (referred to as "Emphasis" and

"NoEmphasis" respectively). In this study, the target words were monosyllabic words in four tones, embedded in sentences like in (18a). To elicit a word in contrastive focus, a target sentence labelled with "correct information" was presented on a computer screen to the speaker; a second sentence differing from the target sentence only in the target word was then presented, and it was labelled with "incorrect information", as in (18b). The speaker was instructed to correct the second sentence, by producing the target sentence. To elicit a word in pre-focus, a question eliciting focus on the sentence-final words was asked, as in (18c). Five native speakers produced the sentences. It was found that the words had a longer duration, a wider pitch span, and higher maximum pitch in contrastive focus than in pre-focus; the minimum pitch only tended to be lower in contrastive focus than in pre-focus, suggesting that the focus-induced pitch span expansion was mainly caused by the rise of the maximum pitch, similar to the findings in Xu (1999). Contrastive focus is thus encoded with more prominence in duration and pitch than non-focus.

(18) a. Zhou1bin1 shuo1 shuo1 TARGET nan2 hen3 duo1
Zhoubin said that to say TARGET is more difficult.

b. (Correct) Zhoubin said that to say miao1 is more difficult.
(Incorrect) Zhoubin said that to say da3 is more difficult.

c. What did Zhoubin say about saying the word miao1?
Zhoubin said that to say miao1 is [more difficult].

Regarding the difference between contrastive focus and narrow focus, Y. Chen and Braun (2006) compared the prosodic realisation of sentence-initial disyllabic words in narrow focus, as in (19a), and in contrastive focus (referred to as corrective rheme focus), as in (19b). It was found that there was no durational difference between the words in these two conditions. As for pitch measurements, the disyllabic T4T2 words had a wider pitch span in both syllables in contrastive focus than in narrow focus; no difference was found between the two conditions in pitch span in the T2T4 words, though the second syllable had a higher maximum pitch in contrastive focus than in narrow focus.

(19) a. A: Who rented a car?
B: [Mona] rented a car.

b. A: Martin rented a car?
B: [Mona] rented a car.

The prosodic realisation of contrastive focus compared to narrow focus was also studied in semi-spontaneous speech in a subsequent study by Greif (2010). In this study, disyllabic target words (names) with certain tonal combinations (i.e., T2T2, T3T2 and T4T4) were elicited sentence-initially in narrow focus, as in (20a), and contrastive focus, as in (20b). Six female native speakers answered the questions based on pictures. It was found that there was no significant difference between contrastive focus and narrow focus in pitch span or duration, though the words in contrastive focus tended to be longer than in narrow focus. Hence, contrastive focus and narrow focus seem to differ slightly in pitch in read speech, but not in semi-spontaneous speech.

(20) a. A: Who has the watermelons?
B: [Ma long] has the watermelons.

b. A: Is it Milo who has the watermelons?
B: [Ma long] has the watermelons.

To sum up, in Mandarin, a word has a longer duration, a wider pitch span, and/or a higher pitch level, and a higher intensity in narrow focus than in non-focus (Xu, 1999; Y. Chen & Braun, 2006) and in broad focus (Shih, 1988; Xu, 1999). Contrastive focus is more prominent than non-focus in pitch and duration (Y. Chen & Gussenhoven, 2008). It is also more prominent than narrow focus in pitch when the focal words contain certain tonal combinations (i.e., T4T2 and T2T4) in read speech (Y. Chen & Braun, 2006), though no evidence for prosodic differences between the two types of focus is found in semi-spontaneous speech (Greif, 2010).

1.5.2 Prosody and prosodic focus marking in Korean

1.5.2.1 Prosody in Korean

Korean does not have pitch accents like West Germanic languages or lexical tones like Mandarin. The model of Seoul Korean intonation (Figure 1-2) proposed and developed by Jun (1993, 1998, 2000, 2005) within the autosegmental metrical framework (Pierrehumbert, 1980; Pierrehumbert & Beckman, 1988) is the most widely accepted model of Seoul Korean prosody (see also earlier studies of Seoul Korean intonation by H. B. Lee, 1964; Koo, 1986; Martin, 1954; S. B. Cho, 1967, as cited in Jun, 1993.). In this model, an utterance consists of one or more Intonation Phrases (IP) which, in turn, consist of one or more Accentual Phrases (AP). An AP contains one or more phonological words (PW). A phonological word contains a lexical word and a case marker or postpositions. In this dissertation, we refer to "phonological word" as "word" (W).

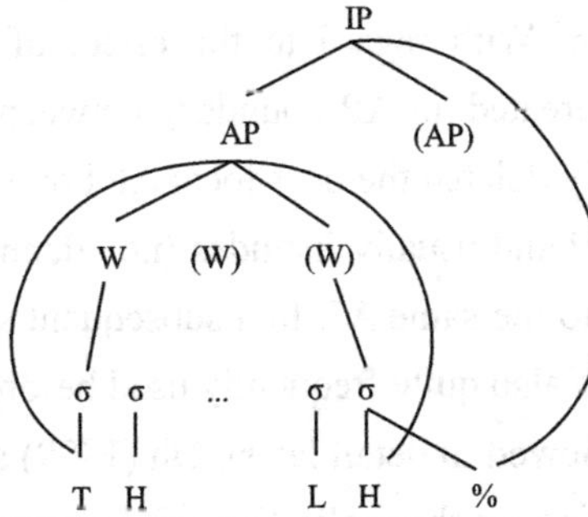

Figure 1-2 Intonation Structure of Seoul Korean. W: phonological word. σ: syllable. %: Intonation phrase boundary tone (taken from Jun, 2005: 205).

The AP is the smallest unit carrying tonal patterns. The most common tonal pattern of an AP is HHLH when the AP-initial segment is aspirated (e.g., /p^h, t^h, k^h/) or fortis① (e.g., /p*, t*, k*/), or a /h/ or a /s/, and is LHLH when the AP-initial segment is lenis (e.g., /p, t, k/) or a sonorant. When an AP has four or more syllables, all four tones are realised, with the first two tones associated with the first two syllables and the last two tones associated with the last two syllables. When an AP has fewer syllables than four, one or both of the two medial tones are not realised. At least 14 AP tonal patterns (i.e., LH, LHH, LLH, LHLH, HH, HLH, HHLH, LL, HL, LHL, HHL, HLL, LHLL and HHLL) have been observed (Jun, 2000), and even more variations in tonal patterns show up as the naturalness of speech increases (S. Y. Kim, 2004). Despite the considerable variation in tonal patterns, AP final high tone is commonly observed (S. Y. Kim, 2004), and is thus a reliable marker of AP (Jun, 2006). A default (vs. focused) phonological word usually forms an AP (Schafer & Jun, 2002; Jun, 2005).

An IP is marked by a boundary tone which is realised on the IP-final syllable and overlaps and overrides the final tone of the last AP in the IP. According to Jun (2000), at

① In Seoul Korean the obstruents are categorized as lenis (i.e., /p, t, k, tʃ, s/), aspirated (i.e., / p^h, t^h, k^h, $tʃ^h$/), and fortis (i.e., /p*, t*, k*, tʃ*, s*/; a.k.a., tense) (T. Cho, Jun & Ladefoged, 2002).

least nine boundary tones (i.e., L%, H%, LH%, HL%, LHL%, HLH%, HLHL%, LHLH%, LHLHL%) have been observed (See Park, 2012, for more variations). An IP is also marked by final-syllable lengthening and is optionally followed by a pause (e.g., Jun, 2005).

1.5.2.2 Prosodic focus marking in Korean

1.5.2.2.1 Prosodic phrasing in focus marking in Korean

Prosodic phrasing (hereafter, phrasing), or grouping of words, is known as the typical focus-marking cue in Korean. With regard to the effect of narrow focus, Jun (1993) described that narrow focus created an AP boundary between the focused word and the preceding word, and frequently deleted the post-focal AP boundaries. In other words, a focused word initiates a new AP and usually includes (i.e., dephrases) the post-focal words up to the next IP boundary into the same AP. In a subsequent study, Jun and colleague reported that IP boundaries were also quite frequently used before the focused words (Jun & Kim, 2007, which will be reviewed in detail later). Oh (1999) studied the effect of narrow focus on phrasing, concentrating on the realisation of pre-focal and post-focal regions. In this study, four speakers repeatedly read two sentences with narrow focus on the modifier, object or verb, and also read the sentences in a "neutral" condition (arguably broad focus), as in (21). It was found that post-focus dephrasing was frequent, but did not always cover up to the next IP boundary as claimed by Jun (1993). In addition, the pre-focal words were also quite often phrased together as one AP.

(21) a. nanɨn pakmariae norerɨl siləhe
I Pakmaria's song dislike.
"I do not like Pakmaria's song."①

b. nanɨn pucawasemi norerɨl norerɨl
I Puca and Semi's song dislike.
"I do not like Puca and Semi's song."

Contrastive focus has an effect on phrasing similar to that of narrow focus, namely, it starts a new phrase, beginning from the focal word and frequently dephrases the post-focal

① In this section, we give the English translation of the Korean sentences in quotation marks, below the word for word English gloss.

words (Jun, 1993; Jun & Lee, 1998). In Jun and Lee (1998), contrastive focus was elicited in a reading task as a correction to a piece of information in a preceding sentence, as in (22). The types (declarative vs. interrogative) and length of the sentences were controlled. Five speakers produced the sentences repeatedly. It was found that the post-focal words were not always dephrased into the same AP as the focused word. The degree of the use of dephrasing varied from always to almost never in the five speakers. Moreover, the use of dephrasing was more frequent when the post-focus sequence became shorter and when in interrogatives than in declaratives.

(22) (miɾaneka onɨl tʃənjəke bananaɾɨl məknɨnke aniɾa,)
(Mira's family this evening bananas eats not)
miɾaneka [neil] tʃənjəke bananaɾɨl məknɨnke
Mira's family [tomorrow] evening bananas eats
"(It is not this evening that Mira's family eats bananas,)
but it is [tomorrow] evening that Mira's family eats bananas."

In a recent study, Jeon & Nolan (2017) investigated the prosodic marking of contrastive focus and analysed the phrasal boundaries in sentences. The target words were a list of two-number sequences (e.g., 20,001; 10,005) with two to four syllables in each number word. They were embedded sentence medially and were elicited with contrastive focus on the first or second number word, as in the second sentence in (23). Four native speakers of Korean read the sentences. The prosodic boundaries before the first number word, after the second number word and between the two number words in the target sentence (e.g., the second sentence in (23)) were annotated as an AP boundary, IP boundary or PW boundary. It was found that AP and IP boundaries were most common before, after and between the two number words in each target sentence, indicating that the number words were most frequently realised as separate APs and IPs. Moreover, the number words in contrastive focus (e.g., "mano (10,005)") always initiated an AP or IP, consistent with previous findings (Jun, 1993). PW boundaries were few in the data, which indicates that the occurrence of dephrasing was rare, and might be optional in short syntactic phrases.

(23) (imanil tsʰʌnili anila)
(20,001, 1,001 is not)
ipʌn sutɯlɯn imanil [mano] twɛkɛs ɯmnita
This time numbers 20,001, [10,005] become

"It is not 20,001, 10,01, but the numbers this time are 20,001, [10,005]."

As for the effect of broad focus on phrasing, researchers have examined broad VP focus, NP focus, and whole-sentence broad focus. Jun and colleagues (Jun, Kim, Lee, et al., 2006; Kim, Jun, Lee, et al., 2006; Jun & Kim, 2007) studied broad VP focus by comparing it to narrow focus and whole-sentence broad focus (referred to as the "neutral" condition in their studies). A set of sentences with controlled structure and length were elicited in the mentioned focus conditions. The speakers were asked to read a sentence to produce a VP in whole-sentence broad focus, as in (24a). They were then asked to answer a question with the same sentence as the one they just read to produce VP focus, as in (24b). Finally, they were asked to answer another question with the same sentence to produce narrow focus on the VP-initial word, as in (24c). It was found that the speakers were inclined to produce each word as an AP in the whole-sentence broad focus condition. However, in the VP focus condition, a new IP boundary was very often inserted before the VP, and the words within the VP were usually not dephrased.

(24) a. Whole-sentence broad focus
[jəŋugɑ minaege ziugæril gənnezuəs'ə]
[Youngu (to) Mina eraser passed]
"[Youngu passed the eraser to Mina]."

b. Broad VP focus
A: What did Youngu do?
B: jəŋugɑ [minaege ziugæril gənnezuəs'ə]
Youngu [(to) Mina eraser passed]
"Youngu [passed the eraser to Mina]."

c. Narrow focus
A: What did Youngu pass to Mina?
B: jəŋugɑ minaege [ziugærhl] gənnezuəs'ə
Youngu (to) Mina [eraser] passed
"Youngu passed the [eraser] to Mina."

Jun (2011) examined the effect of broad NP focus, compared to the effect of whole-sentence broad focus on phrasing. The target NPs, with lengths varying from one noun (e.g., *Yeona*) to four nouns (e.g., *Yeona's tutor's sister's boyfriend*), were embedded into sentences with controlled syntactic structure. The NP focus was elicited via *who*-questions, as in (25), and the whole-sentence broad focus was elicited via reading the sentences out of the blue. It was found that phrasing was influenced by the interaction of focus, syntax, length, and rhythm. In broad focus condition, when a sentence was long and contained a clause or a heavy NP, the clause or NP was usually followed by an IP boundary or an intermediate phrase (ip) boundary①. When a sentence contained five words or fewer, each word tended to form one AP, regardless of the complexity of the sentence structure, similar to the finding on whole-sentence broad focus in H. S. Kim, et al., (2006). When the NP was focused, the NP-final word was most prominent, initiating an ip. The post-focal words were either fully dephrased into the same AP with the NP-final word when the post-focal sequence was short and syntactically simple (e.g., a verb), or were partially dephrased together as one AP but were not included in the same AP with the NP-final word when the post-focal sequence was long or syntactically complex (e.g., a verb clause).

(25) A: Who does Mina like to meet the most?

B: Minanɨn NP-lɨl mannanɨgəl tʃɛil dʒoahejo.

Mina [NP] meet most like

"Mina likes to meet [NP] the most."

1.5.2.2.2 Phonetic use of pitch and duration in focus marking in Korean

In addition to phrasing, previous studies also investigated Korean speakers' use of pitch- and duration- related cues for focus-marking purposes, often independently of phrasing②. The phonetic realisation of narrow focus was examined by Y. C. Lee and Xu (2010). In this study, narrow focus was elicited sentence-medially via a reading task. Six native speakers read both the questions and the answer sentences, as in (26). The lengths of the pre-focal and post-focal sequences were controlled. Narrow focus, pre-focus and post-focus were all compared to broad focus (referred to as the "neutral" condition, elicited via reading). It was found that the words in narrow focus had a higher mean pitch, a higher maximum pitch, a longer duration and a greater intensity than the same words in

① The concept "intermediate phrase (ip)" was proposed in Jun's (2006) revised model of Seoul Korean intonation. An ip is larger than an AP and smaller than an IP. However, demarcating ips in speech data is not straightforward and therefore the ip is excluded from our own analysis of Korean.

② We do not deny that phrasing (or the use of phrasal boundaries) is also realised via phonetic changes in pitch and duration. However, not all phonetic changes lead to a change in the phonological category (i.e., prosodic phrases or prosodic phrasal boundaries). Most of the studies reviewed here analysed the phonetic properties independently of phonological categories.

broad focus; the post-focal words had a lower mean pitch, a lower maximum pitch, a shorter duration and a lower intensity than the same words in broad focus; the pre-focal words did not differ from their counterparts in broad focus in these measurements. Given that the results revealed a "narrow focus > broad focus ⩾ non-focus" trend regarding phonetic prominence, we can interpret the results to mean that narrow focus is more prominent in pitch and duration than non-focus in Korean read speech. Moreover, Y. C. Lee and Xu (2010) mentioned that they did not observe changes in intonational structure due to focus. We thus conjecture that, in their data, the words were produced as separate APs, probably because that the sentences were elicited via reading. We take their findings as weak evidence that Korean speakers vary pitch- and duration-related phonetic cues in a gradient fashion to distinguish narrow focus and non-focus within one phonological category (i.e., the AP category).

(26) A: What is Minsu eating in the evening?
B: Minsuka ʧənjəke [manturɨl] məknɨnta.
Minsu evening [potstickers] eating
"Minsu is eating [potstickers] in the evening."

With respect to the phonetic realisation of broad focus, as mentioned in the preceding paragraph, Y. C. Lee and Xu (2010) found that speakers realise broad focus with a lower mean pitch, a lower maximum pitch, a shorter duration and a lower intensity than narrow focus. Y. C. Lee and Xu's (2010) findings support Jun's (1993) early claim that the words were less prominent in pitch and intensity in broad focus (referred to as "neutral" condition) than in narrow focus. Similarly, Jun and Kim (2007) also reported that words in broad focus had a lower maximum pitch and a shorter duration than the same words in narrow focus.

In addition to whole sentence broad focus, broad VP focus was also examined in previous studies. H. S. Kim, et al. (2006) and Jun, et al. (2006) found that the words in a focused VP generally had a higher maximum pitch and a longer duration than the same words in whole-sentence broad focus; the rise of the maximum pitch was most obvious in the VP initial word, and the lengthening effect was most obvious in the first two words in the VP. Further, substantial lengthening was found in the initial syllable of the initial word in the focused VP but not in the initial syllable of the second word in the focused VP. There findings showed that prosodic prominence increases as the size of focal constituent decrease (from whole sentence broad focus to broad VP focus), and that in broad VP focus the prosody near prosodic boundaries is more prominent than in other regions of the focal constituent. In addition, Jun and Kim (2007) further reported that the lengthening and pitch-rising effects observed on the VP initial words were less robust in the VP focus condition than in narrow focus. Thus the previous studies (Jun & Kim, 2007; Jun, et al., 2006; Kim, et al., 2006; Lee & Xu, 2010) together imply that focus types differing in the size of the focal constituent are phonetically distinguished in Korean read speech, and support that phonetic prominence increases as the size of the focal constituent decreases.

With regard to the phonetic realisation of contrastive focus, previous studies mainly compared contrastive focus to broad focus and non-focus. Jun and Lee (1998) found that the words had a higher maximum pitch in contrastive focus than in broad focus (referred to as "neutral" condition, elicited via reading the target sentences without emphasising any word). Regarding duration-related cues, the word-initial syllable duration was longer in contrastive focus than in broad focus, and the lengthening effect was caused by the lengthening of the initial consonant, indicating that the duration near prosodic boundaries was varied most in contrastive focus. However, the word duration was not consistently lengthened in contrastive focus in all speakers. The post-focal sequence, whether dephrased or not, had a shorter duration than the same sequence in broad focus. It did not always have a lower maximum pitch than the same sequence in broad focus, but had a lower maximum pitch than the preceding focused word in the same sentence, which produced an effect of dephrasing as strongly as actual dephrasing, according to Jun and Lee. A similar observation of post-focus realisation was referred to as *phonetic dephrasing* in Jun (2011). Further, Jun and Lee (1998) reported a trade-off in the use of dephrasing and phonetic cues in individual speakers; that is, speakers (i.e., F1 and M3) who rarely dephrased the post-focal words still used a lower maximum pitch and/or a shorter duration in post-focus than in broad focus. Conversely, speakers who dephrased the post-focal words more consistently than other speakers varied the duration of the post-focus sequence less consistently for sentences of different lengths than other speakers.

Jeon and Nolan (2017) also investigated the phonetic realisation of contrastive focus by comparing it to non-focus and broad focus (over a two-number word sequence). They found that the words were longer in contrastive focus than in broad focus, different from the report in Jun and Lee (1998). In addition, all syllables in the words tend to be longer in contrastive focus than in non-focus (pre-focus and post-focus) or in broad focus, with the word-initial and word-final syllables lengthened more than the word-medial syllables. These findings confirmed that the duration near prosodic boundaries was varied most in contrastive focus. As for pitch, words had a wider pitch span in contrastive focus than in either non-focus or broad focus. Taken together, the previous studies show that contrastive focus is phonetically more prominent than non-focus and broad focus.

1.5.2.2.3 Summarising prosodic focus marking in Korean

In Korean, a word in narrow focus or contrastive focus initiates a new AP or IP (Jun, 1993; Jun & Lee, 1998; Jun & Kim, 2007; Jeon & Nolan, 2017), and optionally dephrases its following word or words (Jun, 1993; Oh, 1999; Jeon & Nolan, 2017). A word is more prominent in pitch and duration in both narrow focus and contrastive focus compared to the same word in non-focus (Lee & Xu, 2010; Jeon & Nolan, 2017), and is also more prominent in pitch than the following word in the same sentence (Jun & Lee, 1998; Jun & Kim, 2007). However, the previous studies did not directly compare contrastive focus and narrow focus, and thus it remains unclear to us whether contrastive focus differs from narrow focus in how frequently it induces pre-focus boundary insertion and post-focus dephrasing, and in how much it induces gradient changes in pitch and duration. As for the distinction of focus types differing in the size of the focal constituent, broad focus has been shown to have a different effect on phrasing than narrow focus. The words in a short sentence or phrase in broad focus tend to form separate APs, though they can be phrased in different ways when the sentence or phrase is long or syntactically complex (Jeon & Nolan, 2017; Jun, 2011; Jun & Kim, 2007; Jun, et al., 2006; Kim, et al, 2006). As for a phonetic distinction according to the size of the focal constituent, we see a trend that the phonetic prominence (in duration and pitch) of the focal words decreases as the size of focal constituent increases: narrow/contrastive focus > broad VP focus > whole-sentence broad focus (Jeon & Nolan, 2017; Jun & Kim, 2007; Jun & Lee, 1998; Lee & Xu, 2010).

Last, as mentioned earlier, most of the studies reviewed in section 1.5.2.2.2 analysed the phonetic properties independently of phonological categories. We thus do not know whether the phonetic differences between two focus conditions were caused by the use of phrasal (AP or IP) boundaries in one condition and the absence of phrasal boundaries (i.e., the use of PW boundaries or dephrasing) in the other. However, the observation that, when the post-focal words were not dephrased, they were produced with reduced pitch (Jun & Lee, 1998), implied the occurrence of phonetic focus marking within one phonological category in Korean.

1.6 Hypotheses and predictions

In section 1.2 of this chapter, we raised the overarching research question, namely, how the differences in prosodic systems and prosodic focus marking between Mandarin and Korean shape the developmental paths to adult-like prosodic focus marking in the two languages. We operationalised this question as two, more specific, research questions, repeated as follows:

> Research question Ⅰ: Does the lexical use of a prosodic parameter (i.e., pitch in Mandarin) influence the acquisition of the same parameter used for focus marking?

> Research question Ⅱ: Does the relative importance of prosodic focus-marking cues in a language (i.e., whether the cues are primary or secondary cues) influence the acquisition of these cues?

As mentioned earlier in section 1.2, we expect that the effects of these factors (i.e., the lexical use of a prosodic parameter and the relative importance of a prosodic focus-marking cue) will manifest in both the rate and route of the acquisition of the prosodic focus-marking cues.

To answer the research questions, we need a comprehensive picture of children's use of prosody for focus-marking purposes in these two languages. We have thus closely examined how children speaking these languages use prosody for three specific focus-marking purposes that have been widely discussed in the literature: first, the use of prosody in distinguishing narrow focus from non-focus, or, pre-focus and post-focus (Effect of narrow focus); second, the use of prosody in distinguishing narrow focus from broad focus (Effect of focal constituent size); third, the use of prosody in distinguishing narrow focus from contrastive focus (Effect of contrastivity). We have conducted cross-sectional studies on four- to five-year-olds, seven- to eight-year-olds and ten- to eleven-year-olds. We chose four- to five-year-olds as the youngest group to examine because we are interested in children's use of prosody in full sentences, and the children under the age of four can differ substantially in their ability to produce full sentences in conversations. We tested children aged four to eleven because we expected that there can be development in children's use of prosody for focus-marking purposes between the ages of five and eleven, as shown in past work on Germanic languages (Wells, et al., 2004, on English; Romøren, 2016, on Swedish). We also tested Mandarin-speaking and Korean-speaking adults as controls to obtain maximally comparable data to the children's data.

Regarding Research question Ⅰ, we have two opposing hypotheses based on different strands of indirect evidence. On the one hand, Mandarin speakers need to maintain the shape of the pitch contour in a word for the sake of the identity of the lexical tone, and thus leave limited acoustic space for pitch variation for focus-marking purposes. This suggests that Mandarin speakers need to execute precise control of pitch to mark focus and to realise tones simultaneously. Previous studies have shown that adult Mandarin speakers expand the pitch span of words to mark focus, without changing the tonal category of words (Xu, 1999). To achieve this, speakers raise the maximum pitch and lower the minimum pitch to different degrees. For example, when words in Tone 2 and Tone 4 are focused, the minimum pitch is lowered to a much less extent than the extent to which the maximum pitch is raised (Xu, 1999), and focused words in Tone 3 are realised with only a modestly lowered minimum pitch (Y. Chen & Gussenhoven, 2008). Research has shown that young children have difficulty in pitch control over a stretch of speech as long as, or longer than, a word (A. Chen, 2009). Mandarin-speaking children may thus take a longer time to become adult-like in the use of pitch than the use of duration for focus-marking purposes, since duration is at most marginally used for lexical purpose in Mandarin. In contrast, pitch in Korean does not have lexical function, and may thus be acquired with less difficulty for focus-marking purposes than in Mandarin. Moreover, the use of pitch is found to be acquired earlier than the use of duration for focus-marking purposes in West Germanic languages, in which pitch does not have lexical function (Wonnacott & Watson, 2008, on English; A. Chen, 2009, on Dutch). Korean-speaking children may resemble children speaking a West Germanic language and show an earlier acquisition of the use of pitch than the use of duration for focus-marking purposes. Along this line of reasoning, we can make the following hypothesis and predictions:

> Hypothesis Ⅰ (a): The lexical use of pitch in a language slows down the acquisition of the use of pitch as a cue to focus.
>
> Predictions: Mandarin-speaking children should acquire the use of pitch later than the use of duration for focus-marking purposes, whereas

Korean-speaking children should acquire the use of pitch earlier than the use of duration for focus-marking purposes.

On the other hand, Mandarin-speaking children can produce lexical tones with considerable accuracy at the age of three (Wong, 2012; Wong, Schwartz & Jenkins, 2005; Zhu, 2002), suggesting that they are sensitive to pitch variation in perception and are competent in pitch control in production for tonal realisation by the age of three, which may facilitate their acquisition of the use of pitch for focus-marking purposes. As for Korean-speaking children, we still expect an earlier acquisition of the use of pitch than the use of duration for the reason that has been stated. However, given that Korean has no lexical use of pitch, we expect that Korean-speaking children's acquisition of the use of pitch for focus-marking purposes may not be as early as that of Mandarin-speaking children. In view of the above considerations, we can make the following hypothesis and predictions:

Hypothesis Ⅰ (b): The lexical use of pitch in a language facilitates the acquisition of the use of pitch as a cue to focus.

Predictions: Both Mandarin-speaking and Korean-speaking children should acquire the use of pitch earlier than the use of duration for focus-marking purposes, but Mandarin-speaking children acquire the use of pitch earlier than Korean-speaking children.

To test Hypotheses Ⅰ (a) and Ⅰ (b) and the corresponding predictions, we compare the acquisition of the use of pitch to the use of duration for focus-marking purposes in Mandarin (see Chapter 3 of this dissertation). We also compare the acquisition of the use of pitch for focus-marking purposes in Mandarin (see Chapter 3 of this dissertation) and Korean (see Chapter 6 of this dissertation) and in previously-studied languages such as West Germanic languages (see Chapter 7 of this dissertation for a cross-linguistic comparison).

Regarding Research question Ⅱ, again we have two opposing hypotheses. On the one hand, the phonetic focus-marking cues are the only and thus the primary prosodic focus-marking cues in Mandarin, and hence Mandarin-speaking children have abundant exposure to phonetic use of prosody, whereas, in Korean, speakers primarily use a phonological cue to mark prosodic focus and rely less on phonetic cues. Thus, Korean-speaking children receive relatively less exposure to phonetic use of prosody. Along this line of reasoning, we make the following hypothesis and prediction:

Hypothesis Ⅱ (a): Phonetic focus marking is acquired early when it is the primary means of prosodic focus marking, but is acquired late when it is a secondary means of prosodic focus marking in languages.

Prediction: Mandarin-speaking children should acquire phonetic focus marking at an earlier age than Korean-speaking children.

On the other hand, children may need a similar amount of time to establish the form-function mapping between prosodic variation and focus in the input, and to develop sufficient control of prosodic parameters in production, regardless of their native language. In view of these considerations, we make the following hypothesis and prediction:

Hypothesis Ⅱ (b): Phonetic use of prosody is equally demanding for children speaking different languages.

Prediction: Mandarin-speaking and Korean-speaking children should acquire phonetic focus marking at a similar age.

To test Hypotheses Ⅱ (a) and Ⅱ (b) and their corresponding predictions, we compare the acquisition of phonetic focus marking in Mandarin (Chapter 3 of this dissertation) to that in Korean (see Chapter 6 of this dissertation), and to that in previously studied West Germanic languages (see Chapter 7 for a cross-linguistic comparison).

1.7 Dissertation outline

The studies on prosodic focus marking in Mandarin-speaking and Korean-speaking children and adult controls are reported in the following five chapters.

Chapter 2 is concerned with Mandarin-speaking adults' use of prosody for focus-marking purposes in semi-spontaneous speech. The purpose of this chapter is to depict the target form of prosodic focus marking that Mandarin-speaking children are supposed to acquire.

Chapter 3 reports how Mandarin-speaking children acquire prosodic focus marking. We will show Mandarin-speaking children's developmental path to adult-like prosodic focus marking on the basis of a cross-sectional study of four- to five-year-olds, seven- to eight-year-olds and ten- to eleven-year-olds.

Chapter 4 discusses how Korean-speaking adults use phonological focus-marking cue of phrasing, as well as duration- and pitch-related phonetic cues for focus-marking purposes in semi-spontaneous speech. The purpose of this chapter is to depict the target form of prosodic focus marking that Korean-speaking children are supposed to acquire.

Chapter 5 and Chapter 6 address how Korean-speaking children use phrasing (Chapter 5) and phonetic cues (Chapter 6) for focus-marking purposes. We will show Korean-speaking children's acquisition of phonological and phonetic focus marking on the basis of a cross-sectional study on four- to five-year-olds, seven- to eight-year-olds and ten- to eleven-year-olds.

Finally, in Chapter 7, we summarise the main findings, and revisit the hypotheses, predictions, and research questions put forward in Chapter 1 by discussing how cross-linguistic differences in the prosodic system and prosodic focus marking affect acquisition of prosodic focus marking in Mandarin and Korean, and suggest directions for future studies.

This dissertation is presented in the form of a series of self-contained articles. This approach has inevitably resulted in some overlap in the sections on the literature reviews and method in chapters 2, 3, 4 and 5. For the sake of completeness and the readability of the individual chapters, we have decided to keep the repeated information in the text. Details on the publishing status are provided for each chapter separately in a footnote.

CHAPTER 2

Prosodic realisation of focus in Mandarin Chinese①

Abstract

This study examines how speakers of Mandarin Chinese vary prosody for focus-marking purposes. Semi-spontaneous productions of short sentences were elicited via a picture-matching task. Narrow focus was realised with a longer duration and larger pitch span than non-focus, as found in read speech. Narrow focus was also realised with a longer duration and a slightly wider pitch span than broad focus, but the pitch span difference was much smaller in our study than in previous studies on read speech. Narrow focus was not distinguished from contrastive focus, different from findings on read speech. Hence, while narrow focus and non-focus are clearly prosodically distinguished, the prosodic differences between different focus types are more pronounced in read speech than in semi-spontaneous speech in Mandarin Chinese.

Keywords

Focus, prosody, semi-spontaneous speech, Mandarin Chinese

2.1 Introduction

When delivering information to listeners, speakers usually make the information that

① Preliminary results of a portion of the data from Chapter 2 were presented at the 4th International Symposium on Tonal Aspects of Languages (TAL), and published in the proceedings (Yang & Chen, 2014a). A version of Chapter 2 is aimed to be submitted in article form to an appropriate journal.

is new to listeners more prominent in their speech than the information that is known (i.e., *given*) to listeners. The new information is generally referred to as *focus* or *comment*, and the given information as *topic* or *(back)ground* (Vallduvi & Engdahl, 1996). The size of the focal constituent can range from one word (narrow focus) to larger constituents (broad focus), including the whole sentence. Focus can also contain contrastive information, e.g., a correction to a certain piece of information introduced previously or an alternative to what has been mentioned already (Gussenhoven, 2004, 2007). Contrastive focus is typically narrow in terms of the size of the constituent. In both theoretical discussions and experimental studies of focus, question-answer pairs are often used to determine what is the focus and what is not the focus (or: what is the topic) in a sentence (Roberts, 2012). For example, a *who*-question (e.g., *Who bought the villa?*) renders the subject focal but the object non-focal or topical in an SVO response (e.g., *The Johnsons bought the villa.*). A *what*-question has the opposite effect (e.g., *What did the Johnsons buy?*). A what-happens question puts the whole sentence in focus. Contrastive focus can be determined by the presence of a limited number of alternatives (e.g., *The Johnsons bought the villa, not the farmhouse.*)

Prosody is a commonly used linguistic device for focus marking in many languages (Gussenhoven, 2007; Vallduvi & Engdahl, 1996). The interface between prosody and focus in adults' speech has been widely discussed in the literature on information structure and prosody. Generally, in languages that use prosody for focus-marking purposes, a word is realised with more prosodic prominence in narrow focus and contrastive focus than when not focused or in broad focus. Contrast may lead to additional prosodic prominence compared to narrow focus. But there are notable differences between languages in the precise realisation of prosodic prominence. Some languages (e.g., English, German, Dutch, Swedish, and Korean) mark focus primarily by making coarse-grained changes in pitch and duration which cause changes in the perceived phonological category, such as by accentuation (i.e., accenting or not accenting a word) in English, Dutch, and German (Baumann, Grice & Steindamm, 2006; A. Chen, 2009, 2011a; Gussenhoven, 2004, 2007; Hanssen, Peters & Gussenhoven, 2008), or by assigning or not assigning a prominence-marking high tone to a word in Swedish (Bruce, 2007; Romøren, 2016), or by prosodic phrasing (i.e., grouping or not grouping words into prosodic phrases) in Korean and Japanese (Jun, 1993; Jun & Lee, 1998). We define these means of focus marking as *phonological focus marking*, following A. Chen (2011a). In addition, speakers of (at least some of) the above mentioned languages also make fine-grained gradient changes in prosodic parameters within a phonological category when phonological means do not suffice in distinguishing focus conditions. For example, in Dutch, in which both focused and non-focused sentence-initial words are frequently realised with a H*L pitch accent (i.e., a falling accent with the fall beginning in the stressed syllable), focused words are realised with a longer duration and lower minimum pitch than non-focused words (A. Chen, 2009). We define the gradient changes in prosodic parameters for focus marking as *phonetic focus marking*, following A. Chen (2011a). In contrast to the aforementioned languages, some other languages mark focus via only phonetic means. Mandarin Chinese (hereafter Mandarin) is a case in point regarding the latter group of languages.

Several studies have examined prosodic realisation of focus in Mandarin in read speech. It has been found that a word in narrow focus is realised with an expanded pitch span, caused by an increase in maximum pitch and/or a decrease in minimum pitch, longer duration, and higher or similar intensity, compared to the same word in a baseline condition, which is operationalised as different conditions in different studies, e.g. a "plain statement", i.e. arguably similar to broad focus over the whole sentence (Shih, 1988), "neutral focus", i.e. broad focus over a whole sentence (Xu, S. W. Chen & Wang, 2012) or over the verb phrase in a SVO sentence (Xu, 1999), and post-focus and pre-focus (Xu, 1999, Y. Chen & Braun, 2006). Broad focus is similar to pre-focus in pitch, but is more prominent than post-focus in pitch span and pitch level (Xu, 1999). Contrastive focus is more prominent than non-focus in pitch span, maximum pitch and duration (Y. Chen & Gussenhoven, 2008), and is also more prominent than narrow focus in pitch span and maximum pitch when the focal words are with certain tonal combinations in read speech (Y. Chen & Braun, 2006).

While the studies on read speech in Mandarin are important in putting forward a first picture of prosodic focus marking in this language, it is premature to conclude that they have depicted the complete picture for two reasons. First, it has been reported for languages, such as English and German, that the use of accentuation and the choice of accent type in spontaneous speech are different from that in read speech (Bard & Aylett, 1999; De Ruiter, 2010). The question arises as to whether prosodic focus marking in (semi-)spontaneous speech differs from that in read speech in languages that only use phonetic means to mark focus. There is initial evidence suggesting that there may be such a difference in Mandarin. For example, Greif (2010) found no evidence that the focal word in contrastive focus was realised with more prosodic prominence than the same word in narrow focus, different from the finding on read speech reported by Y. Chen and Braun (2006). Second, in previous work most authors have assumed that broad focus is a "neutral" condition and comparing the words in narrow focus to the same words in broad focus can show how focus is realised. Because every word in a phrase or a sentence in broad focus is focal, comparing narrow focus to broad focus will only show the prosodic differences between the two types of focus, differing in the size of the focal constituent, instead of how being focal changes the prosody in a word.

To circumvent these limitations in earlier work and shed new light on prosodic focus marking in Mandarin, we elicited semi-spontaneous production of SVO sentences in different focus conditions in an interactive setting and addressed the effect of being focal on prosody and prosodic differences between different types of focus as two separate questions in a large-scale project on prosodic focus marking in children and adults across languages. The present study is concerned with the production of the adult speakers.

2.2 Method

2.2.1 Participants

Twelve adult native speakers of Mandarin (six females and six males, average age 19) participated in this study (See Appendix A for more participant information). They were undergraduates from Beijing Forestry University at the time of testing. All participants spoke Mandarin without any detectable regional accent.

2.2.2 The picture-matching task

We adapted the picture-matching task used in A. Chen (2011a) to elicit semi-spontaneous production. In this task, the participant's role was to help the experimenter put pictures in matched pairs. Three piles of pictures were used. The experimenter and the participant each held a pile of pictures. The third pile lay on the table in a seemingly messy fashion. The experimenter's pictures always missed some information (e.g., the subject, the action, the object, or all three). The participant's pictures always contained all three pieces of information. On each trial, the experimenter showed a picture of hers (e.g., sample picture (a) in Figure 2-1) to the participant, described the picture and asked a question about it or made a remark about the missing information (in the contrastive focus condition). The participant then took a look at the corresponding picture (e.g., sample picture

(b) in Figure 2-1) in his/her pile and responded to the experimenter's question or remark. The experimenter then looked for the right picture (e.g., sample picture (c) in Figure 2-1) in the messy pile and matched it with her own picture to form a pair.

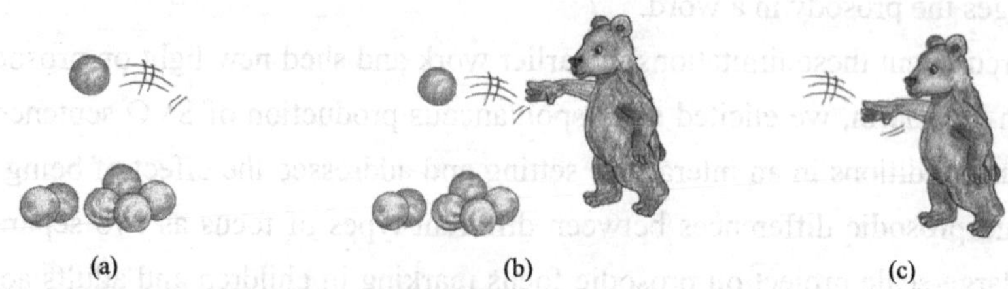

Figure 2-1 Sample pictures for a trial eliciting narrow focus on the sentence-initial word
Picture (a) was the experimenter's picture with the subject missing; picture (b) was the participant's picture containing all the information; and picture (c) contained the information missing from picture (a).

As rules of the task, the participant was asked to answer the experimenter's questions in full sentences and not to reveal his/her pictures to the experimenter. In order to make sure that the experiment was conducted in the same way for all participants, and that adequate background information was equally provided for each trial before a question was asked or a remark was made, scripts containing all words that the experimenters were supposed to say in the experimental sessions were constructed. The experimenters were instructed to follow the scripts closely but were encouraged to make spontaneous remarks that did not affect the information structure of the participants' responses for the purpose of facilitating the conversation. Prior to the picture-matching task, a picture-naming task was conducted to ensure that the participants would use the intended words to refer to the entities in the pictures. This procedure also rendered the entities in the pictures referentially accessible.

2.2.3 Experimental materials

One-hundred and sixty question-answer dialogues were embedded in the experiment to elicit 160 SVO sentences in 5 focus conditions: narrow focus on the subject noun in sentence-initial position (NF-i), responding to *who*-questions; narrow focus on the object noun in sentence-final position (NF-f), responding to *what*-questions; narrow focus on the verb in sentence-medial position (NF-m), responding to *what-does*-X-*do-to*-Y questions; contrastive focus in sentence-medial position (CF-m), correcting the experimenter's remark about the action; broad focus over the whole sentence (BF), responding to *what-happens* questions, as illustrated in (1)[①]. Including narrow focus in three sentence-positions made it possible to study the effect of narrow focus on the sentence-medial target words (NF-m) compared to the same words in pre-focus (or NF-f) and in post-focus (or NF-i). Comparing the target words in NF-m, CF-m and BF allowed us to study the prosodic difference between different focus types.

(1) Examples of question-answer dialogues between the experimenter (E) and participant (P):

(NF-i) E: 看！球。球在空中。看起来有小动物扔球。谁扔球？
Look! The ball, and the ball is in the air. It looks like someone throws the ball. Who throws the ball?
P: [小熊] 扔 球。
[xiao3 xiong2] reng1 qiu2.
[The little bear] throws the ball.

(NF-f) E: 看！小猫，小猫的胳膊伸出去了。看起来小猫扔东西。小猫扔什么？
Look! The little cat, and it stretches out its arm. It looks like the little cat throws something. What does the little cat throw?
P: 小猫 扔 [笔]。
xiao3 mao1 reng1 [bi3].
The little cat throws [the pen].

(NF-m) E: 看！小兔，还有书。看起来小兔要弄书。小兔怎么弄书？
Look! The little rabbit, and the book. It looks like the little rabbit does something to the book. What does the little rabbit do to the book?
P: 小兔 [扔] 书。
xiao3 tu4 [reng1] shu1.
The little rabbit [throws] the book.

① In the examples the digits represent tones, and the referents are referred to with the definite article in the English glossary because they had been introduced in the picture-naming task.

(CF-m) E: 看！小熊，还有菜。看起来小熊要弄菜。我猜：小熊[埋]菜。
Look! The little bear, and the vegetables. It looks like the little bear will do something to the vegetables. I will make a guess: The little bear [buries] the vegetables.
P: 小熊 [扔] 菜。
xiao3 xiong2 [reng1] cai4.
The little bear [throws] the vegetables.

(BF) E: 看！我的图片是模糊的。什么都看不清。你的图片上讲了什么？
Look! My picture is very blurry. I cannot see anything clearly. What happens in your picture?
P: [小狗 扔 菜]。
[xiao3 gou3 reng1 cai4].
[The little dog throws the vegetables].

The SVO sentences were unique combinations of four disyllabic subject-noun phrases starting with the word "xiao3 (little)" (one noun phrase per lexical tone regarding the second word in each phrase), eight monosyllabic verbs (one verb per lexical tone per group), and eight monosyllabic object-nouns (one noun per lexical tone per group), as shown in Table 2-1. Each group-1 verb was combined once with each group-1 object-noun and each group-2 verb was combined once with each group-2 object-noun, leading to one-hundred and sixty verb phrases (4 tones in verbs × 4 tones in objects × 2 groups of verbs and object-nouns × 5 focus conditions = 160 VPs). The subject-nouns were then approximately evenly distributed over the verb phrases, forming one-hundred and sixty SVO sentences (Appendix B). This procedure made sure that in each focus condition, each tone in the verbs was combined with each tone in the preceding subject-noun and with each tone in the following object-noun.

Table 2-1 Words that occurred in the SVO sentences

	Tone 1	Tone 2	Tone 3	Tone 4
Subject nouns	小猫 xiao3 mao1 "little cat"	小熊 xiao3 xiong2 "little bear"	小狗 xiao3 gou3 "little dog"	小兔 xiao3 tu4 "little rabbit"

Continued

	Tone 1	Tone 2	Tone 3	Tone 4
Group-1 verbs	扔 reng1 "throw"	埋 mai2 "bury"	剪 jian3 "cut"	运 yun4 "transport"
Group-2 verbs	浇 jiao1 "water"	闻 wen2 "smell"	舔 tian3 "lick"	卖 mai4 "sell"
Group-1 objects	书 shu1 "book"	球 qiu2 "ball"	笔 bi3 "pen"	菜 cai4 "Vegetable"
Group-2 objects	花 hua1 "flower"	梨 li2 "pear"	草 cao3 "grass"	树 shu4 "tree"

The one-hundred and sixty sentences were then split evenly into two lists (List 1 and List 2) of eighty sentences. Each list contained all verb-object tonal combinations but not all verb-object word combinations. The trials on each list were randomized in a way that trials from the same focus condition did not appear after each other and the focused constituent of a trial was not mentioned on its preceding trial. Half of the participants produced the sentences on List 1 and the other half produced the sentences on List 2.

2.2.4 Experimental procedure

The participants were tested individually in quiet rooms. Four female native speakers administered the experiment after having received intensive training on how to conduct the experiment. Two experimental sessions — one eliciting forty sentences with the group-1 words and the other eliciting forty sentences with the group-2 words — were held on the same day for each participant but with a break in between. Each session lasted about 20 minutes and was both audio and video recorded. Audio recordings were made at a sampling rate of 44.1 kHz with 16 bits using ZOOM H1 recorders. Video recordings were made for training purposes. The participants were informed that the task was of a simple nature because it would also be played with children in separate studies.

2.2.5 Prosodic annotation

The audio recording from each participant was first orthographically annotated in

Praat (Boersma & Weenink, 2013). Then usable sentences were selected for phonetic annotation, and the unusable ones were excluded from further analysis (8%). A target sentence was considered unusable in any of the following cases. First, the participant produced the target sentence before the experimenter asked the question, or the experimenter asked an incorrect question, or the experimenter did not provide an adequate description of the picture before she asked a question. Second, the sentence was produced with strong background noise. Third, the sentence was produced with word insertion, deletion, or replacement. Fourth, the sentence was produced with self-repair or clearly perceivable hesitation.

We were especially interested in whether pitch span and word duration were varied for focus-marking purposes. If pitch span was expanded in certain focus conditions, we wanted to know how the expansion was achieved, namely, by raising the maximum pitch (hereafter the pitch-max), or by lowering the minimum pitch (hereafter the pitch-min), or by varying both. We thus annotated the target words in the usable sentences for word boundaries, pitch-max and pitch-min. Word segmentation was done on the basis of formant intensity, formant contours, waveforms, and auditory perception (Machač & Skarnitzl, 2009; Turk, Nakai & Sugahara, 2006). In the annotation of the pitch-max and pitch-min, care was taken not to confuse local pitch fluctuations with linguistically relevant variation in pitch (e.g., pitch variation due to lexical tone or focus marking). The tonal targets of the lexical tones and the influence from the preceding tone were taken into account when determining the location of pitch-max and pitch-min (Xu, 1997; Xu & Wang, 2001), as illustrated in Figure 2-2. Specifically, Tone 1 is a high level tone and often appears as a slightly rising pitch contour and occasionally as a slightly falling pitch contour sentence-medially. We labelled the pitch-max after the pitch-min in the case of a rising Tone 1 syllable but before the pitch-min in the case of a falling Tone 1 syllable. Tone 2 is a rising tone but appears as a fall-rise contour sentence-medially. The falling part is largely influenced by the preceding tone, and the rising part is taken to contain the tonal targets of Tone 2. We labelled the pitch-max after the pitch-min in the rising part of a Tone 2 syllable. Similarly, Tone 4 is a falling tone but appears as a rise-fall contour sentence-medially. The rising part is subjected to the influence of the preceding tone, and the falling part contains the tonal targets of Tone 4. We labelled the pitch-max of a Tone 4 syllable before the pitch-min in the falling part of a Tone 4 syllable. Tone 3 is a fall-rise tone when produced in isolation or sentence-finally but is realised as a falling pitch contour when followed by Tone 1, Tone 2 or Tone 4 and as a rising contour when followed by another Tone 3. We labelled the pitch-max before the pitch-min in the case of falling Tone 3 but after the pitch-min in the case of rising Tone 3. A small number of trials that were affected by background noise and non-model voice quality (e.g., creakiness) were excluded from pitch annotation.

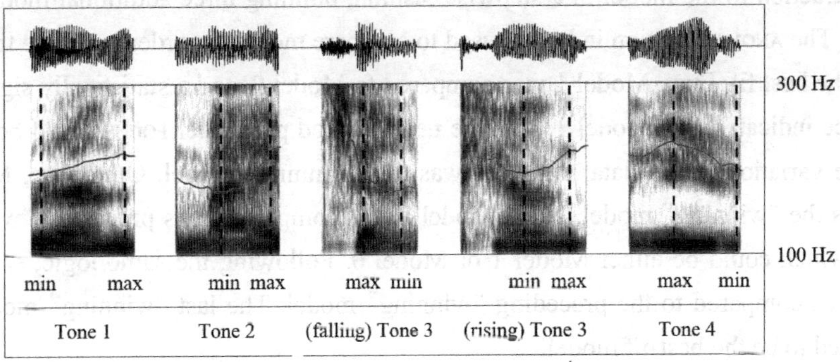

Figure 2-2 Pitch annotation for the four tones. (The four tones were produced by a female speaker in the pre-focus condition. The five words were "reng1 (throw)", "mai2 (bury)", "jian3 (cut)", "tian3 (lick)" and "yun4 (transport)" from the left to the right.)

2.3 Statistical analysis and results

As mentioned earlier, the target words in our analysis were the sentence-medial verbs, which were focal in the NF-m, CF-m and BF conditions and non-focal in the NF-i (or post-focal) and NF-f conditions (or pre-focal). We analysed the effect of focus (narrow focus vs. non-focus) and the differences between focus types differing in size (narrow focus vs. broad focus) and in contrastivity (narrow focus vs. contrastive focus).

Mixed-effects modelling in the programme R with the lme4 package (Bates, Maechler, Bolker, & Walker, 2014) was used to assess the data. The dependent variables were duration, pitch span, pitch-max, and pitch-min of the target words. The independent variables (or fixed factors) were FOCUS and TONE. FOCUS referred to the focus conditions. For each analysis, we compared two or three focus conditions in order to address a specific research question. FOCUS thus had two levels in the models concerning focus effect (narrow focus vs. pre-focus/post-focus) and three levels in the models concerning focus types (narrow focus vs. broad focus vs. contrastive focus). TONE referred to the tones of the target words, and it had four levels (Tone 1, 2, 3, and 4). In addition, two random factors, SPEAKER (i.e., the participants) and SENTENCE (i.e., the target sentences), were included in the analysis.

To find out whether a particular prosodic cue was used to distinguish focus conditions, models were built using the aforementioned factors. Starting from an "empty" model (hereafter Model 0) containing only the random factors, we added FOCUS, TONE and their interaction to the model in a stepwise fashion, building three additional models (Table 2-2). The ANOVA function in R was used to compare models in order to derive the model with the best fit. First, Model 1 was compared to Model 0, and a statistically significant difference indicated that Model 1 with the newly added parameter FOCUS could better explain the variation in the data, and thus was the "winning" model. Otherwise, Model 0 stayed as the "winning" model. Next, Model 2 was compared to its preceding "winning" model, which could be either Model 1 or Model 0. Following the same logic, each later model was compared to the preceding "winning" model. The last "winning" model was considered to be the best-fit model.

Table 2-2　Model build-up procedure

Model	Factor added
Model 0	
Model 1	FOCUS
Model 2	TONE
Model 3	FOCUS : TONE

For each analysis, we report on the best-fit model, according to the model comparisons, and statistical significance of main effects and the interaction, according to the summary of the best-fit model. If the best-fit model contained a significant interaction of FOCUS and TONE, we further discuss how the speakers distinguished the two focus conditions in each tonal category by examining the effect of focus in each tonal category separately. We will not discuss in detail the main effect of TONE, because it is not directly relevant to our research aim. We will also not discuss in detail the main effect of FOCUS when the interaction between FOCUS and TONE proved to be significant.

2.3.1 Realisation of narrow focus

2.3.1.1 Narrow focus vs. pre-focus (NF-m vs. NF-f)

WORD DURATION. The best-fit model for this dependent variable was Model 1 (Table 2-3). The summary of this model (Table 2-4) showed that the main effect of FOCUS was significant, but there was no significant main effect of TONE or significant interaction between FOCUS and TONE, indicating that the words were longer in narrow focus than in pre-focus (19 ms longer, $P < 0.001$), regardless of tone (Figure 2-3).

Table 2-3 Model comparisons regarding the dependent variable word duration in the comparison narrow focus vs. pre-focus

Model comparisons	*Pr*(>Chisq)
0 vs. 1 (adding FOCUS)	0.000***
1 vs. 2 (adding TONE)	0.615
1 vs. 3 (adding FOCUS : TONE)	0.895

Table 2-4 Model summary regarding the dependent variable word duration in the comparison narrow focus vs. pre-focus

Factor	Estimate	Std. Error	*t* value	*Pr*(>|*t*|)
Intercept (Narrow focus)	0.222	0.005	40.939	0.000***
Pre-focus	−0.019	0.005	−3.995	0.000***

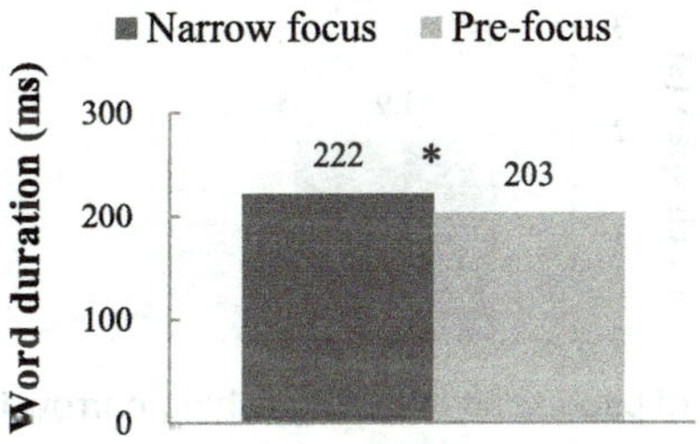

Figure 2-3 The use of word duration in distinguishing narrow focus from pre-focus

PITCH SPAN. The best-fit model for this dependent variable was Model 2 (Table 2-5). The summary of this model (Table 2-6) showed that the main effects of FOCUS and TONE were significant, but there was no significant interaction between FOCUS and TONE, indicating that the pitch span of words was significantly wider in narrow focus than in pre-focus (0.8 st wider, $P < 0.001$), regardless of tone (Figure 2-4).

Table 2-5 Model comparisons regarding the dependent variable pitch span in the comparison narrow focus vs. pre-focus

Model comparisons	*Pr*(>Chisq)
0 vs. 1 (adding FOCUS)	0.014*

Continued

Model comparisons	*Pr*(>Chisq)
1 vs. 2 (adding TONE)	0.000***
2 vs. 3 (adding FOCUS : TONE)	0.303

Table 2-6 Model summary regarding the dependent variable pitch span in the comparison narrow focus vs. pre-focus

Factor	Estimate	Std. Error	*t* value	*Pr*(>|*t*|)
Intercept (Narrow focus. T1)	1.920	0.245	7.838	0.000***
Pre-focus	−0.753	0.201	−3.752	0.000***
T2	0.734	0.276	2.657	0.010*
T3	2.221	0.290	7.647	0.000***
T4	1.721	0.277	6.209	0.000***

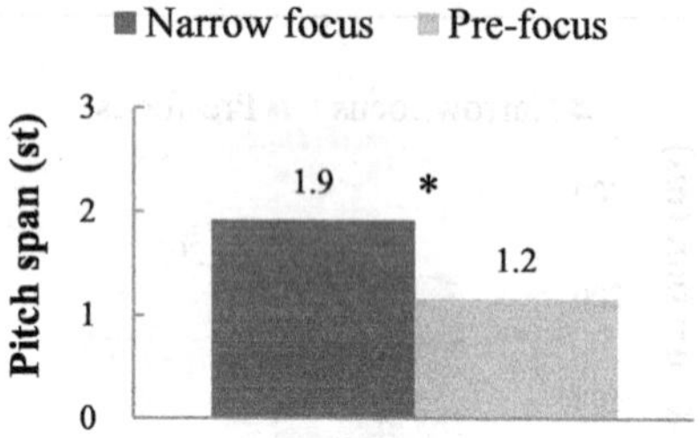

Figure 2-4 The use of pitch span in distinguishing narrow focus from pre-focus

PITCH-MAX. The best-fit model for this dependent variable was Model 2 (Table 2-7). The summary of this model (Table 2-8) showed that the main effect of FOCUS was not significant, and it did not have a significant interaction with TONE. There was thus no evidence that the speakers varied pitch-max to distinguish focus from pre-focus.

Table 2-7 Model comparisons regarding the dependent variable pitch-max in the comparison narrow focus vs. pre-focus

Model comparisons	*Pr*(>Chisq)
0 vs. 1 (adding FOCUS)	0.473
1 vs. 2 (adding TONE)	0.000***
2 vs. 3 (adding FOCUS : TONE)	0.300

Table 2-8 Model summary regarding the dependent variable pitch-max in the comparison narrow focus vs. pre-focus

Factor	Estimate	Std. Error	*t* value	*Pr*(>|*t*|)
Intercept (Narrow focus. T1)	90.432	1.731	52.248	0.000***
Pre-focus	-0.235	0.186	-1.264	0.211
T2	-2.245	0.261	-8.606	0.000***
T3	-1.780	0.265	-6.713	0.000***
T4	0.214	0.261	0.819	0.416

PITCH-MIN. The best-fit model for this dependent variable was Model 2 (Table 2-9). The summary of this model (Table 2-10) showed that the main effects of FOCUS and TONE were significant, but there was no significant interaction of FOCUS and TONE, indicating that the pitch-min of words was lower in narrow focus than in pre-focus (0.5 st lower, $P < 0.05$), regardless of tone (Figure 2-5).

Table 2-9 Model comparisons regarding the dependent variable pitch-min in the comparison narrow focus vs. pre-focus

Model comparisons	*Pr*(>Chisq)
0 vs. 1 (adding FOCUS)	0.301
1 vs. 2 (adding TONE)	0.000***
2 vs. 3 (adding FOCUS : TONE)	0.461

Table 2-10 Model summary regarding the dependent variable pitch-min in the comparison narrow focus vs. pre-focus

Factor	Estimate	Std. Error	*t* value	*Pr*(>|*t*|)
Intercept (Narrow focus. T1)	88.535	1.748	50.665	0.000***
Pre-focus	0.476	0.222	2.148	0.036*
T2	-2.991	0.308	-9.708	0.000***
T3	-4.192	0.317	-13.215	0.000***
T4	-1.532	0.309	-4.966	0.000***

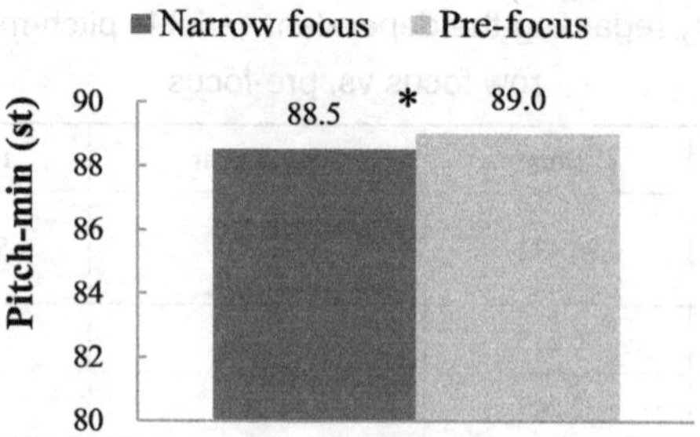

Figure 2-5 The use of pitch-min in distinguishing narrow focus from pre-focus

INTERIM SUMMARY. The speakers used a longer duration and a wider pitch span for words in narrow focus than in pre-focus. The difference in pitch span between the two focus conditions was mainly caused by the lowering of pitch-min in narrow focus.

2.3.1.2 Narrow focus vs. post-focus (NF-m vs. NF-i)

WORD DURATION. The best-fit model for this dependent variable was Model 1 (Table 2-11). The summary of this model (Table 2-12) showed the main effect of FOCUS was significant, but there was no significant main effect of TONE or significant interaction between FOCUS and TONE, indicating that the words were longer in narrow focus than in post-focus (22 ms longer, $P < 0.001$), regardless of tone (Figure 2-6).

Table 2-11 Model comparisons regarding the dependent variable word duration in the comparison narrow focus vs. post-focus

Model comparisons	*Pr*(>Chisq)
0 vs. 1 (adding FOCUS)	0.000***
1 vs. 2 (adding TONE)	0.869
1 vs. 3 (adding FOCUS : TONE)	0.936

Table 2-12 Model summary regarding the dependent variable word duration in the comparison narrow focus vs. post-focus

Factor	Estimate	Std. Error	*t* value	*Pr*(>|*t*|)
Intercept (Narrow focus)	0.222	0.005	45.719	0.000***
Post-focus	−0.022	0.005	−4.706	0.000***

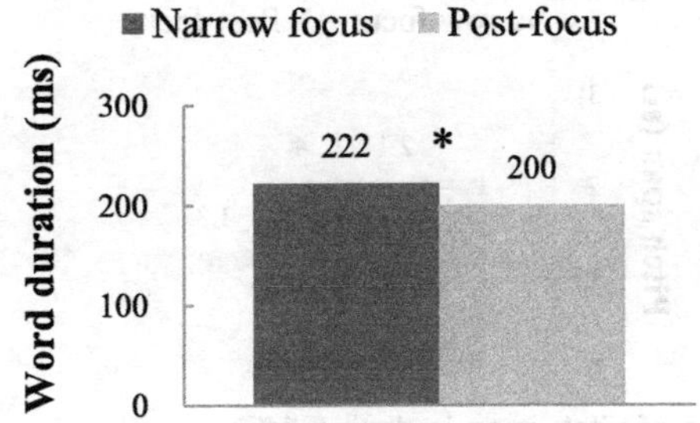

Figure 2-6 The use of word duration in distinguishing narrow focus from post-focus

PITCH SPAN. The best-fit model for this dependent variable was Model 2 (Table 2-13). The summary of this model (Table 2-14) showed that the main effects of FOCUS and tone were significant, but there was no significant interaction between FOCUS and TONE, indicating that the pitch span of words was significantly wider in narrow focus than in post-focus (0.8 st wider, $P < 0.001$), regardless of tone (Figure 2-7).

Table 2-13 Model comparisons regarding the dependent variable pitch span in the comparison narrow focus vs. post-focus

Model comparisons	*Pr*(>Chisq)
0 vs. 1 (adding FOCUS)	0.025*
1 vs. 2 (adding TONE)	0.000***
2 vs. 3 (adding FOCUS : TONE)	0.161

Table 2-14 Model summary regarding the dependent variable pitch span in the comparison narrow focus vs. post-focus

Factor	Estimate	Std. Error	*t* value	*Pr*(>|*t*|)
Intercept (Narrow focus. T1)	2.084	0.284	7.347	0.000***
Post-focus	−0.758	0.233	−3.261	0.002**
T2	0.233	0.323	0.722	0.473
T3	2.149	0.335	6.420	0.000***
T4	1.723	0.321	5.372	0.000***

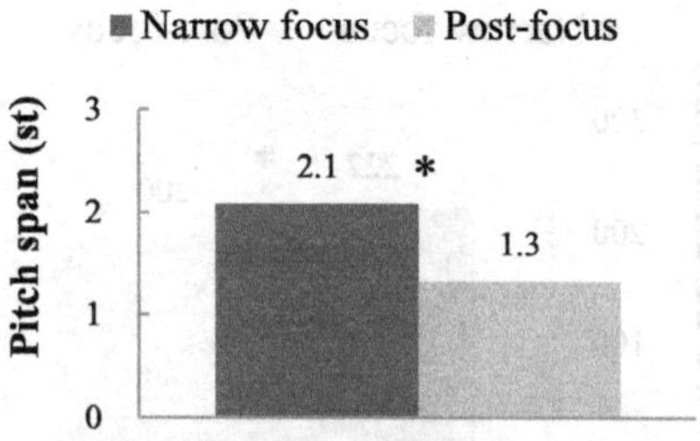

Figure 2-7 The use of pitch span in distinguishing narrow focus from post-focus

PITCH-MAX. The best-fit model for this dependent variable was Model 2 (Table 2-15). The summary of this model (Table 2-16) showed that the main effects of FOCUS and TONE were significant, but there was no significant interaction of FOCUS and TONE, indicating that the pitch-max of words was higher in narrow focus than in post-focus (1.1 st higher, $P < 0.001$), regardless of tone (Figure 2-8).

Table 2-15 Model comparisons regarding the dependent variable pitch-max in the comparison narrow focus vs. post-focus

Model comparisons	Pr(>Chisq)
0 vs. 1 (adding FOCUS)	0.004**
1 vs. 2 (adding TONE)	0.000***
2 vs. 3 (adding FOCUS : TONE)	0.184

Table 2-16 Model summary regarding the dependent variable pitch-max in the comparison narrow focus vs. post-focus

Factor	Estimate	Std. Error	*t* value	Pr(>|*t*|)
Intercept (Narrow focus. T1)	90.355	1.773	50.963	0.000***
Post-focus	-1.089	0.209	-5.214	0.000***
T2	-2.433	0.294	-8.288	0.000***
T3	-1.503	0.297	-5.062	0.000***
T4	0.414	0.292	1.420	0.161

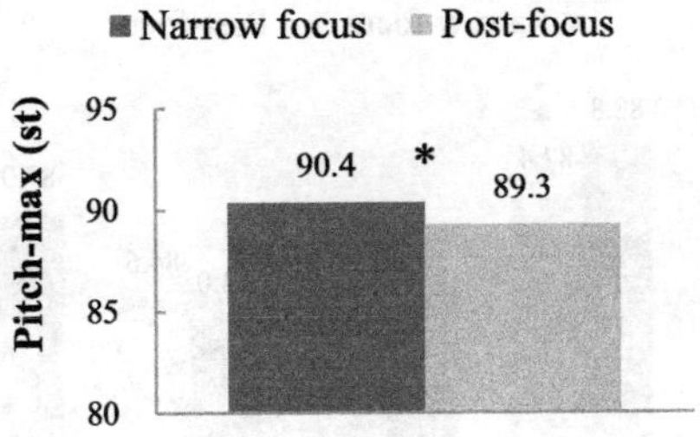

Figure 2-8 The use of pitch-max in distinguishing narrow focus from post-focus

PITCH-MIN. The best-fit model for this dependent variable was Model 3 (Table 2-17). The summary of this model (Table 2-18) showed that the main effects of FOCUS and TONE and the interaction of FOCUS and TONE were all significant. Subsequent analyses on each tonal category showed that the pitch-min of words was lower in narrow focus than in post-focus when the words were in Tone 1 (1.3 st lower in narrow focus, $P < 0.05$), but not in Tone 2 (0.1 st higher in narrow focus, $P > 0.05$), Tone 3 (0.6 st higher in narrow focus, $P > 0.05$), or Tone 4 (0.4 st lower in narrow focus, $P > 0.05$) (Figure 2-9).

Table 2-17 Model comparisons regarding the dependent variable pitch-min in the comparison narrow focus vs. post-focus

Model comparisons	*Pr*(>Chisq)
0 vs. 1 (adding FOCUS)	0.503
1 vs. 2 (adding TONE)	0.000***
2 vs. 3 (adding FOCUS : TONE)	0.020

Table 2-18 Model summary regarding the dependent variable pitch-min in the comparison narrow focus vs. post-focus

Factor	Estimate	Std. Error	*t* value	*Pr*(>|*t*|)
Intercept (Narrow focus. T1)	88.770	1.812	49.003	0.000***
Post-focus	−1.348	0.423	-3.187	0.002**
T2	-3.347	0.428	-7.812	0.000***
T3	−4.723	0.445	10.608	0.000***
T4	−1.767	0.427	-4.140	0.000***
Post-focus : T2	1.449	0.607	2.387	0.020*
Post-focus : T3	1.914	0.625	3.064	0.003**
Post-focus : T4	0.923	0.603	1.531	0.131

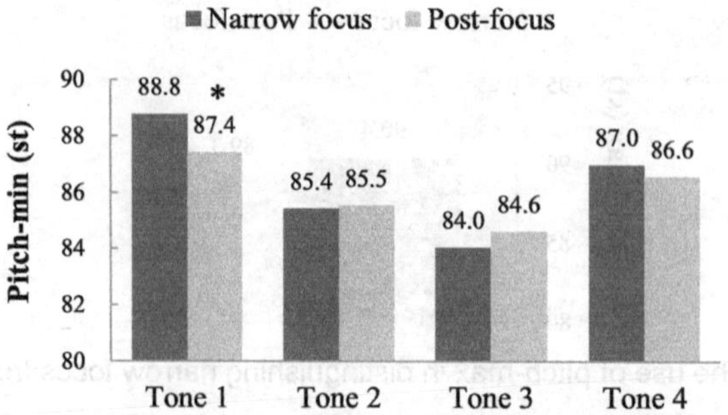

Figure 2-9 The use of pitch-min in distinguishing narrow focus from post-focus in each tone

INTERIM SUMMARY. The speakers used a longer duration and a wider pitch span for words in narrow focus than in post-focus. The difference in pitch span between the two focus conditions was mainly caused by the rising of pitch-max in narrow focus. The Tone 1 words were produced with both a higher pitch-max and a higher pitch-min, that is, a higher overall pitch level, in narrow focus than in post-focus.

2.3.2 Realisation of focus types (Narrow focus vs. broad focus vs. contrastive focus)

WORD DURATION. The best-fit model for this dependent variable was Model 1 (Table 2-19). The summary of this model (Table 2-20) showed that the main effect of FOCUS was significant, but there was no significant main effect of TONE or significant interaction of FOCUS and TONE. The words were longer in narrow focus than in broad focus (13 ms longer, $P < 0.05$), regardless of tone; narrow focus and contrastive focus were not distinguished via word duration (Figure 2-10).

Table 2-19 Model comparisons regarding the dependent variable word duration in the comparison narrow focus vs. broad focus vs. contrastive focus

Model comparisons	*Pr*(>Chisq)
0 vs. 1 (adding FOCUS)	0.025
1 vs. 2 (adding TONE)	0.479
1 vs. 3 (adding focus : TONE)	0.836

Table 2-20 Model summary regarding the dependent variable word duration in the comparison narrow focus vs. broad focus vs. contrastive focus

Factor	Estimate	Std. Error	*t* value	*Pr*(>|*t*|)
Intercept (Narrow focus)	0.222	0.005	43.143	< 2e-16
Broad focus	−0.013	0.005	−2.672	0.009
Contrastive focus	−0.003	0.005	−0.693	0.490

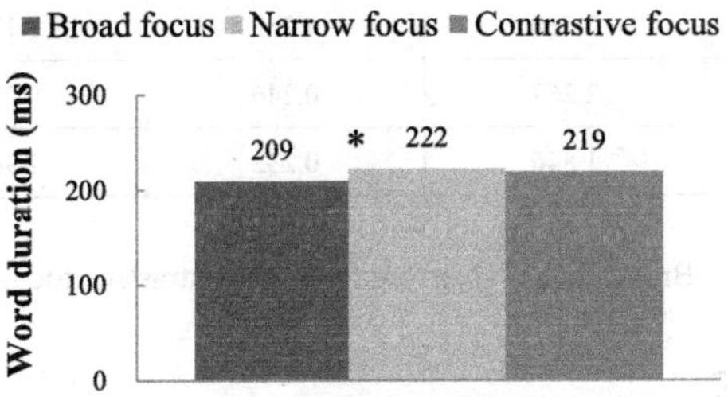

Figure 2-10 The use of word duration in distinguishing narrow focus from broad focus and contrastive focus

PITCH SPAN. The best-fit model for this dependent variable was Model 2 (Table 2-21). The summary of this model (Table 2-22) showed that the main effects of FOCUS and TONE were significant, but there was no significant interaction of FOCUS and TONE. The pitch span of words was wider in narrow focus than in broad focus (0.4 st wider, $P < 0.05$)①, regardless of tone; narrow focus and contrastive focus were not distinguished via pitch span (Figure 2-11).

Table 2-21 Model comparisons regarding the dependent variable pitch span in the comparison narrow focus vs. broad focus vs. contrastive focus

Model comparisons	*Pr*(>Chisq)
0 vs. 1 (adding FOCUS)	0.360
0 vs. 2 (adding TONE)	0.000***
2 vs. 3 (adding FOCUS : TONE)	0.736

① The pitch span difference (0.4st) between narrow focus and broad focus in adults was rather small, and it showed up as an insignificant difference when analysing the adults' data together with the children's in Chapter 3.

Table 2-22 Model summary regarding the dependent variable pitch span in the comparison narrow focus vs. broad focus vs. contrastive focus

Factor	Estimate	Std. Error	*t* value	*Pr*(>|*t*|)
Intercept (Narrow focus. T1)	1.890	0.234	8.070	0.000***
Broad focus	−0.447	0.204	−2.193	0.031*
Contrastive focus	−0.085	0.208	−0.407	0.685
T2	0.730	0.230	3.170	0.002**
T3	2.267	0.246	9.210	0.000***
T4	1.846	0.232	7.969	0.000***

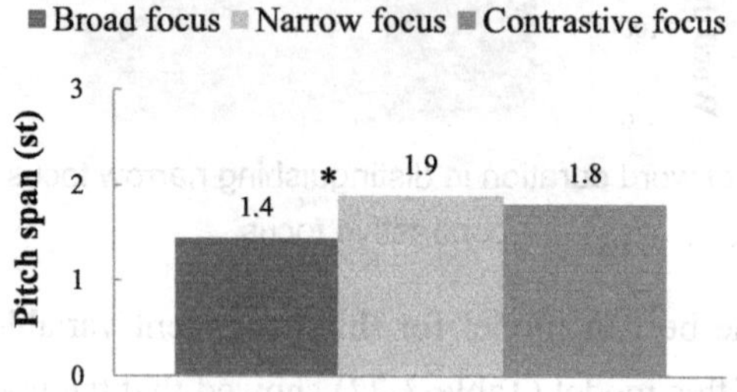

Figure 2-11 The use of pitch span in distinguishing narrow focus from broad focus and contrastive focus

PITCH-MAX. The best-fit model for this dependent variable was Model 2 (Table 2-23). The summary of this model (Table 2-24) showed that the main effect of FOCUS was not significant, and it did not have a significant interaction with TONE. Thus, narrow focus was not distinguished from broad focus or contrastive focus via pitch-max.

Table 2-23 Model comparisons regarding the dependent variable pitch-max in the comparison narrow focus vs. broad focus vs. contrastive focus

Model comparisons	*Pr*(>Chisq)
0 vs. 1 (adding FOCUS)	0.699
0 vs. 2 (adding TONE)	0.000***
2 vs. 3 (adding FOCUS : TONE)	0.942

Table 2-24 Model summary regarding the dependent variable pitch-max in the comparison narrow focus vs. broad focus vs. contrastive focus

Factor	Estimate	Std. Error	*t* value	*Pr*(>|*t*|)
Intercept (Narrow focus. T1)	90.439	1.739	52.006	0.000***
Broad focus	−0.125	0.196	−0.639	0.525
Contrastive focus	−0.312	0.198	−1.572	0.119
T2	−2.430	0.226	−10.767	0.000***
T3	−1.775	0.230	−7.715	0.000***
T4	0.381	0.226	1.686	0.095

PITCH-MIN. The best-fit model for this dependent variable was Model 6 (Table 2-25). The summary of this model (Table 2-26) showed that FOCUS did not have a significant main effect or a significant interaction with TONE. Thus, narrow focus was not distinguished from broad focus or contrastive focus via pitch-min.

Table 2-25 Model comparisons regarding the dependent variable pitch-min in the comparison narrow focus vs. broad focus vs. contrastive focus

Model comparisons	*Pr*(>Chisq)
0 vs. 1 (adding FOCUS)	0.476
0 vs. 2 (adding TONE)	0.000***
2 vs. 3 (adding FOCUS : TONE)	0.908

Table 2-26 Model summary regarding the dependent variable pitch-min in the comparison narrow focus vs. broad focus vs. contrastive focus

Factor	Estimate	Std. Error	*t* value	*Pr*(>|*t*|)
Intercept (Narrow focus. T1)	88.585	1.761	50.311	0.000***
Broad focus	0.303	0.239	1.269	0.207
Contrastive focus	−0.309	0.243	−1.271	0.207
T2	−3.156	0.272	−11.614	0.000***
T3	−4.252	0.284	−14.952	0.000***
T4	−1.506	0.273	−5.522	0.000***

INTERIM SUMMARY. The speakers used a longer duration and a slightly, (yet statistically significantly), wider pitch span for the words in narrow focus than in broad focus. They did not vary word duration, pitch span, pitch-max or pitch-min to distinguish narrow focus from contrastive focus.

2.4 Conclusions

We have shown that in semi-spontaneous speech speakers of Mandarin realised the focused words in narrow focus with a longer duration and wider pitch span than the same words not only in the pre-focus condition but also in the post-focus condition, as reported for read speech (Y. Chen & Braun, 2006; Xu, 1999). The difference in pitch span between words in focus and pre-focus appears to stem from a combined effect of pitch-max rising and pitch-min lowering in the focused words, compared to the same words in the pre-focal condition. The difference in pitch span between focus and post-focus, however, appears to be only related to pitch-max rising in the focused non-Tone 1 words. In Tone 1 words, speakers raise both pitch-max and pitch-min in the focus condition, compared to the post-focus condition, suggesting an increase in pitch register (i.e., overall pitch level) in focal Tone 1 words. Given the limited pitch span of Tone 1 words, it is possible that speakers vary pitch register as an additional focus-marking strategy. Furthermore, we have found that speakers realised the focal words in narrow focus with a longer duration and a slightly wider pitch span than the same words in broad focus, similar to the findings on read speech (Shih, 1988; Xu, 1999). However, the pitch span in our study was varied to a smaller degree (0.4 st, i.e., less than 10 Hz) than in read speech (as much as 66 Hz in Xu, 1999). In addition, we have found no evidence that speakers vary word duration or any of the pitch-related cues to distinguish contrastive focus from narrow focus, similar to the finding on semi-spontaneous speech (Greif, 2010) but different from the findings on read speech (Y. Chen & Braun, 2006).

These results indicate that the realisation of narrow focus in semi-spontaneous speech in our study is similar to the realisation of narrow focus in read speech in previous work on Mandarin. Interestingly, the prosodic differences between focus types are more pronounced in read speech than in semi-spontaneous speech in Mandarin. This is comparable to the sharper prosodic differences between focus conditions in read speech than in (semi-) spontaneous speech in West Germanic languages. For example, in Dutch, focal words are longer than post-focal words in read speech (Cambier-Langeveld, 2000), but not in semi-spontaneous speech (Romøren, 2016). In addition, a study on English read speech has shown that speakers produce contrastive focus with more prosodic prominence than narrow focus if they are made aware that the task is to prosodically distinguishing the two (Breen, Fedorenko, Wagner & Gibson, 2010). Thus, reading sentences repeatedly under explicit instructions in a lab setting may invite speakers to prosodically realise information structural differences that they ordinarily do not realise or realise to a limited degree (Breen, et al., 2010; De Ruiter, 2010; Romøren, 2016).

CHAPTER 3

The developmental path to adult-like prosodic focus marking in Mandarin Chinese-speaking children[1]

Abstract

This study investigates how children acquire prosodic focus marking in Mandarin Chinese. Using a picture-matching game, we elicited semi-spontaneous production of sentences in various focus conditions from children aged four to eleven. We found that Mandarin Chinese-speaking children use some pitch-related cues in some tones and duration in all tones in an adult-like way to distinguish focus from non-focus at the age of four to five. Their use of pitch-related cues is not yet fully adult-like in certain tones at the age of eleven. Further, they are adult-like in the use of duration in distinguishing narrow focus from broad focus at four or five but adult-like in not using the pitch-related cue, pitch-max, for this purpose at seven or eight. The later acquisition of pitch-related cues may be related to the use of pitch for lexical purposes and the differences in the use of pitch in different tones can be explained by differences in how easy it is to vary pitch-related parameters without changing tonal identity.

Keywords

Acquisition, focus, prosody, development, Mandarin Chinese

---

① Chapter 3 is an adapted version of Yang & Chen (2018), published in *First Language*. Preliminary results of a portion of the data from Chapter 3 were presented at the 4th International Symposium on Tonal Aspects of Languages (TAL) and the 7th Speech Prosody Conference, and published in the proceedings (Yang & Chen, 2014a, 2014b).

3.1 Introduction

Speakers use a range of linguistic means to distinguish information that is new to listeners from information that is already known to listeners. Listeners rely on the linguistic expressions of changes in information structure to efficiently process information. Prosody is used for marking information structure in many languages (Gussenhoven, 2007; Vallduvi & Engdahl, 1996). Generally, speakers realise a word with more prosodic prominence when conveying new and/or contrastive information (also known as "focus") than otherwise. However, there are notable differences between languages in the exact realisation of prosodic prominence. Some languages (e.g., Swedish, German, English, Dutch) can vary prosodic prominence via both phonological means, i.e., making coarse-grained variations in prosodic parameters (e.g., accenting or not accenting a word) and phonetic means, i.e. making fine-grained changes in prosodic parameters within a phonological category (e.g. changes in pitch span of a sentence-level accent or a lexical tone). But other languages can only use phonetic means (e.g., Mandarin Chinese, Cantonese). Languages can also differ in the consistency of the form-function mapping between prosody and focus. For example, in Dutch, the subject-noun of a sentence is nearly always accented regardless of whether it is focal or not (A. Chen, 2009); the object-noun is usually unaccented when non-focal in read speech but can be either unaccented or accented in semi-spontaneous speech (A. Chen, 2011a). The relation between accentuation and focus is thus not consistent in Dutch. It changes with the position of the constituent in a sentence and the modality of speech, and is thus probabilistic by nature. In contrast, in Swedish, a word is realised with a prominence-lending high tone only when it is focal (Bruce, 2007). Additionally, the specific prosodic parameters involved in focus marking can be simultaneously used for lexical purposes. For example, pitch is used to distinguish words in tone and pitch-accent languages (e.g., Mandarin Chinese, Cantonese, Swedish).

The question that arises in the context of language development is how the above-mentioned differences between languages influence the acquisition of prosodic focus marking in different languages. Recent years have seen a significant increase in the number of studies examining the use of prosody in focus marking in children acquiring a Germanic language. These studies have shown that children can already use accentuation to mark focus at the age of three to four but not necessarily in an adult-like way, and that they become adult-like in both the placement of accent and the type of accent (i.e., the shape of the pitch pattern) at about the age of eight (Hornby & Hass, 1970; MacWhinney & Bates, 1978; Wells, Peppé & Goulandris, 2004, on English; Müller, Höhle, Schmitz & Weissenborn, 2005, on German; A. Chen, 2011a, 2011b, on Dutch). On the other hand, the use of phonetic means as an alternative to phonological means, especially the use of duration, is not adult-like even at the age of eight (A. Chen, 2009, 2015, on Dutch). However, this developmental path to adult-like prosodic focus marking may not be generalisable to children acquiring a language that differs from West Germanic languages. In the present study, we have investigated children's use of prosody in focus marking in Mandarin Chinese (hereafter Mandarin), in order to shed light on the acquisition of prosodic focus marking from the perspective of a tone language.

Mandarin presents itself as an interesting case for the study of the acquisition of prosodic focus marking for three reasons. First, as mentioned above, Mandarin only uses phonetic means to realise focus, different from West Germanic languages which primarily use phonological means and only use phonetic means when phonological means do not suffice. In Chapter 2, we have examined the prosodic realisation of three types of focus, i.e., (non-contrastive) narrow focus (i.e., focus on one content word in a sentence), contrastive (narrow) focus (i.e., contrast conveyed by one word in a sentence), and whole-sentence focus, or broad focus, in semi-spontaneous speech. It was found that narrow focus was realised with a longer duration and a larger pitch span than non-focus, as found in read speech (Y. Chen & Braun, 2006; Xu, 1999). Narrow focus was also realised with a longer duration and a slightly wider pitch span than broad focus, but was not distinguished from contrastive focus, different from findings on read speech (Y. Chen & Braun, 2006; Shih, 1988; Xu, 1999). Will the extensive use of phonetic means in prosodic focus marking influence the rate of acquisition in Mandarin-speaking children, compared to children acquiring West Germanic languages? There are two plausible but opposing answers to this question. On the one hand, Mandarin-speaking children may learn prosodic focus marking at an earlier age than children acquiring a West Germanic language because of extensive exposure to the use of phonetic means for focus marking in the input. On the other hand, they may learn prosodic focus marking at a similar age to children acquiring a West Germanic language, because children, regardless of their native language, may need a similar amount of time to establish the form-function mapping between prosodic variation and focus in the input, and to develop sufficient control of prosodic parameters in production.

Furthermore, pitch is not only varied to mark focus but also to distinguish words in Mandarin. More specifically, Mandarin has four lexical tones, i.e., a high level tone (Tone

1), a rising tone (Tone 2), a low tone (Tone 3), and a falling tone (Tone 4), which are primarily identified by pitch movements (Chao, 1965; Lin, 2007). For example, the syllable "ma" can mean "mother" in Tone 1, "hemp" in Tone 2, "horse" in Tone 3, and "to scold" in Tone 4. This raises the question of whether lexical uses of pitch will affect the order in which the use of pitch and duration is acquired for focus marking. On the one hand, speakers need to maintain the shape of the pitch contour in a word for the sake of the identity of the lexical tone, and thus leave limited acoustic space for pitch variation for focus-marking purposes. This suggests that speakers need to execute precise control of pitch in order to vary pitch for focus-marking purposes and leave the identity of the lexical tones intact at the same time. Research has shown that young children have difficulty in pitch control over a stretch of speech as long as or longer than a word (A. Chen, 2009). We may thus predict that Mandarin-speaking children take a longer time to become adult-like in the use of pitch than in the use of duration for focus-marking purposes. On the other hand, Mandarin-speaking children produce lexical tones with considerable accuracy as early as three years of age (Wong, 2012; Wong, Schwartz & Jenkins, 2005; Zhu, 2002). They may thus have developed considerable sensitivity to pitch variation and are skillful with pitch control in production, which might in turn facilitate their acquisition of the use of pitch for focus-marking purposes. Along this line of reasoning, we may predict that Mandarin-speaking children master the use of pitch earlier than the use of duration for focus-marking purposes. These conflicting predictions need to be tested experimentally.

Relatedly, although they can produce the four tones with considerable accuracy by the age of three, Mandarin-speaking children do not acquire the four tones at the same rate. Specifically, Tone 1 and Tone 4 have generally been found to be acquired earlier than Tone 2 and Tone 3 by young children (Clumeck, 1977; Li & Thompson, 1977; Wong, 2012; Zhu, 2002). There is no consensus yet on why one tone is acquired later than another. Researchers have attributed the relatively late acquisition of certain tones to production-related difficulties (e.g., the complexity of articulatory control), perception-related challenges (e.g., the difficulty of tonal distinction in perception), or the frequency of the tones in the input received by children in infancy and toddlerhood (Zhu, 2002; Wong, et al., 2005). Whatever the reasons may be, the findings imply that the four tones are not equally easy to acquire. This raises the question of whether Mandarin-speaking children's use of pitch for focus-marking purposes varies between tones, especially at younger ages. Given the relatively late acquisition of Tone 2 and Tone 3, we may predict later adult-like use of pitch for focus marking in Tone 2 and Tone 3 than in Tone 1 and Tone 4.

To address the three above-mentioned issues and resolve conflicting predictions regarding the effects of only using phonetic means to mark focus and lexical use of pitch, we have investigated how Mandarin-speaking four- to eleven-year-olds use pitch and duration for focus-marking purposes in semi-spontaneous speech. Specifically, we have examined how they use pitch and duration to distinguish: (1) Narrow focus from non-focus, i.e., pre-focus and post-focus (Effect of focus); (2) Narrow focus from broad focus (Effect of focal constituent size); and (3) Narrow focus from contrastive focus (Effect of contrastivity).

3.2 Method

3.2.1 Participants

Three groups of children, i.e., twelve four- to five-year-olds (average age: 5;2, range: 4;6-5;10), ten seven- to eight-year-olds (average age: 7;10, range: 7;2-8;3) and twelve ten- to eleven-year-olds (average age: 10;9, range: 10;1-11;5) participated in the experiment (see Appendix A for more participant information). They were recruited and tested in Beijing 21st Century kindergarten and primary school, and came from diverse social-economic backgrounds. They all spoke Mandarin as their native language without detectable regional accent. Twelve adult native speakers of Mandarin (average age: 19, range: 18-20 years; six females and six males) were tested as a control group. They were undergraduates from Beijing Forestry University at the time of testing, and all spoke Mandarin without any detectable regional accent.

3.2.2 The picture-matching game

We adapted the picture-matching game used in A. Chen (2011a) to elicit semi-spontaneous production. In this game, the child was supposed to help the experimenter to put pictures in matched pairs. Three piles of pictures were used. The experimenter and the child each held a pile of pictures. The third pile lay on the table in a seemingly messy fashion. The experimenter's pictures always missed some information (e.g., the subject, the action, the object, or all three). The child's pictures always contained all three pieces of information. On each trial, the experimenter showed one of her pictures to the child, described the picture and asked a question about it or made a remark about the missing information (in the contrastive focus condition). The child then took a look at the corresponding picture in his/her pile and responded to the experimenter's question or remark. The experimenter then looked for the right picture in the messy pile and matched it with her own picture to form a pair.

As rules of the game, the child was asked to answer the experimenter's questions in full sentences and not to reveal his/her pictures to the experimenter. In addition, in order to make sure that the experiment was conducted in the same way for all the children, and that adequate background information was equally provided for each trial before a question was asked or a remark was made, scripts containing all words that the experimenters were supposed to say in the experimental sessions were constructed. The experimenters were instructed to follow the scripts closely but were encouraged to make spontaneous remarks that did not affect the information structure of the child's responses for the purpose of facilitating the conversation. Prior to the picture-matching game, a picture-naming task was conducted to ensure that the children would use the intended words to refer to the entities in the pictures. This procedure also rendered the entities in the pictures referentially accessible.

3.2.3 Experimental materials

One-hundred and sixty question-answer dialogues were embedded in the picture-matching game to elicit one-hundred and sixty SVO sentences in five focus conditions: narrow focus on the subject noun in sentence-initial position (NF-i), responding to *who*-questions; narrow focus on the object-noun in sentence-final position (NF-f), responding to *what*-questions; narrow focus on the verb in sentence-medial position (NF-m), responding to *what-does*-X-*do-to*-Y questions; contrastive focus in sentence-medial position (CF-m), correcting the experimenter's remark about the action; broad focus over the whole sentence (BF), responding to *what-happens* questions, as illustrated in (1). Including narrow focus in three sentence-positions made it possible to study the effect of narrow focus on the sentence-medial verbs (NF-m) compared to the same verbs in pre-focus (or NF-f) and post focus (or NF-i). Comparing the verbs in NF-m, CF-m and BF allowed us to study the prosodic difference between different focus types. Examples of question-answer dialogues in the five focus condition are given in (1), in which the digits represent tones in Mandarin, and the referents are referred to with the definite article in the English glossary because they had been introduced in the picture-naming task.

(1) Examples of question-answer dialogues between the experimenter (E) and participant (P):

(NF-i) E: 看！球。球在空中。看起来有小动物扔球。谁扔球？
Look! The ball, and the ball is in the air. It looks like someone throws the ball. Who throws the ball?
P: [小熊] 扔 球。
[xiao3 xiong2] reng1 qiu2.
[The little bear] throws the ball.

(NF-f) E: 看！小猫，小猫的胳膊伸出去了。看起来小猫扔东西。小猫扔什么？
Look! The little cat, and it stretches out its arm. It looks like the little cat throws something. What does the little cat throw?
P: 小猫 扔 [笔]。
xiao3 mao1 reng1 [bi3].
The little cat throws [the pen].

(NF-m) E: 看！小兔，还有书。看起来小兔要弄书。小兔怎么弄书？
Look! The little rabbit, and the book. It looks like the little rabbit does something to the book. What does the little rabbit do to the book?
P: 小兔 [扔] 书。
xiao3 tu4 [reng1] shu1.
The little rabbit [throws] the book.

(CF-m) E: 看！小熊，还有菜。看起来小熊要弄菜。我猜：小熊[埋]菜。
Look! The little bear, and the vegetables. It looks like the little bear will do something to the vegetables. I will make a guess: The little bear [buries] the vegetables.
P: 小熊 [扔] 菜。
xiao3 xiong2 [reng1] cai4.
The little bear [throws] the vegetables.

(BF) E: 看！我的图片是模糊的。什么都看不清。你的图片上讲了什么？
Look! My picture is very blurry. I cannot see anything clearly.
What happens in your picture?
P: [小狗 扔 菜]。
[xiao3 gou3 reng1 cai4].
[The little dog throws the vegetables].

The SVO sentences were unique combinations of four disyllabic subject-noun phrases starting with the word "xiao3 (little)" (one noun phrase per lexical tone regarding the second word in each phrase), eight monosyllabic verbs (one verb per lexical tone per group), and eight monosyllabic object-nouns (one noun per lexical tone per group), as shown in Table 3-1. Each group-1 verb was combined once with each group-1 object-noun and each group-2 verb was combined once with each group-2 object-noun, leading to one-hundred and sixty verb phrases (4 tones in verbs × 4 tones in objects × 2 groups of verbs and object-nouns × 5 focus conditions = 160 VPs). We used two groups of verbs so that we had two realisations of each tone in the verbs and could avoid data loss regarding the tones in the case that a child mispronounced one verb. As we could not find four nouns representing four tones among the words reported to be acquired by Mandarin-speaking four-year-olds (Y. Liu, Shu & Li, 2007) that could form semantically appropriate VPs with all the eight target verbs, we paired each group of verbs with their "own" object nouns, thus having two groups of object nouns. The subject-nouns were then approximately evenly distributed over the verb phrases, forming one-hundred and sixty SVO sentences (Appendix B). This procedure made sure that in each focus condition, each tone in the verbs was combined with each tone in the preceding subject-noun and with each tone in the following object-noun.

Table 3-1 Words that occurred in the SVO sentences

	Tone 1	Tone 2	Tone 3	Tone 4
Subject nouns	小猫 xiao3 mao1 "little cat"	小熊 xiao3 xiong2 "little bear"	小狗 xiao3 gou3 "little dog"	小兔 xiao3 tu4 "little rabbit"
Group-1 verbs	扔 reng1 "throw"	埋 mai2 "bury"	剪 jian3 "cut"	运 yun4 "transport"

Continued

	Tone 1	Tone 2	Tone 3	Tone 4
Group-2 verbs	浇 jiao1 "water"	闻 wen2 "smell"	舔 tian3 "lick"	卖 mai4 "sell"
Group-1 objects	书 shu1 "book"	球 qiu2 "ball"	笔 bi3 "pen"	菜 cai4 "vegetable"
Group-2 objects	花 hua1 "flower"	梨 li2 "pear"	草 cao3 "grass"	树 shu4 "tree"

The one-hundred and sixty sentences were then split evenly into two lists (List 1 and List 2) of eighty sentences. Each list contained all verb-object tonal combinations but not all verb-object word combinations. The trials on each list were randomized in a way that trials from the same focus condition did not appear after each other and the focused constituent of a trial was not mentioned on its preceding trial. Approximately half of the participants in each age group produced the sentences on List 1 and the other half produced the sentences on List 2.

3.2.4 Experimental procedure

The children were tested individually in quiet rooms in their kindergarten or school. Three female native speakers of Mandarin administered the experiment after having received intensive training on how to conduct the experiment. Two experimental sessions — one eliciting forty sentences with the group-1 words and the other eliciting forty sentences with the group-2 words — were held on two different days for each four- to five-year-old, and on the same day for the older children but with a break in between. The children were also allowed to take a break during an experimental session whenever necessary. Each experimental session lasted about thirty-five minutes and was audio-recorded at a sampling rate of 44.1 kHz with 16 bits using a ZOOM H1 recorder. The four- to five-year-olds were also video-recorded during the experiment for the purpose of training experimenters. The adults were tested following the same experimental procedure, but were informed that the game was of a simple nature because it would also be played with children.

3.2.5 Prosodic annotation

The audio recording from each participant was first orthographically annotated in Praat (Boersma & Weenink, 2013). Then usable sentences were selected for phonetic annotation (59% for the four- to five-year-olds, 82% for the seven- to eight-year-olds, and 90% for the ten- to eleven-year-olds), and unusable ones were excluded from further analysis. A target sentence was considered unusable in any of the following cases: (1) the participant produced the target sentence before the experimenter asked the question; (2) the experimenter asked a different question than the intended question in that trial; (3) the experimenter did not provide an adequate description of the picture before she asked a question; (4) the sentence was produced at a noisy moment of the kindergarten or school; (5) the sentence was produced with word insertion, deletion, or replacement; (6) the sentence was produced with self-repair or clearly perceivable hesitation; or (7) the sentence was produced with perceivable marked intonation, such as chanting-, singing- and howling-like intonation, or with laughter.

We were especially interested in whether pitch span and duration were varied for focus-marking purposes. If pitch span was expanded in certain focus conditions, we wanted to know how the expansion was achieved, namely, by raising the maximum pitch (hereafter the pitch-max), or by lowering the minimum pitch (hereafter the pitch-min), or by varying both. We thus annotated the target words in the usable sentences for word boundaries, pitch-max and pitch-min. Word segmentation was done on the basis of formant intensity, formant contours, waveforms, and auditory perception (Machač & Skarnitzl, 2009; Turk, Nakai & Sugahara, 2006). In the annotation of the pitch-max and pitch min, care was taken not to confuse local pitch fluctuations with linguistically relevant variation in pitch. The tonal targets of the lexical tones and the influence from the preceding tone were taken into account when determining the location of pitch-max and pitch-min (Xu, 1997; Xu & Wang, 2001; see a detailed explanation in section 2.2.5 in Chapter 2 of this dissertation). A small number of trials that were affected by background noise and non-model voice quality were excluded from pitch annotation.

3.3 Statistical analysis and results

As mentioned earlier, the target words were focal in the NF-m, BF and CF-m conditions, post-focal in the NF-i condition, and pre-focal in the NF-f condition. We analysed the effect of focus (i.e., NF-m vs. NF-i/NF-f) and focus types differing in size (i.e., NF-m vs. BF) or contrastivity (i.e., NF-m vs. CF-m) on the use of each duration- or pitch-related prosodic cues. The data of the adult control group (Chapter 2 of this dissertation) was included in the statistical analysis for comparison reasons.

Mixed-effects modelling in the program R with the lme4 package (Bates, et al., 2014) was used to assess the data. The dependent variables were duration, pitch span, pitch-max, and pitch-min of the target words. The random factors were SPEAKER (i.e., the participants) and SENTENCE (i.e., the target sentences). The fixed factors were AGE, FOCUS, and TONE. AGE referred to the four age groups and thus had four levels (i.e., three groups of children and one group of adults. The adults was set as the reference category). FOCUS referred to the focus conditions. For each analysis, two conditions were compared to each other in order to address a specific question. FOCUS thus always had two levels. TONE referred to the tones of the target words, and had four levels (i.e., Tone 1, 2, 3, and 4).

To find out whether a particular prosodic cue was used to distinguish two focus conditions, models were built using the aforementioned factors. Starting from an "empty" model (hereafter Model 0) containing only the random factors, we added the main effects of the fixed factors, the two-way interactions between each two fixed factors, and the three-way interaction between all of them to the model in a stepwise fashion, building seven additional models (Table 3-2). The ANOVA function in R was used to compare models in order to derive the model with the best fit. First, Model 1 was compared to Model 0, and a statistically significant difference indicated that Model 1 with the newly added parameter FOCUS could better explain the variation in the data, and thus was the "winning" model. Otherwise, Model 0 stayed as the "winning" model. Next, Model 2 was compared to its preceding "winning" model, which could be either Model 1 or Model 0. Following the same logic, each later model was compared to the preceding "winning" model. The last "winning" model was considered to be the best-fit model.

Table 3-2 Model build-up procedure

Model	Factor added
Model 0	
Model 1	FOCUS
Model 2	AGE
Model 3	TONE
Model 4	FOCUS : AGE
Model 5	FOCUS : TONE
Model 6	AGE : TONE
Model 7	FOCUS : AGE : TONE

For each analysis, we report on the best-fit model, according to the model comparisons, and statistical significance of main effects and interactions, according to the summary of the best-fit model. As the model summary does not straightforwardly show the difference between two focus conditions in the use of a particular prosodic cue in each age group, we did additional analysis of each age group to obtain a clearer picture on interactions involving the factor AGE. If the best-fit model contained the three-way interaction of FOCUS, AGE and TONE, we discuss how the speakers in each age group distinguished the two focus conditions in each tonal category by examining the interaction of FOCUS and TONE in each age group. If the best-fit model contained the two-way interaction of FOCUS and AGE, we discuss how the speakers in each age group distinguished the two focus conditions by examining the main effect of FOCUS in each age group. We do not discuss in detail the main effects of the factors when the interactions involving these factors are significant, two-way interactions when three-way interactions involving the same factors are significant, and interactions that do not involve the factors FOCUS and AGE.

3.3.1 Realisation of narrow focus

3.3.1.1 Narrow focus vs. pre-focus (NF-m vs. NF-f)

WORD DURATION. The best-fit model for this dependent variable was Model 4 (Table 3-3). The summary of this model (Table 3-4) showed that the main effects of FOCUS, AGE and their interaction were significant. Subsequent analysis of the main effect of FOCUS in each age group separately revealed that the word duration was significantly longer in narrow focus than in pre-focus in each group of children (69 ms longer in the four- to five-year-olds, 61 ms longer in the seven- to eight-year-olds, 33 ms longer in the ten- to eleven-year-olds; $P < 0.001$ in all cases), as in the adults (19 ms longer, $P < 0.001$) (Figure 3-1). However, the children varied word duration to a much larger extent than the adults. Among the children, the four- to five-year-olds and seven- to eight-year-olds tended to vary word duration to a larger degree than the ten- to eleven-year-olds.

Table 3-3 Model comparisons regarding the dependent variable word duration in the comparison narrow focus vs. pre-focus

Model comparisons	***Pr*(>Chisq)**
0 vs. 1 (adding FOCUS)	0.000***
1 vs. 2 (adding AGE)	0.000***
2 vs. 3 (adding TONE)	0.730
2 vs. 4 (adding FOCUS : AGE)	0.000***
4 vs. 5 (adding FOCUS : TONE)	0.667
4 vs. 6 (adding AGE : TONE)	0.904
4 vs. 7 (adding FOCUS : AGE : TONE)	0.917

Table 3-4 Model summary regarding the dependent variable word duration in the comparison narrow focus vs. pre-focus

Factor	**Estimate**	**Std. Error**	***t* value**	***Pr*(>|*t*|)**
Intercept (Adults. Narrow focus. T1)	0.218	0.010	21.831	0.000***
Pre-focus	−0.019	0.006	−3.010	0.003**
Age 4-5	0.112	0.012	9.659	0.000***
Age 7-8	0.097	0.012	8.084	0.000***
Age 10-11	0.052	0.011	4.532	0.000***
T2	0.009	0.008	1.135	0.261
T3	0.003	0.008	0.415	0.679
T4	0.003	0.008	0.366	0.715
Pre-focus : Age 4-5	−0.050	0.007	−7.609	0.000***
Pre-focus : Age 7-8	−0.042	0.006	−6.775	0.000***
Pre-focus : Age 10-11	−0.014	0.006	−2.343	0.019*

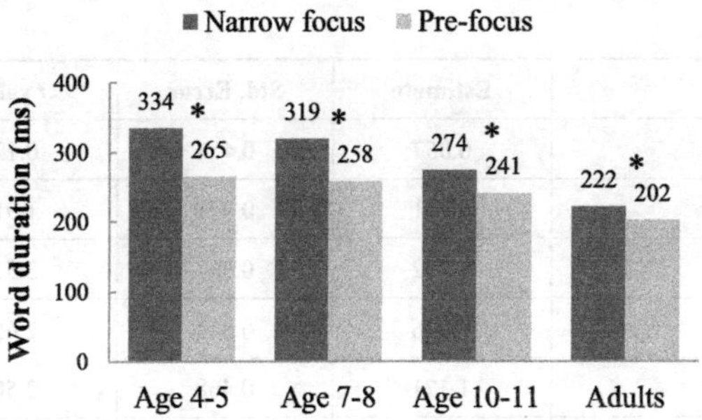

Figure 3-1 The use of word duration in distinguishing narrow focus from pre-focus

PITCH SPAN. The best-fit model for this dependent variable was Model 6 (Table 3-5). The summary of this model (Table 3-6) showed that the main effect of FOCUS was not significant, but the interaction of FOCUS and AGE and the interaction of FOCUS and TONE were significant. In addition, the main effects of AGE and TONE and their interaction were also significant. Regarding the interaction of FOCUS and AGE, subsequent analysis of the main effect of FOCUS in each age group separately revealed that the pitch span was significantly wider in narrow focus than in pre-focus in the seven- to eight-year-olds (1.8 st wider; $P < 0.001$) and ten- to eleven-year-olds (1.5 st wider, $P < 0.001$), similar to the adults (0.7 st wider; $P < 0.05$), but not in the four- to five-year-olds (Figure 3-2).

Table 3-5 Model comparisons regarding the dependent variable pitch span in the comparison narrow focus vs. pre-focus

Model comparisons	Pr(>Chisq)
0 vs 1 (adding FOCUS)	0.000***
1 vs. 2 (adding AGE)	0.000***
2 vs. 3 (adding TONE)	0.000***
3 vs. 4 (adding FOCUS : AGE)	0.000***
4 vs. 5 (adding FOCUS : TONE)	0.128
4 vs. 6 (adding AGE : TONE)	0.000***
6 vs. 7 (adding FOCUS : AGE : TONE)	0.556

Table 3-6 Model summary regarding the dependent variable pitch span in the comparison narrow focus vs. pre-focus

Factor	Estimate	Std. Error	*t* value	Pr(>|*t*|)
Intercept (Adults. Narrow focus. T1)	1.529	0.385	3.976	0.000***

Continued

Factor	Estimate	Std. Error	*t* value	*Pr*(>|*t*|)
Pre-focus	0.057	0.454	0.126	0.900
Age 4-5	0.711	0.371	1.918	0.058
Age 7-8	1.292	0.367	3.519	0.001**
Age 10-11	0.926	0.348	2.658	0.009**
T2	1.171	0.468	2.500	0.015*
T3	2.732	0.491	5.561	0.000***
T4	2.430	0.469	5.178	0.000***
Pre-focus : Age 4-5	−0.457	0.251	−1.826	0.068
Pre-focus : Age 7-8	−1.292	0.230	−5.622	0.000***
Pre-focus : Age 10-11	−0.797	0.208	−3.821	0.000***
Pre-focus : T2	−0.944	0.619	−1.526	0.133
Pre-focus : T3	−0.849	0.640	−1.326	0.189
Pre-focus : T4	−1.463	0.620	−2.360	0.022*
Age 4-5 : T2	0.809	0.325	2.488	0.013*
Age 7-8 : T2	1.296	0.300	4.324	0.000***
Age 10-11 : T2	0.660	0.280	2.360	0.018*
Age 4-5 : T3	0.789	0.406	1.945	0.052
Age 7-8 : T3	1.212	0.365	3.318	0.001**
Age 10-11 : T3	0.361	0.313	1.151	0.250
Age 4-5 : T4	0.731	0.332	2.201	0.028**
Age 7-8 : T4	1.532	0.305	5.031	0.000***
Age 10-11 : T4	0.616	0.281	2.190	0.029**

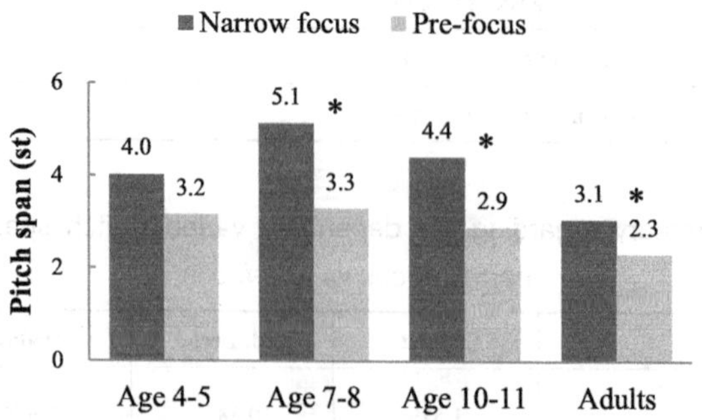

Figure 3-2 The use of pitch span in distinguishing narrow focus from pre-focus

PITCH-MAX. The best-fit model for this dependent variable was Model 7 (Table 3-7). The summary of this model (Table 3-8) showed that the main effect of FOCUS was not significant, but the interaction of FOCUS and AGE and the interaction of FOCUS, AGE and TONE were significant. In addition, the main effects of AGE and TONE and their interaction were also significant. Subsequent analysis revealed no significant main effect of FOCUS or significant interaction of FOCUS and TONE in the four- to five-year-olds, indicating that they did not use pitch-max to distinguish narrow focus from pre-focus (0.7 st higher in narrow focus, $P > 0.05$), regardless of tone, similar to the adults (0.2 st higher in narrow focus, $P > 0.05$). In the seven- to eight-year-olds, there was a significant interaction of FOCUS and TONE. They used a significantly higher pitch-max in narrow focus than in pre-focus for words in Tone 1 (1.4 st higher, $P < 0.05$) and Tone 4 (2.2 st higher, $P < 0.001$), but not for words in Tone 2 or Tone 3 (Figure 3-3). In the ten- to eleven-year-olds, there were significant main effects of FOCUS and TONE, but no significant interaction, suggesting that they used a higher pitch-max in narrow focus than in pre-focus (0.7 st higher, $P < 0.05$), regardless of tone.

Table 3-7 Model comparisons regarding the dependent variable pitch-max in the comparison narrow focus vs. pre-focus

Model comparisons	***Pr*(>Chisq)**
0 vs. 1 (adding FOCUS)	0.123
0 vs. 2 (adding AGE)	0.000***
2 vs. 3 (adding TONE)	0.000***
3 vs. 4 (adding FOCUS : AGE)	0.035*
4 vs. 5 (adding FOCUS : TONE)	0.014*
5 vs. 6 (adding AGE : TONE)	0.000***
6 vs. 7 (adding FOCUS : AGE : TONE)	0.039*

Table 3-8 Model summary regarding the dependent variable pitch-max in the comparison narrow focus vs. pre-focus

Factor	**Estimate**	**Std. Error**	***t* value**	***Pr*(>|*t*|)**
Intercept (Adults. Narrow focus. T1)	90.450	1.043	86.687	0.000***
Pre-focus	−0.281	0.462	−0.608	0.545
Age 4-5	10.050	1.439	6.985	0.000***
Age 7-8	9.790	1.501	6.522	0.000***

Continued

Factor	Estimate	Std. Error	*t* value	*Pr*(>|*t*|)
Age 10-11	8.043	1.432	5.615	0.000***
T2	−2.466	0.465	−5.308	0.000***
T3	−1.971	0.471	−4.182	0.000***
T4	0.484	0.462	1.047	0.297
Pre-focus : Age 4-5	−1.599	0.465	−3.441	0.001**
Pre-focus : Age 7-8	−1.124	0.442	−2.541	0.011*
Pre-focus : Age 10-11	−0.861	0.411	−2.095	0.036*
Pre-focus : T2	0.390	0.654	0.596	0.553
Pre-focus : T3	0.371	0.666	0.558	0.578
Pre-focus : T4	−0.525	0.654	−0.802	0.424
Age 4-5 : T2	0.573	0.465	1.233	0.218
Age 7-8 : T2	−0.265	0.441	−0.601	0.548
Age 10-11 : T2	−0.199	0.420	−0.474	0.636
Age 4-5 : T3	−0.153	0.485	−0.316	0.752
Age 7-8 : T3	−1.683	0.446	−3.774	0.000***
Age 10-11 : T3	−1.119	0.422	−2.651	0.008**
Age 4-5 : T4	0.227	0.463	0.490	0.624
Age 7-8 : T4	0.364	0.438	0.830	0.407
Age 10-11 : T4	−0.050	0.413	−0.122	0.903
Pre-focus : Age 4-5 : T2	1.882	0.663	2.841	0.005**
Pre-focus : Age 7-8 : T2	0.669	0.629	1.063	0.288
Pre-focus : Age 10-11 : T2	0.621	0.586	1.061	0.289
Pre-focus : Age 4-5 : T3	1.883	0.682	2.764	0.006**
Pre-focus : Age 7-8 : T3	1.546	0.644	2.401	0.017*
Pre-focus : Age 10-11 : T3	0.710	0.593	1.197	0.231
Pre-focus : Age 4-5 : T4	1.082	0.665	1.627	0.104
Pre-focus : Age 7-8 : T4	−0.261	0.630	−0.415	0.678
Pre-focus : Age 10-11 : T4	0.328	0.582	0.563	0.573

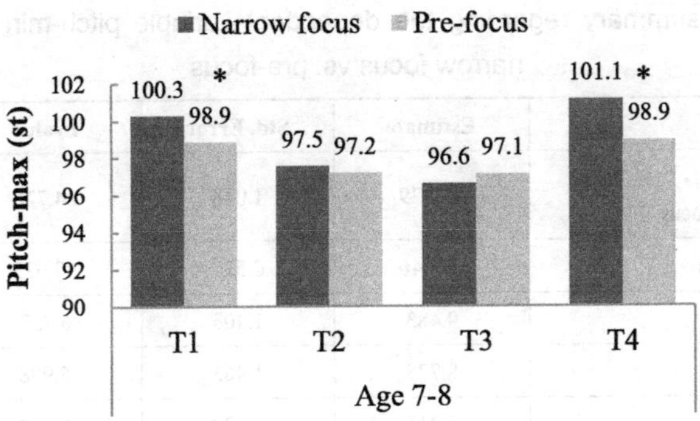

Figure 3-3 The use of pitch-max in distinguishing narrow focus from pre-focus in different tones in the seven- to eight-year-olds

PITCH-MIN. The best-fit model for this dependent variable was Model 7 (Table 3-9). The summary of this model (Table 3-10) showed that the main effect of FOCUS was not significant, but the interaction of FOCUS and AGE and the interaction of FOCUS, AGE and TONE were significant. In addition, the main effects of AGE and TONE and their interaction were also significant. Subsequent analysis revealed a significant main effect of FOCUS, but no significant interaction of FOCUS and TONE in the ten- to eleven-year-olds, indicating that they used a lower pith-min in narrow focus than in pre-focus (0.9 st lower, $P < 0.05$), regardless of tone, similar to the adults (0.5 st lower, $P < 0.05$). In both the four- to five-year-olds and the seven- to eight-year-olds we found a significant interaction of FOCUS and TONE. The four- to five-year-olds used a lower pitch-min in narrow focus than in pre-focus for words in Tone 2 (1.8 st lower, $P < 0.05$), but not for words in the other tones (Figure 3-4). The seven- to eight-year-olds used a lower pitch-min in narrow focus than in pre-focus for words in Tone 2 (2.0 st lower, $P < 0.05$) and Tone 3 (1.9 st lower, $P < 0.05$), but not for words in the other tones (Figure 3-4).

Table 3-9 Model comparisons regarding the dependent variable pitch-min in the comparison narrow focus vs. pre-focus

Model comparisons	*Pr*(>Chisq)
0 vs. 1 (adding FOCUS)	0.142
0 vs. 2 (adding AGE)	0.000***
2 vs. 3 (adding TONE)	0.000***
3 vs. 4 (adding FOCUS : AGE)	0.203
3 vs. 5 (adding FOCUS : TONE)	0.025*
5 vs. 6 (adding AGE : TONE)	0.000***
6 vs. 7 (adding FOCUS : AGE : TONE)	0.010*

Table 3-10 Model summary regarding the dependent variable pitch-min in the comparison narrow focus vs. pre-focus

Factor	Estimate	Std. Error	*t* value	*Pr*(>|*t*|)
Intercept (Adults. Narrow focus. T1)	88.779	1.048	84.726	0.000***
Pre-focus	−0.046	0.577	−0.079	0.937
Age 4-5	9.483	1.403	6.757	0.000***
Age 7-8	8.778	1.463	5.998	0.000***
Age 10-11	7.311	1.397	5.235	0.000***
T2	−3.441	0.582	−5.909	0.000***
T3	−4.805	0.606	−7.932	0.000***
T4	−1.740	0.582	−2.991	0.004**
Pre-focus : Age 4-5	−1.408	0.465	−3.028	0.003**
Pre-focus : Age 7-8	−0.475	0.439	−1.081	0.280
Pre-focus : Age 10-11	−0.495	0.409	−1.210	0.227
Pre-focus : T2	0.838	0.819	1.024	0.309
Pre-focus : T3	1.037	0.846	1.226	0.223
Pre-focus : T4	0.454	0.821	0.553	0.582
Age 4-5 : T2	−0.645	0.481	−1.341	0.180
Age 7-8 : T2	−2.070	0.442	−4.689	0.000***
Age 10-11 : T2	−1.197	0.422	−2.838	0.005**
Age 4-5 : T3	−0.485	0.641	−0.756	0.450
Age 7-8 : T3	−2.639	0.584	−4.517	0.000***
Age 10-11 : T3	−1.284	0.483	−2.657	0.008**
Age 4-5 : T4	−0.458	0.490	−0.936	0.350
Age 7-8 : T4	−1.833	0.449	−4.083	0.000***
Age 10-11 : T4	−0.988	0.421	−2.345	0.019*
Pre-focus : Age 4-5 : T2	2.740	0.683	4.012	0.000***
Pre-focus : Age 7-8 : T2	1.743	0.628	2.777	0.006**
Pre-focus : Age 10-11 : T2	1.559	0.585	2.665	0.008**
Pre-focus : Age 4-5 : T3	1.963	0.854	2.298	0.022*
Pre-focus : Age 7-8 : T3	1.986	0.771	2.578	0.010*
Pre-focus : Age 10-11 : T3	0.891	0.651	1.367	0.172
Pre-focus : Age 4-5 : T4	1.316	0.693	1.899	0.058
Pre-focus : Age 7-8 : T4	0.919	0.637	1.443	0.149

Continued

Factor	Estimate	Std. Error	*t* value	*Pr*(>|*t*|)
Pre-focus : Age 10-11 : T4	1.046	0.589	1.775	0.076

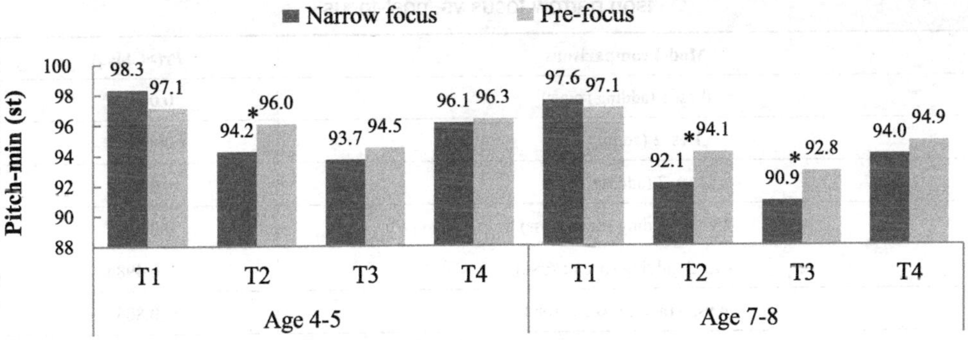

Figure 3-4 The use of pitch-min in distinguishing narrow focus from pre-focus in different tones in the four- to five-year-olds and seven- to eight-year-olds

INTERIM SUMMARY. To distinguish narrow focus from pre-focus, the three groups of children all used a longer duration for the focused words than for the pre-focal ones, similar to the adults. But only the seven- to eight-year-olds and ten- to eleven-year olds used a wider pitch span for the focused words than for the pre-focal ones, as the adults did. Different from the adults who expanded the pitch span mainly by lowering the pitch-min, the ten- to eleven-year-olds did that by both raising the pitch-max and lowering the pitch-min. The way in which the seven- to eight-year-olds expanded the pitch span of the focused words was conditioned by tones. They expanded the pitch span of the Tone 1 and Tone 4 words mainly by raising the pitch-max and expanded the pitch span of the Tone 2 and Tone 3 words mainly by lowering the pitch-min.

3.3.1.2 Narrow focus vs. post-focus (NF-m vs. NF-i)

WORD DURATION. The best-fit model for this dependent variable was Model 4 (Table 3-11). The summary of this model (Table 3-12) showed that the main effects of FOCUS, AGE and their interaction were significant. Subsequent analysis of each age group showed that the word duration was significantly longer in narrow focus than in post-focus in all the four age groups (64 ms longer in the four- to five-year-olds, 71 ms longer in the seven- to eight-year-olds, 49 ms longer in the ten- to eleven-year-olds, and 22 ms longer in the adults; $P < 0.001$ in all cases.) (Figure 3-5). However, the children varied word duration to a much larger extent than the adults. Among the children, the four- to five-year-olds and seven- to eight-year-olds tended to vary word duration to a larger degree than the ten- to eleven-year-olds.

Table 3-11 Model comparisons regarding the dependent variable word duration in the comparison narrow focus vs. post-focus

Model comparisons	*Pr*(>Chisq)
0 vs. 1 (adding FOCUS)	0.000***
1 vs. 2 (adding AGE)	0.000***
2 vs. 3 (adding TONE)	0.874
2 vs. 4 (adding FOCUS : AGE)	0.000***
4 vs. 5 (adding FOCUS : TONE)	0.498
4 vs. 6 (adding AGE : TONE)	0.806
4 vs. 7 (adding FOCUS : AGE : TONE)	0.784

Table 3-12 Model summary regarding the dependent variable word duration in the comparison narrow focus vs. post-focus

Factor	Estimate	Std. Error	*t* value	*Pr*(>|*t*|)
Intercept (Adults. Narrow focus. T1)	0.219	0.010	21.348	0.000***
Post-focus	−0.022	0.006	−3.380	0.001**
Age 4-5	0.112	0.012	9.339	0.000***
Age 7-8	0.097	0.012	7.804	0.000***
Age 10-11	0.052	0.012	4.348	0.000***
T2	0.006	0.008	0.774	0.442
T3	0.003	0.008	0.326	0.746
T4	0.005	0.008	0.677	0.501
Post-focus : Age 4-5	−0.043	0.006	−6.851	0.000***
Post-focus : Age 7-8	−0.049	0.006	−8.187	0.000***
Post-focus : Age 10-11	−0.027	0.006	−4.741	0.000***

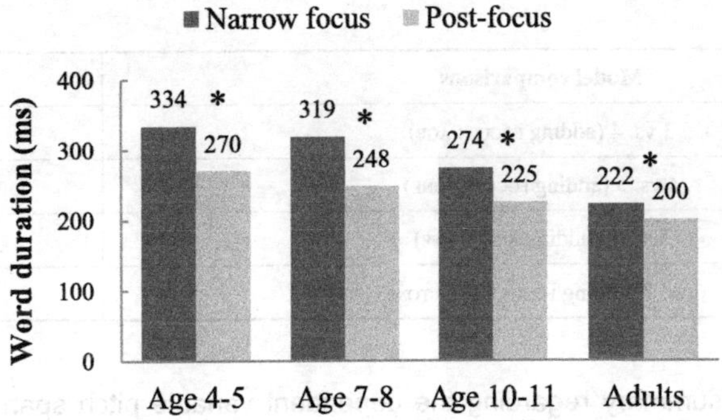

Figure 3-5 The use of word duration in distinguishing narrow focus from post-focus

PITCH SPAN. The best-fit model for this dependent variable was Model 7 (Table 3-13). The summary of this model (Table 3-14) showed that the main effect of FOCUS was not significant, but the interaction of FOCUS, AGE and TONE was significant. In addition, the main effects of AGE and TONE and their interaction were also significant. Sebsequent analysis showed no significant main effect of FOCUS or significant interaction of FOCUS and TONE in the four- to five-year-olds, indicating they did not use pitch span to distinguish narrow focus from post-focus (0.7 st wider in narrow focus, $P > 0.05$), different from the adults, who used a wider pitch span in narrow focus than in post-focus regardless of tones (0.8 st wider, $P < 0.05$). In both the seven- to eight-year-olds and ten- to eleven-year-olds, we found a significant interaction of FOCUS and TONE. The seven- to eight-year-olds used a significantly wider pitch span in narrow focus than in post-focus for words in Tone 2 (4.0 st wider, $P < 0.001$) and Tone 4 (2.0 st wider, $P < 0.05$). They also tended to use a wider pitch span in narrow focus than in post-focus for words in Tone 3 (1.9 st wider), but this tendency only approached statistical significance ($P = 0.05$). They did not vary pitch span for the same distinction for Tone 1 (Figure 3-6). The ten- to eleven-year-olds used a significantly wider pitch span in narrow focus than in post-focus for words in Tone 2 (2.8 st wider, $P < 0.001$), Tone 3 (1.6 st wider, $P < 0.05$) and Tone 4 (1.4 st wider, $P < 0.05$), but not in Tone 1(Figure 3-6).

Table 3-13 Model comparisons regarding the dependent variable pitch span in the comparison narrow focus vs. post-focus

Model comparisons	*Pr*(>Chisq)
0 vs. 1 (adding FOCUS)	0.005**
1 vs. 2 (adding AGE)	0.000***
2 vs. 3 (adding TONE)	0.000***

Continued

Model comparisons	*Pr*(>Chisq)
3 vs. 4 (adding FOCUS : AGE)	0.000***
4 vs. 5 (adding FOCUS : TONE)	0.009**
5 vs. 6 (adding AGE : TONE)	0.006**
6 vs. 7 (adding FOCUS : AGE : TONE)	0.005**

Table 3-14 Model summary regarding the dependent variable pitch span in the comparison narrow focus vs. post-focus

Factor	Estimate	Std. Error	*t* value	*Pr*(>|*t*|)
Intercept (Adults. Narrow focus. T1)	1.690	0.467	3.622	0.000***
Post-focus	0.027	0.593	0.046	0.963
Age 4-5	0.730	0.447	1.631	0.105
Age 7-8	0.997	0.437	2.282	0.024*
Age 10-11	0.646	0.422	1.529	0.129
T2	0.829	0.599	1.385	0.170
T3	2.748	0.626	4.390	0.000***
T4	2.204	0.599	3.680	0.000***
Post-focus : Age 4-5	0.339	0.502	0.675	0.500
Post-focus : Age 7-8	0.077	0.447	0.172	0.863
Post-focus : Age 10-11	0.378	0.440	0.859	0.391
Post-focus : T2	−1.239	0.850	−1.457	0.149
Post-focus : T3	−0.836	0.880	−0.950	0.344
Post-focus : T4	−0.968	0.845	−1.145	0.255
Age 4-5 : T2	1.050	0.502	2.094	0.037*
Age 7-8 : T2	1.891	0.460	4.109	0.000***
Age 10-11 : T2	1.210	0.439	2.757	0.006**
Age 4-5 : T3	0.340	0.668	0.509	0.611
Age 7-8 : T3	1.569	0.608	2.581	0.010*
Age 10-11 : T3	0.483	0.505	0.957	0.339
Age 4-5 : T4	0.822	0.515	1.595	0.111
Age 7-8 : T4	2.018	0.470	4.295	0.000***
Age 10-11 : T4	0.995	0.439	2.268	0.024*

Continued

Factor	Estimate	Std. Error	*t* value	*Pr*(>|*t*|)
Post-focus : Age 4-5 : T2	−1.160	0.733	−1.584	0.114
Post-focus : Age 7-8 : T2	−2.774	0.662	−4.191	0.000***
Post-focus : Age 10-11 : T2	−2.081	0.650	−3.201	0.001**
Post-focus : Age 4-5 : T3	0.417	0.886	0.471	0.638
Post-focus : Age 7-8 : T3	−1.880	0.812	−2.314	0.021*
Post-focus : Age 10-11 : T3	−1.242	0.705	−1.761	0.079
Post-focus : Age 4-5 : T4	0.162	0.729	0.223	0.824
Post-focus : Age 7-8 : T4	−1.105	0.663	−1.667	0.096
Post-focus : Age 10-11 : T4	−0.802	0.622	−1.291	0.197

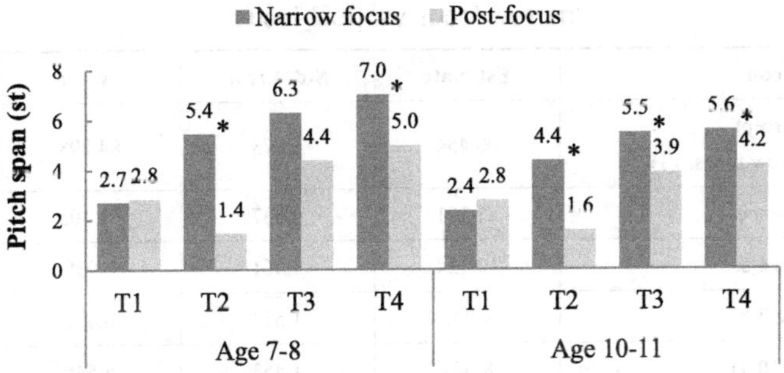

Figure 3-6 The use of pitch span in distinguishing narrow focus from post-focus in different tones in the seven- to eight-year-olds and ten- to eleven-year-olds

PITCH-MAX. The best-fit model for this dependent variable was Model 7 (Table 3-15). The summary of this model (Table 3-16) showed that the main effect of FOCUS, the interaction of FOCUS and AGE and the interaction of FOCUS, AGE and TONE were significant. In addition, the main effects of AGE and TONE and their interaction were also significant. Subsequent analysis showed a significant interaction of FOCUS and TONE in each group of children. The three groups of children all used a significantly higher pitch-max in narrow focus than in post-focus for words in Tone 1, Tone 2 and Tone 4 (Figure 3-7, $P < 0.05$ in all cases), but not for words in Tone 3, different from the adults, who used a significantly higher pitch-max in narrow focus than in post-focus regardless of tones (1.1 st higher, $P < 0.001$).

Table 3-15 Model comparisons regarding the dependent variable pitch-max in the comparison narrow focus vs. post-focus

Model comparisons	*Pr*(>Chisq)
0 vs. 1 (adding FOCUS)	0.000***
1 vs. 2 (adding AGE)	0.000***
2 vs. 3 (adding TONE)	0.000***
3 vs. 4 (adding FOCUS : AGE)	0.000***
4 vs. 5 (adding FOCUS : TONE)	0.003**
5 vs. 6 (adding AGE : TONE)	0.000***
6 vs. 7 (adding FOCUS : AGE : TONE)	0.004**

Table 3-16 Model summary regarding the dependent variable pitch-max in the comparison narrow focus vs. post-focus

Factor	Estimate	Std. Error	*t* value	*Pr*(>|*t*|)
Intercept (Adults. Narrow focus. T1)	90.454	1.073	84.298	0.000***
Post-focus	−1.291	0.537	−2.405	0.018*
Age 4-5	10.134	1.461	6.938	0.000***
Age 7-8	9.796	1.523	6.432	0.000***
Age 10-11	8.044	1.453	5.535	0.000***
T2	−2.475	0.540	−4.580	0.000***
T3	−2.010	0.547	−3.676	0.000***
T4	0.485	0.538	0.902	0.369
Post-focus : Age 4-5	−1.588	0.504	−3.147	0.002**
Post-focus : Age 7-8	−2.541	0.459	−5.539	0.000***
Post-focus : Age 10-11	−1.660	0.448	−3.707	0.000***
Post-focus : T2	0.022	0.766	0.029	0.977
Post-focus : T3	1.005	0.775	1.297	0.197
Post-focus : T4	−0.138	0.761	−0.181	0.857
Age 4-5 : T2	0.528	0.493	1.070	0.285
Age 7-8 : T2	−0.229	0.467	−0.490	0.624
Age 10-11 : T2	−0.189	0.445	−0.426	0.670
Age 4-5 : T3	−0.115	0.515	−0.224	0.823
Age 7-8 : T3	−1.621	0.473	−3.429	0.001**
Age 10-11 : T3	−1.085	0.447	−2.424	0.015*

Continued

Factor	Estimate	Std. Error	*t* value	*Pr*(>|*t*|)
Age 4-5 : T4	0.297	0.492	0.604	0.546
Age 7-8 : T4	0.362	0.465	0.778	0.437
Age 10-11 : T4	−0.063	0.438	−0.143	0.886
Post-focus : Age 4-5 : T2	1.386	0.723	1.917	0.056
Post-focus : Age 7-8 : T2	0.311	0.670	0.464	0.643
Post-focus : Age 10-11 : T2	0.042	0.652	0.064	0.949
Post-focus : Age 4-5 : T3	2.428	0.732	3.316	0.001**
Post-focus : Age 7-8 : T3	2.684	0.672	3.994	0.000***
Post-focus : Age 10-11 : T3	1.169	0.646	1.810	0.071
Post-focus : Age 4-5 : T4	1.393	0.702	1.983	0.048*
Post-focus : Age 7-8 : T4	1.008	0.659	1.530	0.126
Post-focus : Age 10-11 : T4	0.865	0.624	1.387	0.166

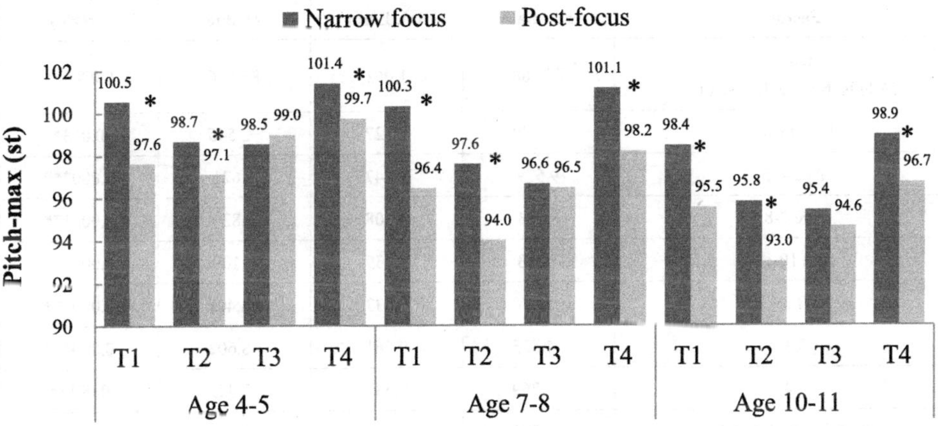

Figure 3-7 The use of pitch-max in distinguishing narrow focus from post-focus in different tones in the three groups of children

PITCH-MIN. The best-fit model for this dependent variable was Model 7 (Table 3-17). The summary of this model (Table 3-18) showed that the main effects of FOCUS, AGE and TONE, and all the two-way and three-way interactions were significant. Subsequent analysis showed a significant interaction of FOCUS and TONE in each age group. The four age groups all used a higher pitch-min in narrow focus than in post-focus for words in Tone 1 (3.8 st higher for the four- to five-year-olds, 4.0 st higher for the seven- to eight-year-olds, 3.2 st higher for the ten- to eleven-year-olds, and 1.3 st higher for the adults;

$P < 0.05$ in all cases) but not for words in the other tones (Figure 3-8).

Table 3-17 Model comparisons regarding the dependent variable pitch-min in the comparison narrow focus vs. post-focus

Model comparisons	*Pr*(>Chisq)
0 vs. 1 (adding FOCUS)	0.169
0 vs. 2 (adding AGE)	0.000***
2 vs. 3 (adding TONE)	0.000***
3 vs. 4 (adding FOCUS : AGE)	0.005**
4 vs. 5 (adding FOCUS : TONE)	0.000***
5 vs. 6 (adding AGE : TONE)	0.067
5 vs. 7 (adding FOCUS : AGE : TONE)	0.000***

Table 3-18 Model summary regarding the dependent variable pitch-min in the comparison narrow focus vs. post-focus

Factor	Estimate	Std. Error	*t* value	*Pr*(>|*t*|)
Intercept (Adults. Narrow focus. T1)	88.768	1.061	83.676	0.000***
Post-focus	−1.340	0.527	−2.545	0.013*
Age 4-5	9.579	1.447	6.621	0.000***
Age 7-8	8.783	1.508	5.826	0.000***
Age 10-11	7.353	1.439	5.109	0.000***
T2	−3.416	0.533	−6.407	0.000***
T3	−4.825	0.561	−8.602	0.000***
T4	−1.769	0.533	−3.322	0.001**
Post-focus : Age 4-5	−2.285	0.500	−4.571	0.000***
Post-focus : Age 7-8	−2.604	0.454	−5.733	0.000***
Post-focus : Age 10-11	−1.987	0.448	−4.438	0.000***
Post-focus : T2	1.485	0.759	1.957	0.053
Post-focus : T3	1.938	0.786	2.466	0.015*
Post-focus : T4	0.910	0.752	1.210	0.229
Age 4-5 : T2	−0.673	0.509	−1.322	0.187
Age 7-8 : T2	−2.072	0.466	−4.449	0.000***
Age 10-11 : T2	−1.258	0.445	−2.828	0.005**
Age 4-5 : T3	−0.235	0.674	−0.348	0.728

Continued

Factor	Estimate	Std. Error	*t* value	*Pr*(>|*t*|)
Age 7-8 : T3	−2.561	0.615	−4.168	0.000***
Age 10-11 : T3	−1.376	0.510	−2.700	0.007**
Age 4-5 : T4	−0.302	0.517	−0.585	0.559
Age 7-8 : T4	−1.753	0.474	−3.702	0.000***
Age 10-11 : T4	−0.964	0.445	−2.167	0.030*
Post-focus : Age 4-5 : T2	2.853	0.736	3.874	0.000***
Post-focus : Age 7-8 : T2	2.927	0.669	4.376	0.000***
Post-focus : Age 10-11 : T2	1.821	0.660	2.758	0.006**
Post-focus : Age 4-5 : T3	1.508	0.890	1.694	0.091
Post-focus : Age 7-8 : T3	3.631	0.815	4.454	0.000***
Post-focus : Age 10-11 : T3	2.039	0.711	2.870	0.004**
Post-focus : Age 4-5 : T4	1.604	0.733	2.188	0.029*
Post-focus : Age 7-8 : T4	2.314	0.668	3.463	0.001**
Post-focus : Age 10-11 : T4	1.558	0.631	2.469	0.014*

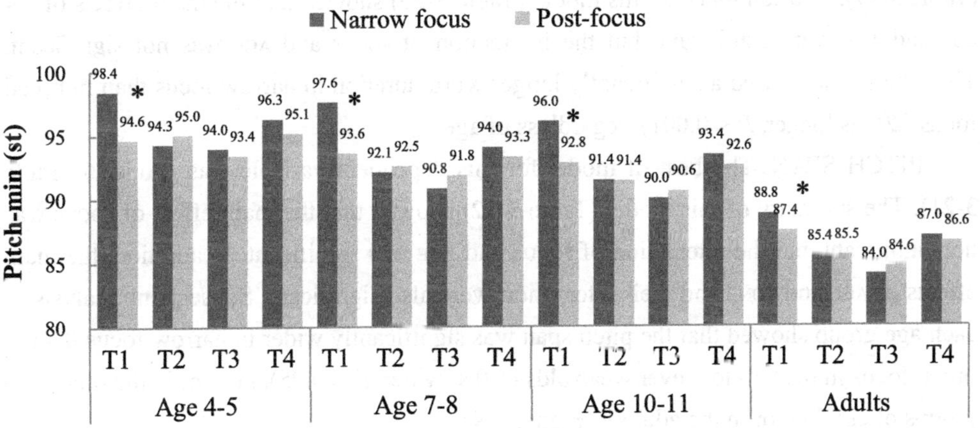

Figure 3-8 The use of pitch-min in distinguishing narrow focus from post-focus in different tones in each age group

INTERIM SUMMARY. To distinguish narrow focus from post-focus, the three groups of children all used a longer duration in narrow focus than in post-focus, similar to the adults. However, different from the adults, who used a wider pitch span in narrow focus than in post-focus, the ten- to eleven-year-olds used pitch span in this manner for words in Tone 2, Tone 3, and Tone 4, and the seven- to eight-year-olds used pitch span in this manner for words in Tone 2 and Tone 4. The four- to five-year-olds, however, did not vary pitch span for this purpose. Further, different from the adults, who used a higher pitch-max in narrow focus than in post-focus, the three groups of children only used pitch-max in this manner for words in Tone 1, Tone 2, and Tone 4. In addition, the children all used a higher pitch-min in narrow focus than in post-focus for words in Tone 1, similar to the adults. Thus, in the two groups of older children, the pitch span difference between narrow focus and post-focus for words in Tone 2 and Tone 4 was caused by a difference between focus and post-focus in pitch-max, similar as in the adults' production. Last, the three groups of children all used a higher pitch register (i.e., a higher pitch-max and a higher pitch-min) in narrow focus than in post-focus for words in Tone 1, similar to the adults.

3.3.2 Realisation of focus types

3.3.2.1 Narrow focus vs. broad focus (NF-m vs. BF)

WORD DURATION. The best-fit model for this dependent variable was Model 2 (Table 3-19). The summary of this model (Table 3-20) showed that the main effects of FOCUS and AGE were significant, but the interaction of FOCUS and AGE was not significant. Thus the speakers used a significantly longer word duration in narrow focus than in broad focus (20 ms longer, $P < 0.001$), regardless of age.

PITCH SPAN. The best-fit model for this dependent variable was Model 6 (Table 3-21). The summary of this model (Table 3-22) showed that the main effect of FOCUS was not significant, but the interaction of FOCUS and AGE was significant. In addition, the main effects of AGE and TONE and their interaction were also significant. Subsequent analysis of each age group showed that the pitch span was significantly wider in narrow focus than in broad focus in the ten- to eleven-year-olds (1.0 st wider, $P < 0.05$), but not in the other two groups of children or in the adults① (Figure 3-9).

Table 3-19 Model comparisons regarding the dependent variable word duration in the comparison narrow focus vs. broad focus

Model comparisons	Pr(>Chisq)
0 vs. 1 (adding FOCUS)	0.001**

① The pitch span difference (0.4 st) between narrow focus and broad focus in adults was rather small and was not significant according to the best-fit model for the adult data, i.e., the model with only the main effect of focus, though it was significant when analysing the adults' data in Chapter 2, involving both focus and tone in the model.

Continued

Model comparisons	*Pr*(>Chisq)
1 vs. 2 (adding AGE)	0.000***
2 vs. 3 (adding TONE)	0.958
2 vs. 4 (adding FOCUS : AGE)	0.354
2 vs. 5 (adding FOCUS : TONE)	0.352
2 vs. 6 (adding AGE : TONE)	0.658
2 vs. 7 (adding FOCUS : AGE : TONE)	0.508

Table 3-20 Model summary regarding the dependent variable word duration in the comparison narrow focus vs. broad focus

Factor	Estimate	Std. Error	*t* value	*Pr*(>|*t*|)
Intercept (Narrow focus. Adults)	0.226	0.010	23.290	0.000***
Broad focus	−0.020	0.006	−3.540	0.001**
Age 4-5	0.104	0.013	8.180	0.000***
Age 7-8	0.093	0.013	7.018	0.000***
Age 10-11	0.048	0.013	3.842	0.000***

Table 3-21 Model comparisons regarding the dependent variable pitch span in the comparison narrow focus vs. broad focus

Model comparisons	*Pr*(>Chisq)
0 vs. 1 (adding FOCUS)	0.030*
1 vs. 2 (adding AGE)	0.000***
2 vs. 3 (adding TONE)	0.000***
3 vs. 4 (adding FOCUS : AGE)	0.023*
4 vs. 5 (adding FOCUS : TONE)	0.444
4 vs. 6 (adding AGE : TONE)	0.000***
6 vs. 7 (adding FOCUS : AGE : TONE)	0.267

Table 3-22 Model summary regarding the dependent variable pitch span in the comparison narrow focus vs. broad focus

Factor	Estimate	Std. Error	*t* value	*Pr*(>|*t*|)
Intercept (Adults. Narrow focus. T1)	1.701	0.414	4.104	0.000***

Continued

Factor	Estimate	Std. Error	*t* value	*Pr*(>|*t*|)
Broad focus	0.060	0.473	0.126	0.900
Age 4-5	0.593	0.418	1.419	0.159
Age 7-8	0.976	0.418	2.333	0.022*
Age 10-11	0.683	0.396	1.722	0.089
T2	0.963	0.487	1.977	0.052
T3	2.507	0.511	4.910	0.000***
T4	2.165	0.488	4.438	0.000***
Broad focus : Age 4-5	−0.559	0.277	−2.022	0.043*
Broad focus : Age 7-8	−0.755	0.254	−2.970	0.003**
Broad focus : Age 10-11	−0.602	0.224	−2.691	0.007**
Broad focus : T2	−0.794	0.645	−1.230	0.224
Broad focus : T3	−0.337	0.671	−0.502	0.617
Broad focus : T4	−0.811	0.647	−1.253	0.215
Age 4-5 : T2	0.772	0.357	2.162	0.031*
Age 7-8 : T2	1.478	0.324	4.560	0.000***
Age 10-11 : T2	1.187	0.297	3.993	0.000***
Age 4-5 : T3	1.000	0.422	2.370	0.018*
Age 7-8 : T3	1.959	0.426	4.604	0.000***
Age 10-11 : T3	0.624	0.336	1.853	0.064
Age 4-5 : T4	0.958	0.365	2.622	0.009**
Age 7-8 : T4	2.166	0.332	6.523	0.000***
Age 10-11 : T4	0.849	0.301	2.816	0.005**

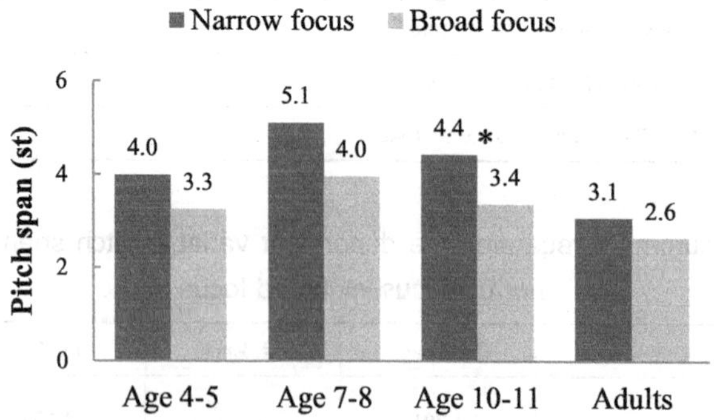

Figure 3-9 The use of pitch span in distinguishing narrow focus from broad focus

PITCH-MAX. The best-fit model for this dependent variable was Model 6 (Table 3-23). The summary of this model (Table 3-24) showed that the main effect of FOCUS was not significant, but the interaction of FOCUS and AGE was significant. In addition, the effects of AGE and TONE and their interaction were also significant. Subsequent analysis of each age group showed that the pitch-max was significantly higher in narrow focus than in broad focus in the four- to five-year-olds (1.3 st higher, $P < 0.05$), but not in the other two groups of older children or in the adults (Figure 3-10).

Table 3-23 Model comparisons regarding the dependent variable pitch-max in the comparison narrow focus vs. broad focus

Model comparisons	***Pr*(>Chisq)**
0 vs. 1 (adding FOCUS)	0.156
0 vs. 2 (adding AGE)	0.000***
2 vs. 3 (adding TONE)	0.000***
3 vs. 4 (adding FOCUS : AGE)	0.002**
4 vs. 5 (adding FOCUS : TONE)	0.152
4 vs. 6 (adding AGE : TONE)	0.000***
6 vs. 7 (adding FOCUS : AGE : TONE)	0.652

Table 3-24 Model summary regarding the dependent variable pitch-max in the comparison narrow focus vs. broad focus

Factor	**Estimate**	**Std. Error**	***t* value**	***Pr*(>|*t*|)**
Intercept (Adults. Narrow focus. T1)	90.537	1.037	87.308	0.000***
Broad focus	−0.274	0.399	−0.687	0.494
Age 4-5	9.866	1.430	6.897	0.000***
Age 7-8	9.669	1.495	6.469	0.000***
Age 10-11	7.922	1.424	5.562	0.000***
T2	−2.621	0.418	−6.278	0.000***
T3	−2.198	0.421	−5.219	0.000***
T4	0.502	0.417	1.206	0.231
Broad focus : Age 4-5	−1.044	0.265	−3.944	0.000***
Broad focus : Age 7-8	−0.478	0.243	−1.963	0.050
Broad focus : Age 10-11	−0.494	0.221	−2.238	0.025*
Broad focus : T2	0.289	0.537	0.539	0.592

Continued

Factor	Estimate	Std. Error	*t* value	*Pr*(>|*t*|)
Broad focus : T3	0.739	0.537	1.377	0.174
Broad focus : T4	−0.446	0.537	−0.830	0.410
Age 4-5 : T2	0.730	0.360	2.028	0.043*
Age 7-8 : T2	−0.200	0.337	−0.593	0.554
Age 10-11 : T2	0.192	0.309	0.621	0.535
Age 4-5 : T3	0.210	0.363	0.579	0.563
Age 7-8 : T3	-1.217	0.341	-3.571	0.000***
Age 10-11 : T3	-0.937	0.311	-3.015	0.003**
Age 4-5 : T4	0.220	0.364	0.605	0.545
Age 7-8 : T4	0.349	0.337	1.036	0.300
Age 10-11 : T4	-0.092	0.309	-0.297	0.767

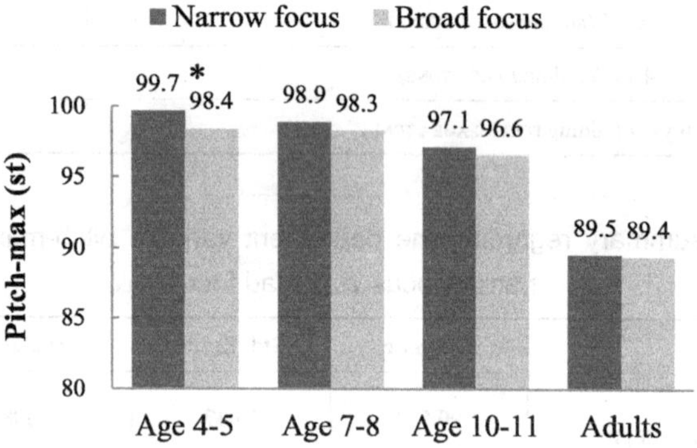

Figure 3-10 The use of pitch-max in distinguishing narrow focus from broad focus

PITCH-MIN. The best-fit model for this dependent variable was Model 6 (Table 3-25). The summary of this model (Table 3-26) showed that the main effect of FOCUS was not significant, and it was not involved in any interaction. Thus, the speakers did not use pitch-min to distinguish narrow focus from broad focus, regardless of age.

Table 3-25 Model comparisons regarding the dependent variable pitch-min in the comparison narrow focus vs. broad focus

Model comparisons	*Pr*(>Chisq)
0 vs. 1 (adding FOCUS)	0.554
0 vs. 2 (adding AGE)	0.000***

Continued

Model comparisons	*Pr*(>Chisq)
2 vs. 3 (adding TONE)	0.000***
3 vs. 4 (adding FOCUS : AGE)	0.296
3 vs. 5 (adding FOCUS : TONE)	0.268
3 vs. 6 (adding AGE : TONE)	0.000***
6 vs. 7 (adding FOCUS : AGE : TONE)	0.669

Table 3-26 Model summary regarding the dependent variable pitch-min in the comparison narrow focus vs. broad focus

Factor	Estimate	Std. Error	*t* value	*Pr*(>|*t*|)
Intercept (Adults. Narrow focus. T1)	88.861	1.051	84.567	0.000***
Broad focus	−0.369	0.554	−0.666	0.508
Age 4-5	9.388	1.402	6.698	0.000***
Age 7-8	8.679	1.464	5.930	0.000***
Age 10-11	7.228	1.395	5.183	0.000***
T2	−3.753	0.568	−6.602	0.000***
T3	−4.837	0.591	−8.180	0.000***
T4	−1.717	0.569	−3.016	0.004**
Broad focus : Age 4-5	−0.508	0.299	−1.698	0.090
Broad focus : Age 7-8	0.200	0.275	0.727	0.467
Broad focus : Age 10-11	0.025	0.242	0.103	0.918
Broad focus : T2	1.301	0.760	1.712	0.092
Broad focus : T3	1.076	0.785	1.371	0.175
Broad focus : T4	0.462	0.762	0.607	0.547
Age 4-5 : T2	−0.088	0.387	−0.228	0.820
Age 7-8 : T2	−1.624	0.351	−4.627	0.000***
Age 10-11 : T2	−0.886	0.322	−2.748	0.006**
Age 4-5 : T3	−0.075	0.454	−0.166	0.868
Age 7-8 : T3	−2.490	0.463	−5.383	0.000***
Age 10-11 : T3	−1.340	0.363	−3.690	0.000***
Age 4-5 : T4	−0.608	0.396	−1.537	0.125
Age 7-8 : T4	−1.793	0.359	−4.997	0.000***
Age 10-11 : T4	−0.951	0.327	−2.913	0.004**

INTERIM SUMMARY. The three groups of children all used a longer duration in narrow focus than in broad focus, similar to the adults. The seven- to eight-year-olds did not vary the pitch-related cues for this distinction, similar to the adults. The ten- to eleven-year-olds used a wider pitch span and the four- to five-year-olds used a higher pitch-max for the words in narrow focus than in broad focus, different from the adults.

3.3.2.2 Narrow focus vs. contrastive focus (NF-m vs. CF-m)

WORD DURATION. The best-fit model for this dependent variable was Model 2 (Table 3-27). The summary of this model (Table 3-28) showed that the main effect of FOCUS was not significant, and it was not involved in any interaction. Thus, the speakers did not use word duration to distinguish narrow focus from broad focus, regardless of age.

Table 3-27 Model comparisons regarding the dependent variable word duration in the comparison narrow focus vs. contrastive focus

Model comparisons	*Pr*(>Chisq)
0 vs. 1 (adding FOCUS)	0.959
0 vs. 2 (adding AGE)	0.000***
2 vs. 3 (adding TONE)	0.386
2 vs. 4 (adding FOCUS : AGE)	0.360
2 vs. 5 (adding FOCUS : TONE)	0.650
2 vs. 6 (adding AGE : TONE)	0.506
2 vs. 7 (adding FOCUS : AGE : TONE)	0.646

Table 3-28 Model summary regarding the dependent variable word duration in the comparison narrow focus vs. contrastive focus

Factor	Estimate	Std. Error	*t* value	*Pr*(>|*t*|)
Intercept (Adults. Narrow focus)	0.220	0.011	20.694	0.000***
Contrastive focus	0.000	0.006	0.039	0.969
Age 4-5	0.116	0.014	8.381	0.000***
Age 7-8	0.099	0.014	6.821	0.000***
Age 10-11	0.054	0.014	3.893	0.000***

PITCH SPAN. The best-fit model for this dependent variable was Model 6 (Table 3-29). The summary of this model (Table 3-30) showed that the main effect of FOCUS was not significant, and it was not involved in any interaction. Thus, the speakers did not use pitch span to distinguish narrow focus from contrastive focus, regardless of age.

Table 3-29 Model comparisons regarding the dependent variable pitch span duration in the comparison narrow focus vs. contrastive focus

Model comparisons	***Pr*(>Chisq)**
0 vs. 1 (adding FOCUS)	0.687
0 vs. 2 (adding AGE)	0.000***
2 vs. 3 (adding TONE)	0.000***
3 vs. 4 (adding FOCUS : AGE)	0.168
3 vs. 5 (adding FOCUS : TONE)	0.533
3 vs. 6 (adding AGE : TONE)	0.000***
6 vs. 7 (adding FOCUS : AGE : TONE)	0.727

Table 3-30 Model summary regarding the dependent variable pitch span duration in the comparison narrow focus vs. contrastive focus

Factor	**Estimate**	**Std. Error**	***t* value**	***Pr*(>|*t*|)**
Intercept (Adults. Narrow focus. T1)	1.733	0.443	3.907	0.000***
Contrastive focus	−0.120	0.491	−0.244	0.808
Age 4-5	0.552	0.465	1.186	0.239
Age 7-8	0.992	0.466	2.127	0.037*
Age 10-11	0.655	0.445	1.471	0.145
T2	0.864	0.506	1.708	0.092
T3	2.625	0.539	4.875	0.000***
T4	2.077	0.507	4.093	0.000***
Contrastive focus : Age 4-5	0.442	0.292	1.513	0.131
Contrastive focus : Age 7-8	0.516	0.272	1.900	0.058
Contrastive focus : Age 10-11	0.222	0.251	0.886	0.376
Contrastive focus : T2	0.108	0.663	0.163	0.871
Contrastive focus : T3	−0.027	0.714	−0.038	0.970
Contrastive focus : T4	0.074	0.666	0.112	0.911
Age 4-5 : T2	1.128	0.367	3.069	0.002**

Continued

Factor	Estimate	Std. Error	*t* value	*Pr*(>|*t*|)
Age 7-8 : T2	1.802	0.346	5.214	0.000***
Age 10-11 : T2	1.003	0.325	3.087	0.002**
Age 4-5 : T3	0.797	0.502	1.588	0.113
Age 7-8 : T3	1.525	0.473	3.226	0.001**
Age 10-11 : T3	0.507	0.401	1.265	0.206
Age 4-5 : T4	1.158	0.389	2.977	0.003**
Age 7-8 : T4	1.805	0.355	5.089	0.000***
Age 10-11 : T4	1.204	0.331	3.644	0.000***

PITCH-MAX. The best-fit model for this dependent variable was Model 6 (Table 3-31). The summary of this model (Table 3-32) showed that the main effect of FOCUS was not significant, and it was not involved in any interaction. Thus, the speakers did not use pitch-max to distinguish narrow focus from contrastive focus, regardless of age.

Table 3-31 Model comparisons regarding the dependent variable pitch-max in the comparison narrow focus vs. contrastive focus

Model comparisons	*Pr*(>Chisq)
0 vs. 1 (adding FOCUS)	0.411
0 vs. 2 (adding AGE)	0.000***
2 vs. 3 (adding TONE)	0.000***
3 vs. 4 (adding FOCUS : AGE)	0.632
3 vs. 5 (adding FOCUS : TONE)	0.938
3 vs. 6 (adding AGE : TONE)	0.000***
6 vs. 7 (adding FOCUS : AGE : TONE)	0.963

Table 3-32 Model summary regarding the dependent variable pitch-max in the comparison narrow focus vs. contrastive focus

Factor	Estimate	Std. Error	*t* value	*Pr*(>|*t*|)
Intercept (Adults. Narrow focus. T1)	90.430	1.040	86.917	0.000***
Contrastive focus	−0.372	0.391	−0.949	0.345
Age 4-5	10.250	1.438	7.128	0.000***

Continued

Factor	Estimate	Std. Error	*t* value	*Pr*(>|*t*|)
Age 7-8	9.760	1.503	6.494	0.000***
Age 10-11	8.086	1.433	5.643	0.000***
T2	-2.455	0.411	-5.970	0.000***
T3	-1.929	0.418	-4.614	0.000***
T4	0.544	0.410	1.325	0.188
Contrastive focus : Age 4-5	-0.147	0.262	-0.559	0.576
Contrastive focus : Age 7-8	0.196	0.249	0.787	0.431
Contrastive focus : Age 10-11	-0.104	0.233	-0.447	0.655
Contrastive focus : T2	0.069	0.517	0.133	0.894
Contrastive focus : T3	0.096	0.520	0.184	0.855
Contrastive focus : T4	-0.029	0.518	-0.055	0.956
Age 4-5 : T2	0.364	0.357	1.018	0.309
Age 7-8 : T2	-0.101	0.346	-0.292	0.771
Age 10-11 : T2	-0.302	0.324	-0.932	0.352
Age 4-5 : T3	-0.227	0.378	-0.600	0.548
Age 7-8 : T3	-1.654	0.353	-4.688	0.000***
Age 10-11 : T3	-1.248	0.334	-3.739	0.000***
Age 4-5 : T4	-0.061	0.367	-0.166	0.868
Age 7-8 : T4	0.287	0.344	0.834	0.404
Age 10-11 : T4	-0.005	0.322	-0.014	0.989

PITCH-MIN. The best-fit model for this dependent variable was Model 6 (Table 3-33). The summary of this model (Table 3-34) showed that the effect of FOCUS was not significant, but it had a two-way interaction with AGE. In addition, the effects of age and tone and their interaction were also significant. Subsequent analysis of each age group showed that the pitch-min was significantly lower in contrastive focus than in narrow focus in the four- to five-year-olds (1.4 st lower, $P < 0.05$), but not in the other two groups of children or in the adults.

Table 3-33 Model comparisons regarding the dependent variable pitch-min in the comparison narrow focus vs. contrastive focus

Model comparisons	***Pr*(>Chisq)**
0 vs. 1 (adding FOCUS)	0.465
0 vs. 2 (adding AGE)	0.000***
2 vs. 3 (adding TONE)	0.000***
3 vs. 4 (adding FOCUS : AGE)	0.200
3 vs. 5 (adding FOCUS : TONE)	0.496
3 vs. 6 (adding AGE : TONE)	0.000***
6 vs. 7 (adding FOCUS : AGE : TONE)	0.588

Table 3-34 Model summary regarding the dependent variable pitch-min in the comparison narrow focus vs. contrastive focus

Factor	**Estimate**	**Std. Error**	***t* value**	***Pr*(>|*t*|)**
Intercept (Adults. Narrow focus. T1)	88.764	1.022	86.811	0.000***
Contrastive focus	−0.391	0.457	−0.854	0.396
Age 4-5	9.642	1.395	6.914	0.000***
Age 7-8	8.660	1.456	5.947	0.000***
Age 10-11	7.390	1.389	5.322	0.000***
T2	-3.419	0.473	-7.227	0.000***
T3	-4.775	0.506	-9.437	0.000***
T4	-1.620	0.475	-3.414	0.001**
Contrastive focus : Age 4-5	-0.633	0.292	-2.169	0.030*
Contrastive focus : Age 7-8	−0.092	0.272	−0.338	0.736
Contrastive focus : Age 10-11	−0.160	0.251	−0.638	0.523
Contrastive focus : T2	0.110	0.612	0.180	0.858
Contrastive focus : T3	0.431	0.665	0.648	0.519
Contrastive focus : T4	−0.070	0.616	−0.113	0.910
Age 4-5 : T2	−0.695	0.368	−1.889	0.059
Age 7-8 : T2	−1.917	0.347	−5.531	0.000***
Age 10-11 : T2	−1.295	0.326	3.975	0.000***
Age 4-5 : T3	−0.633	0.504	−1.257	0.209
Age 7-8 : T3	−1.899	0.474	−4.002	0.000***
Age 10-11 : T3	−1.270	0.401	−3.166	0.002**

Continued

Factor	Estimate	Std. Error	*t* value	*Pr*(>|*t*|)
Age 4-5 : T4	−0.918	0.389	−2.363	0.018*
Age 7-8 : T4	−1.474	0.355	−4.153	0.000***
Age 10-11 : T4	−1.215	0.331	−3.665	0.000***

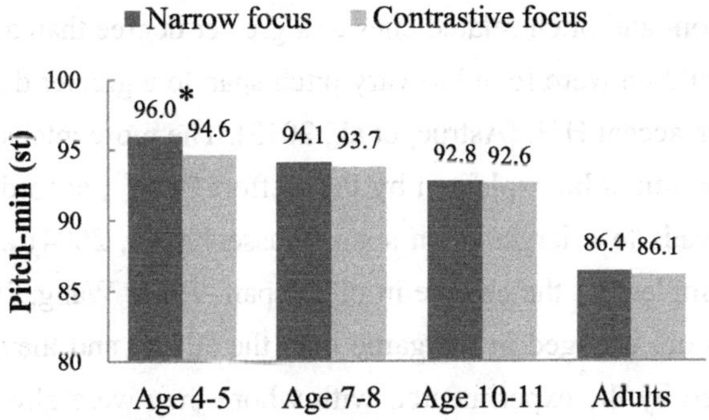

Figure 3-11 The use of pitch-min in distinguishing narrow focus from contrastive focus

INTERIM SUMMARY. The seven- to eight-year-olds and ten- to eleven-year-olds did not use any of the four phonetic cues to distinguish narrow focus from contrastive focus, similar to the adults. The four- to five-year-olds used a lower pitch-min for contrastive focus than for narrow focus, different from the adults.

3.4 Discussion and conclusions

We have examined how Mandarin-speaking four- to five-year-olds, seven- to eight-year-olds, and ten- to eleven-year-olds use duration and pitch to distinguish narrow focus from non-focus and two other types of focus, compared to adults in semi-spontaneous speech.

With regard to the prosodic realisation of narrow focus, we have observed adult-like use of duration in distinguishing narrow focus from both pre-focus and post-focus at the age of four to five. However, children make no systematic use of pitch span for the same purposes at this age, unlike adults. Nevertheless, they can vary pitch-max and pitch-min to distinguish focus from post-focus and vary pitch-min to distinguish focus from pre-focus in an adult-like way in certain tonal categories. By the age of seven to eight, they can vary pitch span in an adult-like way to distinguish focus from pre-focus regardless of tone, and to distinguish focus from post-focus in Tone 2 and Tone 4. By the age of ten- to eleven, they become adult-like in the use of pitch span in distinguishing focus from post-focus in all but Tone 1. In addition, children's use of pitch-max and pitch-min is still not fully adult-like at the age of seven to eleven, thus unadult-like in how they realise the difference in pitch span between different focus conditions. Additionally, it is worth noting that children vary the duration- and pitch-related cues to a greater degree than adults do. Similarly, English-speaking children were found to vary pitch span to a greater degree than adults in producing the falling accent H*L (Astruc, et al., 2013). The more intensive use of duration and pitch in children might be explained by the "Effort Code", according to which more articulatory effort leads to a larger pitch span (Gussenhoven, 2004) and consequently a longer duration to implement the change in pitch span (Xu & Wang, 2001). The children in our study were more engaged in the game than the adults, and they were eager to answer questions asked by the experimenter, with whom they were already familiar. Thus, they may have taken more effort in speech production, especially when offering new information, which might have led to a more intensive use of the prosodic cues, in line with the "Effort Code".

As for the distinction of focus types differing in focal constituent size, we have found that four- to five-year-olds can already vary duration in an adult-like way in distinguishing narrow focus from broad focus. However, they also use a higher pitch-max for narrow focus than for broad focus, different from adults. By the age of seven to eight, children no longer distinguish these two types of focus using the pitch-related cues, similar to adults. Unexpectedly, at the age of ten to eleven, children use a wider pitch span for narrow focus than for broad focus, different from adults. Ten- to eleven-year-olds' use of pitch span in distinguishing these two conditions is similar to adult's use of prosody for the same purpose in read speech (Xu, 1999), suggesting more careful manner of speaking in this age group than in the other age groups.

Regarding the distinction of focus types differing in contrastivity, adults do not use any of the four prosodic cues to distinguish narrow focus from contrastive focus. At the age of four to five, children do not use duration to make the distinction but use a lower pitch-min in contrastive focus than in narrow focus, different from adults. At the age of seven to eight and onwards, they do not prosodically distinguish narrow focus from contrastive focus, like adults. A similar observation that children at the age of three use prosody to mark contrast while adults do not has been reported in German (Grünloh, Lieven &

Tomasello, 2015). It is thus possible that at least some young children (e.g., the four- to five-year-olds in our study and the three-year-olds in Grunloh and colleagues' study) may find it exciting to correct an adult with whom they are already familiar, and thus mark contrastive focus with more prosodic prominence.

Furthermore, we have seen evidence that Mandarin-speaking children's use of pitch for focus-marking purposes varies between tones at younger ages. First, as mentioned earlier, to distinguish narrow focus from pre-focus, seven- to eight-year-olds expand the pitch span in Tone 1 and Tone 4 by raising the pitch-max, and expand the pitch span in Tone 2 and Tone 3 by lowering the pitch-min in narrow focus. Given that Tone 1 and Tone 4 start with a high tonal onset, while Tone 2 and Tone 3 start with a relatively low tonal onset (Xu, 1997), seven- to eight-year-olds might have chosen to expand the pitch span by raising the high tonal onset in Tone 1 and Tone 4, which led to an even higher pitch-max in Tone 1 and Tone 4, and lowering the low tonal onset in Tone 2 and Tone 3, which led to an even lower pitch-min in Tone 2 and Tone 3. This approach is not adult-like but may still be effective in achieving more prosodic prominence in focus. It has been shown that listeners associate a higher pitch of a high tone and a lower pitch of low tone with more prominence in Dutch (Gussenhoven & Rietveld, 2000). Further, in distinguishing focus from post-focus, ten- to eleven-year-olds' use of pitch span in Tone 1 and their use of pitch span in terms of variation in pitch-max in Tone 3 are not adult-like. The later acquisition of the use of pitch span for Tone 1 and Tone 3 than for Tone 2 and Tone 4 post-focally may be related to tonal properties. Specifically, Tone 2 and Tone 4 are characterised by a sharp rise and a steep fall respectively, whereas Tone 1 is a flat tone and Tone 3 is usually realised as a low tone with a slightly falling pitch contour. Adult speakers vary the pitch span in Tone 1 and Tone 3 to a lesser degree than in Tone 2 and Tone 4 in focus marking, probably to keep the tonal identities of Tone 1 and Tone 3 intact. Thus, the perceivable changes in pitch span in post-focal regions may also be relatively small in Tone 1 and Tone 3 in the input available to children. Accordingly, children may need more time to grasp these small changes from input in Tone 1 and Tone 3 than in Tone 2 and Tone 4. As discussed in the introduction, given children's later acquisition of Tone 2 and Tone 3 than Tone 1 and Tone 4, we predicted a later adult-like use of pitch for focus-marking purposes in Tone 2 and Tone 3 than in Tone 1 and Tone 4. This prediction is not borne out. Thus, the acquisition of the use of pitch to mark focus in different lexical tones does not follow the order of the acquisition of the lexical tones, implying that the acquisition of prosodic focus marking does not closely correlate with the acquisition of lexical tones in Mandarin.

Comparing Mandarin-speaking children with children acquiring a West Germanic language, we have found that Mandarin-speaking children begin to use phonetic means at an earlier age and become adult-like in the use of certain phonetic means at an earlier age, in line with our prediction based on the more extensive exposure to phonetic focus marking in Mandarin. Specifically, Mandarin-speaking children can already vary duration to distinguish narrow focus from non-focus as well as from broad focus in an adult-like way by the age of four to five. In contrast, English-speaking children do not vary duration to distinguish contrastive (i.e., "Given-Shift" and "New") from non-contrastive (i.e., "Given-NonShift") words when they are both accented with a falling pitch accent at the age of three to four (Wonnacott & Watson, 2008), different from adults (Watson, Arnold & Tanenhaus, 2005, as cited by Wonnacott & Watson, 2008). Dutch-speaking children do not vary duration to distinguish sentence-initial focus from non-focus when a falling accent is used in both cases at the age of seven to eight, different from adults (A. Chen, 2009). Furthermore, English- and German-speaking children vary pitch-related cues in a adult-like way to mark focus at the age of four to five when focus is contrastive (Wonnacott & Watson, 2008; Müller, et al., 2005), while Dutch-speaking children of this age range do not show adult-like use of pitch in distinguishing focus from non-focus when focus is not contrastive (A. Chen, 2009). These findings imply that children's phonetic use of pitch in West Germanic languages is very likely related to the expression of contrast (A. Chen, 2015). However, Mandarin-speaking children at a similar age can vary pitch-max and pitch-min of certain lexical tones for focus-marking purposes even when the focused words do not carry contrast.

We have also found that the use of pitch for lexical purposes in Mandarin influences the order in which Mandarin-speaking children learn to use pitch and duration in focus marking. We have predicted that the lexical use of pitch can either speed up the acquisition of pitch for focus-marking purposes (because children need to pay close attention to pitch from an early age in word learning) or slow it down (because there is limited acoustic space left for focus-related manipulation in pitch), compared to the acquisition of duration. Our results provide evidence for the latter prediction. Mandarin-speaking children have fully mastered the use of duration for focus-marking purposes by the age of four to five. At this age, they have also started to use pitch for focus-marking purposes for words in certain tones in an adult-like way, but their use of this cue is still developing after the age of eleven. In contrast, children acquiring Dutch acquire the use of pitch earlier than the use of duration in phonetic focus marking (A. Chen, 2009). As we know, pitch is not used to distinguish words in Dutch. Our findings on Mandarin and previous findings on Dutch together imply that the lexical use of pitch in a language influences the acquisition of the use of pitch as compared to the acquisition of the use of duration for focus-marking purposes. Interestingly, the acquisition of the use of pitch in Mandarin is still earlier than that in Dutch, which starts after the age of five (A. Chen, 2009). We thus speculate that Mandarin-speaking children's early competence in the use of pitch for lexical purpose induces an early use of pitch for focus-marking purposes, but does not lead to an early mastery of the use of pitch for such purpose.

CHAPTER 4

Prosodic realisation of focus in Seoul Korean: the use of prosodic phrasing and phonetic cues①

Abstract

This study examines how Seoul Korean speakers use phonological (i.e., prosodic phrasing) and phonetic (i.e., gradient changes in pitch and duration) cues for focus-marking purposes. Semi-spontaneous productions of short sentences were elicited via a picture-matching task. Regarding phonological focus marking, Seoul Korean speakers use prosodic phrasing to distinguish narrow focus from non-focus (i.e., pre-focus and post-focus) and from two other types of focus (i.e., broad focus and contrastive focus). As for phonetic focus marking, when the target words were AP-initial words, they used a longer word duration, longer initial-syllable duration, and a higher maximum pitch for words in narrow focus than in non-focus. They did not distinguish narrow focus from broad focus or contrastive focus using phonetic cues.

Keywords

Focus, prosodic phrasing, phonetic cues, Seoul Korean

---

① Preliminary results of a portion of the data from Chapter 4 were presented at the 18th International Congress of Phonetic Sciences (ICPhS), and published in the proceedings (Yang, Cho, Kim, & Chen, 2015). A version of Chapter 4 is aimed to be submitted in article form to an appropriate journal.

4.1 Introduction

The prosodic encoding of focus in Seoul Korean (hereafter, Korean) has long been studied (Jeon & Nolan, 2017; Jun, 1993; Jun & H. J. Lee, 1998; Y. C. Lee & Xu, 2010). It is well known that Korean uses both phonological (i.e., prosodic phrasing) and phonetic (i.e., gradient changes in pitch and duration) cues for focus-marking purposes. However, the previous studies were all based on read speech, and most analysed the use of prosodic phrasing (hereafter, phrasing) in a descriptive way. The analysis of phonetic focus marking was usually independent of phonological category. In order to have a better understanding of the prosodic encoding of focus in Korean, we have examined phonological and phonetic focus marking in semi-spontaneous speech.

In what follows, we will first briefly review phonological and phonetic focus marking in Korean (section 4.1.1), and then discuss the limitations of past work (section 4.1.2). Finally, we will state the purpose of the current study (section 4.1.3).

4.1.1 Phonological and phonetic focus marking in Korean

Korean has no word-level use of prosody. Pitch movement in this language is aligned to larger prosodic units, namely, prosodic phrases (Jun, 1993, 1998, 2000, 2005). According to Jun (1993, 1998, 2000, 2005), the Accentual Phrase (AP) and the Intonation Phrase (IP) are two prosodic units above the Phonological Word (PW) (i.e., a lexical item followed by a case marker or postpositions). The PW does not have any prosodic specification. The AP is the smallest unit carrying a phrasal tone sequence, T(HL)H, where the initial tone (T) is realised as either a high tone (H) or a low tone (L) depending on the laryngeal feature of the initial segment of the AP, and the tones in the brackets are either realised or deleted, depending on the number of syllables in the AP. An AP consists of one or more PWs and is marked by the sequential tonal pattern. An IP consists of one or more APs and is marked by a phrase-final boundary tone and phrase-final lengthening (see more details of the intonational structure of Korean in Chapter 1 or in Jun 1993, 1998, 2000, 2005). Phrasing, or grouping of words, is the phonological focus-marking cue in Korean. It has been found that, in read speech, a word in narrow focus starts a new AP or IP, and usually causes the words following it to lose their status as separate phrases and to be incorporated into the same phrase as the focused word (i.e., dephrasing) (Jeon & Nolan, 2017; Jun, 1993; Jun & Kim, 2007; Oh, 1999). Contrastive focus resembles narrow focus in that it also starts a new prosodic phrase from the focused word and usually dephrases the post-focal words in read speech (Jun & H. J. Lee, 1998; but see a non-frequent use of post-focus dephrasing in Jeon & Nolan, 2017). When a short syntactic phrase (e.g., a verb phrase or noun phrase) or a short sentence is in focus (i.e., broad focus), each word in it tends to form an AP (Jun, 2011; Jun & H. S. Kim, 2007; H. S. Kim, et al., 2006).

In addition to phrasing, phonetic cues are also used to mark focus. A word in narrow focus or contrastive focus is more prominent in pitch, duration, and intensity than the same word in a "neutral" condition (which is arguably a broad focus condition) (Jeon & Nolan, 2017; Jun & Kim, 2007; Jun & H. J. Lee, 1998; Y. C. Lee & Xu, 2010), while the pre-focal and post-focal words are either less prominent than or similar to the "neutral" counterparts in pitch, duration and intensity (Jeon & Nolan, 2017; Jun & H. J. Lee, 1998; Y. C. Lee & Xu, 2010).

4.1.2 Limitations of past work

Whereas previous studies on prosodic focus marking in Korean are extensive, some crucial questions on this topic remain to be explored. First of all, studies have shown that Korean speakers do not always use phrasing to mark focus in read speech (Jun & H. J. Lee, 1998; Oh, 1999), inconsistent with Jun's (1993) early claim. However, it is still unclear to what extent phrasing is used to mark focus in (semi-)spontaneous speech. Studies have revealed that prosodic differences between (semi-)spontaneous speech and read speech are present in many languages (Bard & Aylett, 1999; De Ruiter, 2010; Chapter 2 of this dissertation). For example, contrastive focus and narrow focus are not prosodically distinguished in semi-spontaneous speech in Mandarin (Chapter 2 of this dissertation; Grief, 2010), but are distinguished in Mandarin read speech (Y. Chen & Braun, 2006). Thus, a re-examination of the effect of focus on phrasing in semi-spontaneous Korean is needed. Second, among previous studies, only one (Jeon & Nolan, 2017) used statistical methods to verify how phrasal boundaries were used to distinguish between focus conditions. Jeon and Nolan (2017) found that, in highly-controlled read speech, IP boundaries were used more frequently to initiate target number words in contrastive focus than in broad focus and than in pre-focus in certain contexts. However, we still do not have a complete understanding of whether a certain type of focus differs from non-focus and other types of focus in how frequently it starts a new AP or IP, or induces post-focus dephrasing. Hence, a thorough statistical analysis of the use of phrasal boundaries in different focus conditions is needed. Last, very few studies have examined prosodic focus marking in Korean from both a phonological and a phonetic perspective (Jeon & Nolan, 2017; Jun & H. J. Lee 1998; Oh, 1999). The examination of phonetic focus marking in previous studies was usually independent of phonological category. One study (Jun & H. J. Lee, 1998) mentioned that an individual speaker who rarely dephrased the post-focal words lowered the maximum pitch and reduced the duration of them to distinguish focus from non-focus. This was similar to an observation on Dutch that, when speakers produced both sentence-initial focus and non-focus, frequently with the same falling pitch accent, they varied phonetic cues to distinguish focus from non-focus within the same phonological category (A. Chen, 2009). To explore whether Korean-speakers vary phonetic cues to mark focus within a certain phonological category, a study based on quantitative data is needed.

4.1.3 The current study

The current study aims at obtaining a clearer picture of phonological and phonetic focus marking in Korean semi-spontaneous speech. To this end, we have examined how the speakers vary prosody to distinguish (1) Narrow focus from non-focus (Effect of focus); (2) Narrow focus from broad focus (Effect of focal constituent size); and (3) Narrow focus from contrastive focus (Effect of contrastivity).

4.2 Method

4.2.1 Participants

Twelve native adult speakers of Korean participated in this study (six females and six males, average age: twenty-four years. See more details in Appendix C). They were students at Hanyang University in Seoul at the time of testing, and all spoke Seoul Korean as their native language.

4.2.2 The picture-matching task

We adapted the picture-matching task used in A. Chen (2011a) to elicit semi-spontaneous production of sentences. In this task, the participant's role was to help the experimenter put pictures in matched pairs. Three piles of pictures were used. The experimenter and the participant each held a pile of pictures. The third pile lay on the table in a seemingly messy fashion. The experimenter's pictures always missed some information (e.g., the subject, the action, the object, or all three). The participant's pictures always contained all three pieces of information. On each trial, the experimenter showed a picture of hers to the participant, described the picture and asked a question about it or, in the contrastive focus condition, made a remark about the missing information. The participant took a look at the corresponding picture in his/her pile and responded to the experimenter's question or remark. The experimenter then looked for the right picture in the messy pile and matched it with her own picture to form a pair.

As rules of the task, the participant was asked to answer the experimenter's questions in full sentences and not to reveal his/her pictures to the experimenter. In order to make sure that the experiment was conducted in the same way for all participants, and that adequate background information was equally provided for each trial before a question was asked or a remark was made, we constructed a script containing what the experimenter was supposed to say and how she was supposed to respond in each trial. The experimenter was instructed to follow the script closely but was encouraged to make spontaneous remarks that did not affect the information structure of the participant's responses for the purpose of facilitating the conversation. Prior to the picture-matching task, a picture-naming task was conducted to ensure that the participant would use the intended words to refer to the entities in the pictures. This procedure also rendered all the entities in the pictures referentially accessible.

4.2.3 Experimental materials

Sixty question-answer dialogues were embedded in the picture-matching task to elicit sixty SOV sentences in five focus conditions: narrow focus on the sentence-initial subject-noun (NF-i), responding to *who*-questions; narrow focus on the sentence-medial object-noun (NF-m), responding to *what*-questions; narrow focus on the sentence-final verb (NF-f), responding to *what-does*-X-*do-to*-Y questions; contrastive focus in sentence-medial position (CF-m), correcting the experimenter's remark about the object; broad focus over the whole sentence (BF), responding to *what-happens* questions, as illustrated in (1). Including narrow focus in three sentence-positions made it possible to study the effect of narrow focus on the sentence-medial object-nouns (NF-m) compared to the same medial words in pre-focus (or NF-f) and post focus (or NF-i). Comparing the object-nouns in NF-m, CF-m and BF allowed us to study the prosodic difference between different focus types. Examples of question-answer dialogues in the five focus conditions are given in (1), in which the referents are referred to with the definite article in the English glossary because they had been introduced in the picture-naming task.

(1) Examples of question-answer dialogues between the experimenter (E) and participant (P):

(NF-i) E: Look! The bread, and someone looks a bit puzzled. It looks like someone looks for the bread. Who looks for the bread?

P: [소가] 빵을 찾아요 .
soka p*aŋɨl tɕʰatɕajo
[The cow] the bread looks for.

(NF-m) E: Look! The dog, and it holds a painting brush. It looks like the dog draws something. What does the dog draw?

P: 개가 [빵을] 그려요 .
kɛka p*aŋɨl kɨljʌjo
The dog [the bread] draws.

(NF-f) E: Look! The rat, and the bread. It looks like the rat does something to the bread. What does the rat do to the bread?

P: 쥐가 빵을 [만져요].
tɕuka p*aŋɨl mantʃʌjo
The rat the bread [touches].

(CF-m) E: Look! The bear. The bear looks a bit puzzled. It looks like the bear looks for something. I will make a guess: the bear looks for the egg.

P: 곰이 [빵을] 찾아요 .
komi p*aŋɨl tɕʰatɕajo

The bear [the bread] looks for.

(BF) E: Look! My picture is very blurry. I cannot see anything clearly. What happens in your picture?

P: [말이 빵을 그려요].

mali p*aŋɨl kɨljʌjo

[The horse the bread draws].

The sixty SOV sentences were unique combinations of five subject-nouns, twelve target object-nouns, and three verbs (Table 4-1, see the sentences in Appendix D). Each subject-noun was a monosyllabic lexical word followed by a nominative case marker, 가 (/ka/) or 이 (/i/). The target object-nouns included six two-syllable (or "short") words and six four-syllable (or "long") words, because APs① with two to four syllables tend to occur frequently in Korean. Each "short" word was a monosyllabic lexical word followed by an accusative case marker, 을 (/ɨl/) or 를 (/lɨl/). As for the "long" words, except for 까마귀를 (/k*amakwilɨl/), which consisted of a three-syllable lexical word and the accusative case marker 를 (/lɨl/), each of the other words consisted of a disyllabic lexical word, a monosyllabic suffix 들 (/tɨl/) indicating the plural form of the lexical word, and the accusative case marker 을 (/ɨl/). Each target word was initiated with either a high-tone-triggering aspirated stop (i.e., /pʰ/ or /kʰ/) or fortis stop (i.e., /p*/ or /k*/) or a low-tone-triggering lenis stop (i.e., /p/ or /k/) or a vowel (i.e., /a/), so that there would be varied AP tonal patterns in the data. Each target word appeared once in five focus conditions (twelve targets × five focus conditions), leading to sixty "sentences" but without subject-nouns and verbs. The five subject-nouns and three verbs were then nearly evenly distributed to the "sentences", forming sixty SOV sentences. Each sentence was completed with the particle 요 (/jo/), a common politeness marker in informal Korean.

Table 4-1 Words that occurred in the SOV sentences

Subjects	개가 /kɛka/ "dog"	쥐가 /tɕuka/ "rat"	곰이 /komi/ "bear"	말이 /mali/ "horse"	소가 /soka/ "cow"	
Short objects	발을 /palɨl/ "foot"	비를 /pilɨl/ "rain"	불을 /pulɨl/ "fire"	팔을 /pʰalɨl/ "arm"	빵을 /p*aŋɨl/ "bread"	알을 /alɨl/ "egg"

① The AP is a word-sized unit by default (vs. focused) (Schafer & Jun, 2002; Jun, 2005).

Continued

Long objects	가방들을 /kapaŋtɨlɨl/ "bags"	기둥들을 /kituŋtɨlɨl/ "pillars"	구두들을 /kututɨlɨl/ "shoes"	카드들을 /kʰatɨtɨlɨl/ "cards"	까마귀를 /k*amakwilɨl/ "crow"	안경들을 /ankjʌŋtɨlɨl/ "pairs of glasses"
Verbs	그려 /kɨljʌ/ "draw"	만져 /mantʃʌ/ "touch"	찾아 /tɕʰatɕa/ "look for"			

The sixty sentences were elicited in two experimental sessions: the thirty sentences with "short" target words in Session A and the other thirty sentences with "long" target words in Session B. The trials in each session were randomised in such a way that trials from the same focus condition did not appear next to each other and the focused constituent of a trial was not mentioned on its preceding trial.

4.2.4 Experimental procedure

The participants were tested individually in Hanyang Phonetics and Psycholinguistics Laboratory at Hanyang University. They were informed that the task was of a simple nature because it would also be carried out by children in separate studies. A female native speaker administered the experiment after having received intensive training on how to conduct the experiment. Each participant took about 40 minutes to complete the experiment, including a short casual chat between the experimenter and the participant before the first experimental session, and a short break between the two sessions. Each participant was audio recorded with a sampling rate of 44.1 kHz with 16 bits. Video recordings were also made for some of the participants for training purposes.

4.3 Analysis and results, part 1: prosodic phrasing

We first investigated how Korean speakers vary prosodic boundaries, or phrasing, for focus-marking purposes. As mentioned earlier, the target words were focal in the NF-m, CF-m and BF conditions, post-focal in the NF-i condition, and pre focal in the NF-f condition. The two boundaries immediately before the target words (i.e., between the subject-noun and object-noun) and after the target words (i.e., between the object-noun and verb) were analysed. To examine the effect of narrow focus, the boundaries before/after the target words in narrow focus (NF-m) were compared to those in pre-focus (NF-f) and post-focus (NF-i). To look at the effect of focal constituent size, the boundaries before/after the target words in narrow focus (NF-m) were compared to those in broad focus (BF). To observe the effect of contrastivity, the boundaries before/after the target words in narrow focus (NF-m) were compared to those in contrastive focus (CF-m).

4.3.1 Prosodic annotation

The audio recordings from the participants were first orthographically annotated in Praat (Boersma & Weenink, 2013). Then, usable sentences were selected, and unusable ones were excluded from further analysis (9%; see the percentage of included sentences for each participant in Appendix C). A target sentence was considered unusable in any of the following cases: (1) the participant produced the target sentence before the experimenter asked the question; (2) the experimenter asked an incorrect question; (3) the experimenter did not provide an adequate description of the picture before she asked a question; (4) the sentence was produced with strong background noise; (5) the sentence was produced with word insertion, deletion or replacement; (6) the sentence was produced with self-repair or clearly perceivable hesitation.

The usable sentences were then annotated for phrasing, following the Korean Tones and Break Indices (K-ToBI) transcription conventions (Jun, 2000, 2005). That is, the two boundaries before and after the target word in a sentence were annotated as an AP boundary, an IP boundary, or a phrase-internal phonological word boundary (hereafter, PW boundary) by combining auditory impression and close inspection of prosodic cues to phrasing (e.g., tonal patterns, boundary tones and breaks). The AP boundary is "a minimal phrasal disjuncture, with no strong subjective sense of pause" and is associated with AP tonal patterns as described in K-ToBI (Jun, 2005). Word-final (i.e., pre-boundary) high tone and word-initial (i.e., post-boundary) low tone are taken as the typical AP boundary markers. The absence of voicing in word-initial lenis stops is also an informative indicator of an AP boundary (Jun, 1993; T. Cho, Jun & Ladefoged, 2002). Moreover, word-initial (or post-boundary) strengthening in terms of perceptual clarity in the initial segment or syllable may also indicate an AP boundary, unless this cue contradicts another important cue such as a tonal cue. The IP boundary refers to phrasal boundaries that are demarcated by boundary tones and "a strong phrasal disjuncture, with a strong subjective sense of pause", that is, either an "objective visible pause" or a "virtual pause" cued by final lengthening, as described in K-ToBI (Jun, 2005). The PW boundary refers to word boundaries that are not demarcated by perceivable prosodic disjuncture in K-ToBI.

The annotation for phrasing was conducted in three steps to maximise the reliability of the annotation. First, the usable sentences were annotated by the first transcriber (i.e. the author), following the above-described K-ToBI conventions, while a portion of the sentences (i.e., 106 sentences produced by two randomly selected participants[①]) were jointly transcribed by two expert K-ToBI transcribers and native speakers of Korean. The Cohen's Kappa test on the annotation of the first transcriber and the expert transcribers for the 106 sentences revealed a good inter-rater agreement for the boundaries before the target words ($K = 0.747$, $P < 0.0005$), and after the target words ($K= 0.780$, $P < 0.0005$) (Landis & Koch, 1977). The cases of disagreements were primarily concerned with the distinction between the AP boundary and PW boundary. Second, the first transcriber and the expert transcribers discussed the cases of the disagreement, and decided that the first transcriber should give more weight to three cues in her decision on AP and PW boundaries; namely, the word-initial and word-final tones and word-initial strengthening. Lastly, the first transcriber re-annotated all the usable sentences without access to her previous annotation, following the expert transcribers' recommendation. The expert transcribers jointly transcribed 18% of the usable sentences (i.e., 10 sentences randomly selected from each speaker). The Cohen's Kappa test on the new annotation for 18% of the usable sentences revealed a very good inter-rater agreement between the first transcriber and the expert transcribers for the boundaries before the targets ($K = 0.916$, $P < 0.0005$), and after the targets ($K= 0.985$, $P < 0.0005$) (Landis & Koch, 1977). Our statistical analysis of the adults' use of phrasing was based on the second round of annotation by the first transcriber.

4.3.2 Results on the varying of phrasal boundaries

The composition of boundaries before and after the target words in each focus condition is summarised in Table 4-2. Descriptively, we found that AP boundaries were predominant before the target words across focus conditions, and were also frequent after the target words in certain focus conditions. In both the NF-m and CF-m conditions, the speakers always produced an AP or IP boundary before the focused target word, and frequently used a PW boundary after the focused target word, dephrasing the post-focal verb. They also quite often phrased the subject-noun, object-noun and verb into three APs. In the NF-f

① The two participants were kaap08 and kaap13.

condition, the speakers almost always produced an AP or IP before the focused verb. As for the pre-focal subject-noun and object-noun, the speakers most frequently produced them as two APs and occasionally phrased them together as one AP. In the NF-i condition, the speakers frequently produced the post-focal object-noun and verb as one AP, but rarely included them into the same AP as the focused subject-noun. They also quite often phrased the subject-noun, object-noun and verb as three APs. In the BF condition, the speakers most frequently phrased the subject-noun, object-noun and verb as three APs, sometimes phrased the object-noun and verb together as one AP, and never phrased all three into one AP.

Table 4-2 The use of boundaries in each focus condition

Focus condition		Boundary before the target			Boundary after the target		
		AP	IP	PW	AP	IP	PW
NF-m	N	118	15	0	56	6	71
	%	88.7%	11.3%	0.0%	42.1%	4.5%	53.4%
NF-f	N	110	3	17	115	14	1
	%	84.6%	2.3%	13.1%	88.5%	10.8%	0.8%
NF-i	N	97	21	10	55	6	67
	%	75.8%	16.4%	7.8%	43.0%	4.7%	52.3%
BF	N	93	33	2	97	9	22
	%	72.7%	25.8%	1.6%	75.8%	7.0%	17.2%
CF-m	N	110	24	0	36	3	95
	%	82.1%	17.9%	0.0%	26.9%	2.2%	70.9%

To examine the use of boundaries in different focus conditions statistically, we conducted multinomial logistic regression (MLR) analyses in SPSS (IBM SPSS Statistics 22). The dependent variable (or the outcome variable) was BOUNDARY with three categories: AP boundary, IP boundary, and PW boundary. The AP and PW boundaries were set, in turn, as the reference category in order to get the comparisons between each two categories. The independent variables (or the predictor variables) were FOCUS, referring to the five focus conditions①, and LENGTH, referring to the "short" and "long" contrast in the target words. The main effects of FOCUS and LENGTH and their interaction were entered into the model in

① We have done the analyses in which focus was defined as having two levels (narrow focus vs. one of the other focus conditions). To make the report on statistical results less cumbersome, we report the output of the model with focus as a five-level fixed factor, which had the same parameter estimates as the models with focus as a two-level fixed factor.

a stepwise fashion using a forward entry, meaning that only significant items showed up in the final model and were provided with parameter estimates. The boundaries before and after the target words were analysed separately. The significance level was set at 0.05. In the data, the PW boundary was absent in the NF-m and CF-m conditions before the target word (Table 4-2), which made it impossible to obtain interpretable parameter estimates in relevant analyses. We therefore introduced one fictive instance to each absent category, by changing one instance of an AP boundary to a PW boundary. This operation only caused a subtle change to the Wald statistics but generated interpretable results. This method was adopted from Braun and Chen (2010) in which a similar situation was dealt with in this way.

4.3.2.1 Boundary before the target word

Analysing the boundaries before the target words, we found that only the main effect of FOCUS significantly improved the model fitting ($\chi^2 = 55.82$, df = 8, $P < 0.05$), indicating that FOCUS had a similar effect on the boundaries before the target words, regardless of the length of the target words.

NF-m vs. NF-f. The parameter estimates (Table 4-3) showed that whether a target word was in the narrow focus condition (NF-m) or in the pre-focus condition (NF-f) significantly predicted whether the boundary before the target word was an IP boundary or an AP boundary ($P < 0.05$), whether it was a PW boundary or an AP boundary ($P < 0.05$), and whether it was an IP boundary or a PW boundary ($P < 0.05$). The odds ratios (i.e., Exp (B)) indicated that the odds of the boundary before the target word being an IP boundary compared to being an AP boundary in the NF-m condition were 3.57 (1/0.28) times as high as in the NF-f condition. The odds of the boundary before the target word being a PW boundary compared to being an AP boundary in the NF-m condition were 0.11 (1/9.05) times as high as in the NF-f condition, The odds of the boundary before the target word being an IP boundary compared to being a PW boundary in the NF-m condition were 33.33 (1/0.03) times as high as in the NF-f condition. In other words, the speakers were more likely to produce an IP boundary, but less likely to produce a PW boundary before the target word in narrow focus (NF-m) than in pre-focus (NF-f).

NF-m vs. NF-i. The parameter estimates (Table 4-3) showed that whether a target word was in the narrow focus condition (NF-m) or in the post-focus condition (NF-i) significantly predicted whether the boundary before the target word was a PW boundary or an AP boundary ($P < 0.05$). The odds ratio indicated that the odds of the boundary before the target word being a PW boundary compared to being an AP boundary in the NF-m condition were 0.17 (1/5.98) times as high as in the NF-i condition. In other words, the speakers were less likely to produce a PW boundary before the target word in narrow focus (NF-m) than in post-focus (NF-i).

NF-m vs. BF. The parameter estimates (Table 4-3) showed that whether a target word was in the narrow focus condition (NF-m) or the broad focus condition (BF) significantly predicted whether the boundary before the target word was an IP boundary or an AP boundary ($P < 0.05$). The odds ratio indicated that the odds of the boundary before the target word being an IP boundary compared to being an AP boundary in the NF-m condition were 0.36 (1/2.77) times as high as in the BF condition. In other words, the speakers were more likely to produce an IP boundary before the target word in broad focus (BF) than in narrow focus (NF-m).

NF-m vs. CF-m. The parameter estimates (Table 4-3) showed that whether a target word was in the narrow focus condition (NF-m) or the contrastive focus condition (CF-m) did not significantly predict the composition of boundaries before the target word.

Table 4-3 Parameter estimates for the boundary before the target word

Boundary before the target		***B***	**Std. Error**	**Wald**	**df**	**Sig.**	**Exp (*B*)**
	NF-m (Intercept)	−2.05	0.27	55.58	1	0.00**	
	NF-f	−1.26	0.58	4.74	1	0.03*	0.28
IP (vs. AP)	NF-i	0.52	0.37	1.99	1	0.16	1.67
	BF	1.02	0.34	8.94	1	0.00**	2.77
	CF-m	0.54	0.36	2.32	1	0.13	1.72
	NF-m (Intercept)	−4.06	0.71	32.42	1	0.00**	
	NF-f	2.20	0.76	8.41	1	0.00**	9.05
PW (vs. AP)	NF-i	1.79	0.79	5.17	1	0.02	5.98
	BF	0.64	0.92	0.48	1	0.49	1.89
	CF-m	0.07	1.01	0.01	1	0.94	1.07
IP (vs. PW)	NF-m (Intercept)	2.02	0.75	7.16	1	0.01*	
	NF-f	−3.46	0.94	13.69	1	0.00**	0.03
	NF-i	−1.27	0.85	2.27	1	0.13	0.28
IP (vs PW)	BF	0.38	0.97	0.16	1	0.69	1.47
	CF-m	0.47	1.05	0.20	1	0.66	1.60

4.3.2.2 Boundary after the target word

Analysing the boundaries after the target words, we found that the main effects of FOCUS ($\chi^2 = 215.10$, df = 8, $P < 0.05$) and LENGTH ($\chi^2 = 19.35$, df = 2, $P < 0.05$) significantly improved the model fitting, but the interaction of FOCUS and LENGTH did not, indicating that FOCUS had a similar effect on the boundaries after the target words, regardless of the length of the target words.

NF-m vs. NF-f. The parameter estimates (Table 4-4) showed that whether a target word was in the narrow focus condition (NF-m) or in the pre-focus condition (NF-f) significantly predicted whether the boundary after the target word was a PW boundary or an AP boundary ($p < 0.05$), and whether it was an IP boundary or a PW boundary ($P < 0.05$). The odds ratios indicated that the odds of the boundary after the target word being a PW boundary compared to being an AP boundary in the NF-m condition were 100 (1/0.01) times as high as in the NF-f condition. The odds of the boundary after the target word being an IP boundary compared to being a PW boundary in the NF-m condition were 0.01 (1/81.82) times as high as in the NF-f condition. In other words, the speakers were more likely to produce a PW boundary but less likely to produce an IP boundary after the target word in narrow focus (NF-m) than in pre-focus (NF-f).

NF-m vs. NF-i. The parameter estimates (Table 4-4) showed that whether a target word was in the narrow focus condition (NF-m) or in the post-focus condition (NF-i) did not significantly predict the boundary category before the target word.

NF-m vs. BF. The parameter estimates (Table 4-4) showed that whether a target word was in the narrow focus condition (NF-m) or in the broad focus condition (BF) significantly predicted whether the boundary after the target word was a PW boundary or an AP boundary ($P < 0.05$), and whether it was an IP boundary or a PW boundary ($P < 0.05$). The odds ratios indicated that the odds of the boundary after the target word being a PW boundary compared to being an AP boundary in the NF-m condition were 5.56 (1/0.18) times as high as in the BF condition. The odds of the boundary after the target word being an IP boundary compared to being a PW boundary in the NF-m condition were 0.22 (1/4.55) times as high as in the BF condition. In other words, the speakers were more likely to produce an IP boundary but less likely to produce a PW boundary after the target word in broad focus (BF) than in narrow focus (NF-m).

NF-m vs. CF-m. The parameter estimates (Table 4-4) showed that whether a target word was in the narrow focus condition (NF-m) or in the contrastive focus condition (CF-m) significantly predicted whether the boundary after the target word was a PW boundary or an AP boundary ($P < 0.05$). The odds ratios indicated that the odds of the boundary after the target word being a PW boundary compared to being an AP boundary in the NF-m condition were 0.47 (1/2.14) times as high as in the CF-m condition. In other words, the speakers were more likely to produce a PW boundary after the target word in contrastive focus (CF-m) than in narrow focus (NF-m).

Table 4-4 Parameter estimates for the boundary after the target word

Boundary after the target		*B*	Std. Error	Wald	df	Sig.	Exp (*B*)
IP (vs. AP)	NF-m (Intercept)	−1.66	0.44	13.98	1	0.00**	
	NF-f	0.12	0.52	0.06	1	0.81	1.13
	NF-i	0.19	0.60	0.10	1	0.75	1.21
	BF	−0.21	0.56	0.14	1	0.71	0.81
	CF-m	0.04	0.69	0.00	1	0.95	1.04
PW (vs. AP)	NF-m (Intercept)	0.26	0.21	1.52	1	0.22	
	NF-f	−4.28	0.74	33.89	1	0.00**	0.01
	NF-i	−0.02	0.25	0.01	1	0.93	0.98
	BF	−1.72	0.30	33.79	1	0.00**	0.18
	CF-m	0.76	0.27	8.14	1	0.00**	2.14
IP (vs. PW)	NF-m (Intercept)	−1.92	0.44	18.91	1	0.00**	
	NF-f	4.41	0.87	25.50	1	0.00**	81.82
	NF-i	0.21	0.59	0.13	1	0.72	1.24
	BF	1.52	0.59	6.66	1	0.01*	4.55
	CF-m	−0.72	0.67	1.15	1	0.28	0.49

4.4 Analysis and results, part 2: the varying of phonetic cues

We found that phrasal boundaries were varied to distinguish focus conditions. Nonetheless, we could not ignore the fact that the AP boundaries were predominant before the sentence-medial target words. The focus effects on the AP-initial target words were not captured by the boundary type before them. We thus decided to do phonetic analyses on the AP-initial target words. The purpose was to find out whether and how phonetic cues were used to distinguish focus conditions within the same phonological category (i.e., AP-initial words).

4.4.1 Phonetic annotation

We phonetically annotated the sentence-medial AP-initial target words (88.7%, 84.6%, 75.8%, 72.7% and 82.1% from the NF-m, NF-f, NF-i, BF, and CF-m conditions respectively) in Praat (Boersma & Weenink, 2013). We were especially interested in the varying of duration- and pitch-related cues for focus-marking purposes, and thus examined a selection of these cues, including word duration, word initial syllable duration (hereafter initial-syllable duration), maximum pitch (hereafter pitch-max), minimum pitch (hereafter pitch-min), and pitch span (i.e., pitch-max minus pitch-min). Segmentation of words and syllables was done on the basis of formant intensity, formant contours, waveforms, and auditory perception (Machač & Skarnitzl, 2009; Turk, Nakai & Sugahara, 2006). In the annotation of pitch-max and pitch-min, care was taken to avoid voiced lenis stops and not to confuse local pitch fluctuations with linguistically relevant variation in pitch. A small number of trials affected by background noise and non-model voice quality were excluded from pitch annotation.

4.4.2 Statistical analysis and results

We used mixed-effects modelling in the programme R with the lme4 package (Bates, Maechler, Bolker & Walker, 2014) to assess the realisation of narrow focus (i.e., narrow focus vs. non-focus) and focus types differing in size (i.e., narrow focus vs. broad focus), and contrastivity (i.e., narrow focus vs. contrastive focus). The dependent variables were word duration, initial-syllable duration, pitch span, pitch-max, and pitch-min of the AP-initial words. The independent variables (or fixed factors) were FOCUS and LENGTH. FOCUS referred to the focus conditions. For each analysis, we compared two or three focus conditions in order to address a specific research question. FOCUS thus had two levels in the models concerning focus effect (narrow focus vs. pre-focus/post-focus) and three levels in the models concerning focus types (narrow focus vs. broad focus vs. contrastive focus). LENGTH referred to the "short vs. long" distinction in the target words, and thus had two levels. In addition, two random factors, SPEAKER (i.e., the participants) and SENTENCE (i.e., the target sentences), were included in the analysis.

To find out whether a particular cue was used to distinguish certain focus conditions, models were built using the aforementioned factors. Starting from an "empty" model (hereafter Model 0) containing only the random factors, we added FOCUS, LENGTH and their interaction to the model in a stepwise fashion, building three additional models (Table 4-5). The ANOVA function in R was used to compare models in order to derive the model with the best fit. First, Model 1 was compared to Model 0, and a statistically significant difference indicated that Model 1 with the newly added parameter FOCUS could better explain the variation in the data, and thus was the "winning" model. Otherwise, Model 0 stayed as the "winning" model. Next, Model 2 was compared to its preceding "winning" model, which could be either Model 1 or Model 0. Following the same logic, Model 3 was compared to the preceding "winning" model. The last "winning" model was considered to be the best-fit model.

Table 4-5 Model build-up procedure

Model	Factor added
Model 0	
Model 1	FOCUS
Model 2	LENGTH
Model 3	FOCUS : LENGTH

For each analysis, we report on the best-fit model, according to the model comparisons, and statistical significance of main effects and the interaction, according to the summary of the best-fit model. If the best-fit model contained a significant interaction of FOCUS and LENGTH, we further discuss how the speakers distinguished the two focus conditions in the "short" words and in the "long" words by examining the effect of FOCUS in the "short" words and "long" words separately. We will not discuss in detail the main effects of the factors when the interaction between them proved to be significant.

4.4.2.1 Realisation of narrow focus

4.4.2.1.1 Narrow focus vs. pre-focus (NF-m vs. NF-f)

WORD DURATION. The best-fit model for the analysis of word duration was Model 2 (Table 4-6). The summary of this model (Table 4-7) showed that the main effects of FOCUS and LENGTH were significant. Thus the target words were significantly longer in narrow focus than in pre-focus (34 ms longer, $P < 0.05$), whether they were two-syllable "short" words or four-syllable "long" words (Figure 4-1).

Table 4-6 Model comparisons regarding the dependent variable word duration in the comparison narrow focus vs. pre-focus

Model comparisons	Pr(>Chisq)
0 vs. 1 (adding FOCUS)	0.557
0 vs. 2 (adding LENGTH)	0.000***
2 vs. 3 (adding FOCUS : LENGTH)	0.360

Table 4-7 Model summary regarding the dependent variable word duration in the comparison narrow focus vs. pre-focus

Factor	Estimate	Std. Error	*t* value	Pr(>|*t*|)
Intercept (Narrow focus. Short)	0.283	0.016	17.496	0.000***
Pre-focus	–0.034	0.016	-2.074	0.049*
Long	0.267	0.016	16.362	0.000***

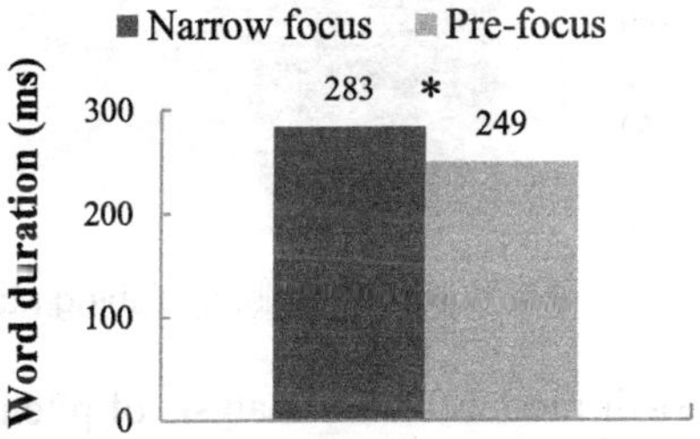

Figure 4-1 The use of word duration in distinguishing narrow focus from pre-focus

INITIAL-SYLLABLE DURATION. The best-fit model for the analysis of initial-syllable duration was Model 1 (Table 4-8). The summary of this model (Table 4-9) showed that the main effect of FOCUS was significant. Thus, the initial-syllable of the words were significantly longer in narrow focus than in pre-focus (23 ms longer, $P < 0.05$), whether the words were "short" or "long" (Figure 4-2).

Table 4-8 Model comparisons regarding the dependent variable initial-syllable duration in the comparison narrow focus vs. pre-focus

Model comparisons	*Pr*(>Chisq)
0 vs. 1 (adding FOCUS)	0.046*
1 vs. 2 (adding LENGTH)	0.781
1 vs. 3 (adding focus : LENGTH)	0.843

Table 4-9 Model summary regarding the dependent variable initial-syllable duration in the comparison narrow focus vs. pre-focus

Factor	Estimate	Std. Error	*t* value	*Pr*(>|*t*|)
Intercept (Narrow focus)	0.144	0.009	16.655	0.000***
Pre-focus	−0.023	0.011	−2.081	0.048*

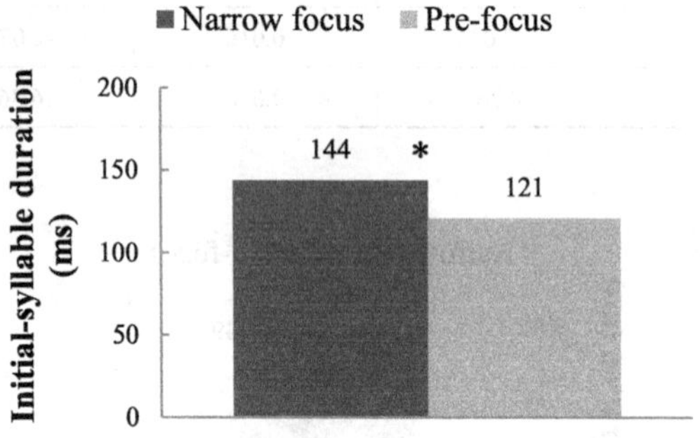

Figure 4-2 The use of initial-syllable duration in distinguishing narrow focus from pre-focus

PITCH SPAN. The best-fit model for the analysis of pitch span was Model 3 (Table 4-10). The summary of this model (Table 4-11) showed that the main effect of FOCUS was not significant, but the interaction of FOCUS and LENGTH was significant. The main effect of LENGTH was also significant. Subsequent analysis showed that the pitch span was significantly wider in narrow focus than in pre-focus in the four-syllable "long" words (2.5 st wider, $P < 0.05$), but not in the two-syllable "short" words (Figure 4-3).

Table 4-10 Model comparisons regarding the dependent variable pitch span in the comparison narrow focus vs. pre-focus

Model comparisons	*Pr*(>Chisq)
0 vs. 1 (adding FOCUS)	0.106

Continued

Model comparisons	*Pr*(>Chisq)
1 vs. 2 (adding LENGTH)	0.000***
2 vs. 3 (adding FOCUS : LENGTH)	0.003**

Table 4-11 Model summary regarding the dependent variable pitch span in the comparison narrow focus vs. pre-focus

Factor	Estimate	Std. Error	*t* value	*Pr*(>|*t*|)
Intercept (Narrow focus. Short)	2.922	0.417	7.005	0.000***
Pre-focus	0.035	0.553	0.064	0.950
Long	3.890	0.550	7.077	0.000***
Pre-focus : Long	-2.506	0.781	-3.209	0.004**

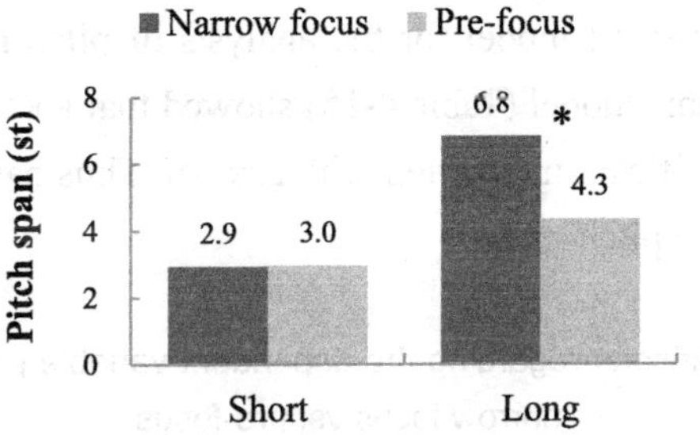

Figure 4-3 The use of pitch span in distinguishing narrow focus from pre-focus

PITCH-MAX. The best-fit model for the analysis of pitch-max was Model 1 (Table 4-12). The summary of this model (Table 4-13) showed that the main effect of FOCUS was significant. Thus pitch-max was significantly higher in narrow focus than in pre-focus (2.0 st higher, $P < 0.05$), regardless of word length (Figure 4-4).

Table 4-12 Model comparisons regarding the dependent variable pitch-max in the comparison narrow focus vs. pre-focus

Model comparisons	*Pr*(>Chisq)
0 vs. 1 (adding FOCUS)	0.039*
1 vs. 2 (adding LENGTH)	0.489
1 vs. 3 (adding FOCUS : LENGTH)	0.753

Table 4-13 Model summary regarding the dependent variable pitch-max in the comparison narrow focus vs. pre-focus

Factor	Estimate	Std. Error	*t* value	*Pr*(>|*t*|)
Intercept (Narrow focus)	91.454	1.699	53.834	0.000***
Pre-focus	-1.990	0.923	-2.156	0.042

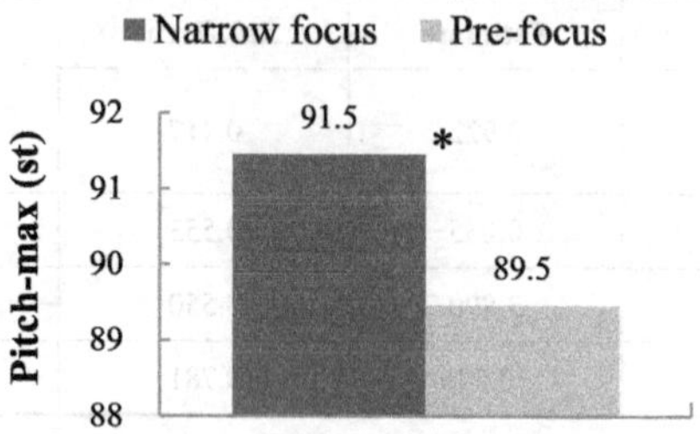

Figure 4-4 The use of pitch-max in distinguishing narrow focus from pre-focus

PITCH-MIN. The best-fit model for the analysis of pitch-min was Model 2 (Table 4-14). The summary of this model (Table 4-15) showed that FOCUS did not show a significant main effect or a significant interaction with LENGTH. Thus narrow focus and pre-focus were not distinguished via pitch-min.

Table 4-14 Model comparisons regarding the dependent variable pitch-min in the comparison narrow focus vs. pre-focus

Model comparisons	*Pr*(>Chisq)
0 vs. 1 (adding FOCUS)	0.401
0 vs. 2 (adding LENGTH)	0.042*
2 vs. 3 (adding FOCUS : LENGTH)	0.186

Table 4-15 Model summary regarding the dependent variable pitch-min in the comparison narrow focus vs. pre-focus

Factor	Estimate	Std. Error	*t* value	*Pr*(>|*t*|)
Intercept (Narrow focus. Short)	87.511	1.673	52.311	0.000***
Pre-focus	−0.728	0.774	−0.940	0.357
Long	−1.956	0.774	−2.527	0.019*

INTERIM SUMMARY. The speakers used a longer word duration, initial-syllable duration, and a higher pitch-max for the words in narrow focus than in pre-focus. They also used a wider pitch span for the four-syllable "long" words in narrow focus than in pre-focus.

4.4.2.1.2 Narrow focus vs. post-focus (NF-m vs. NF-i)

WORD DURATION. The best-fit model for the analysis of word duration was Model 2 (Table 4-16). The summary of this model (Table 4-17) showed that the main effects of FOCUS and LENGTH were significant. Thus the target words were significantly longer in narrow focus than in post-focus (55 ms longer, $P < 0.05$), whether they were two-syllable "short" words or four-syllable "long" words (Figure 4-5).

Table 4-16 Model comparisons regarding the dependent variable word duration in the comparison narrow focus vs. post-focus

Model comparisons	***Pr*(>Chisq)**
0 vs. 1 (adding FOCUS)	0.309
0 vs. 2 (adding LENGTH)	0.000***
2 vs. 3 (adding FOCUS : LENGTH)	0.961

Table 4-17 Model summary regarding the dependent variable word duration in the comparison narrow focus vs. post-focus

Factor	**Estimate**	**Std. Error**	***t* value**	***Pr*(>|*t*|)**
Intercept (Narrow focus. Short)	0.290	0.014	20.581	0.000***
Post-focus	-0.055	0.014	-3.994	0.001**
Long	0.251	0.014	18.356	0.000***

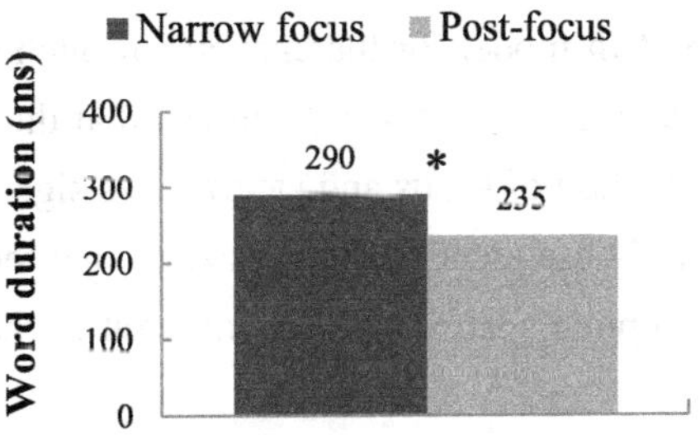

Figure 4-5 The use of word duration in distinguishing narrow focus from post-focus

INITIAL-SYLLABLE DURATION. The best-fit model for the analysis of initial-syllable duration was model 1 (Table 4-18). The summary of this model showed that the main effect of FOCUS was significant. Thus the initial syllable was significantly longer in narrow focus than in post-focus (28 ms longer, $P < 0.05$), whether the words were "short" or "long" (Figure 4-6).

Table 4-18 Model comparisons regarding the dependent variable initial-syllable duration in the comparison narrow focus vs. post-focus

Model comparisons	*Pr*(>Chisq)
0 vs. 1 (adding FOCUS)	0.006**
0 vs. 2 (adding LENGTH)	0.232
2 vs. 3 (adding FOCUS : LENGTH)	0.476

Table 4-19 Model summary regarding the dependent variable initial-syllable duration in the comparison narrow focus vs. post-focus

Factor	Estimate	Std. Error	*t* value	*Pr*(>|*t*|)
Intercept (Narrow focus)	0.144	0.008	18.960	0.000***
Post-focus	-0.028	0.010	-2.945	0.007**

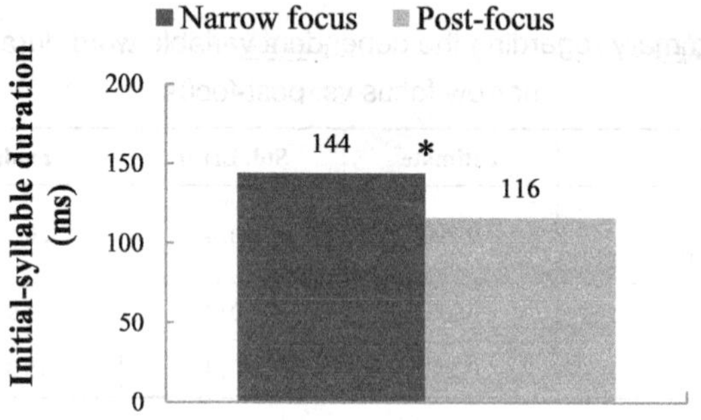

Figure 4-6 The use of initial-syllable duration in distinguishing narrow focus from post-focus

PITCH SPAN. The best-fit model for the analysis of pitch span was Model 3 (Table 4-20). The summary of this model (Table 4-21) showed that the main effect of FOCUS was not significant, but the interaction of FOCUS and LENGTH was significant. The main effect of LENGTH was also significant. Subsequent analysis showed that the difference between narrow focus and post-focus in pitch span was not significant in the "short" words or in the "long" words.

Table 4-20 Model comparisons regarding the dependent variable pitch span in the comparison narrow focus vs. post-focus

Model comparisons	Pr(>Chisq)
0 vs. 1 (adding FOCUS)	0.339
1 vs. 2 (adding LENGTH)	0.000***
2 vs. 3 (adding FOCUS : LENGTH)	0.045*

Table 4-21 Model summary regarding the dependent variable pitch span in the comparison narrow focus vs. post-focus

Factor	Estimate	Std. Error	*t* value	Pr(>|*t*|)
Intercept (Narrow focus. Short)	2.940	0.412	7.130	0.000
Post-focus	0.112	0.523	0.214	0.833
Long	3.883	0.527	7.373	0.000
Post-focus : Long	−1.593	0.767	−2.077	0.049

PITCH-MAX. The best-fit model for the analysis of pitch-max was Model 1 (Table 4-22). The summary of this model (Table 4-23) showed that the main effect of FOCUS was significant. Thus the pitch-max of the words was significantly higher in narrow focus than in post-focus (2.7 st higher, $P < 0.05$), regardless of the length of the words (Figure 4-7).

Table 4-22 Model comparisons regarding the dependent variable pitch-max in the comparison narrow focus vs. post-focus

Model comparisons	Pr(>Chisq)
0 vs. 1 (adding FOCUS)	0.006**
1 vs. 2 (adding LENGTH)	0.212
1 vs. 3 (adding FOCUS : LENGTH)	0.449

Table 4-23 Model summary regarding the dependent variable pitch-max in the comparison narrow focus vs. post-focus

Factor	Estimate	Std. Error	*t* value	Pr(>|*t*|)
Intercept (Narrow focus)	91.457	1.663	55.000	0.000***
Post-focus	−2.668	0.889	−3.002	0.006

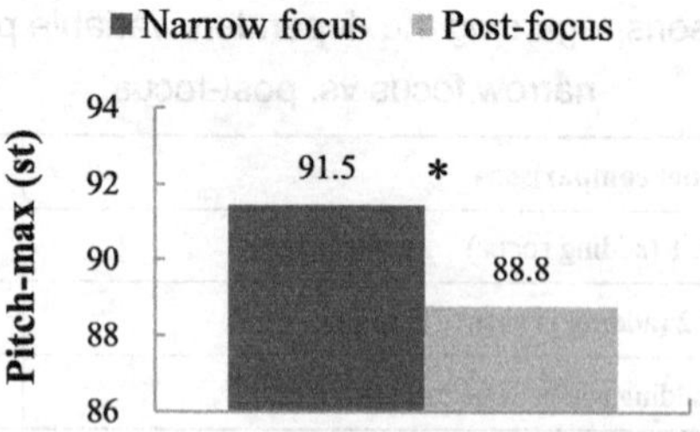

Figure 4-7 The use of pitch-max in distinguishing narrow focus from post-focus

PITCH-MIN. The best-fit model for the analysis of pitch-min was Model 2 (Table 4-24). The summary of this model (Table 4-25) showed that the main effects of FOCUS and LENGTH were significant. Thus the pitch-min of the words was significantly higher in narrow focus than in post-focus (1.9 st higher, $P < 0.05$), regardless of the length of the words (Figure 4-8).

Table 4-24 Model comparisons regarding the dependent variable pitch-min in the comparison narrow focus vs. post-focus

Model comparisons	***Pr*(>Chisq)**
0 vs. 1 (adding FOCUS)	0.031*
1 vs. 2 (adding LENGTH)	0.014*
2 vs. 3 (adding FOCUS : LENGTH)	0.149

Table 4-25 Model summary regarding the dependent variable pitch-min in the comparison narrow focus vs. post-focus

Factor	**Estimate**	**Std. Error**	***t* value**	***Pr*(>|*t*|)**
Intercept (Narrow focus. Short)	87.475	1.635	53.508	0.000***
Post-focus	−1.915	0.735	-2.605	0.016
Long	−1.929	0.737	-2.617	0.015

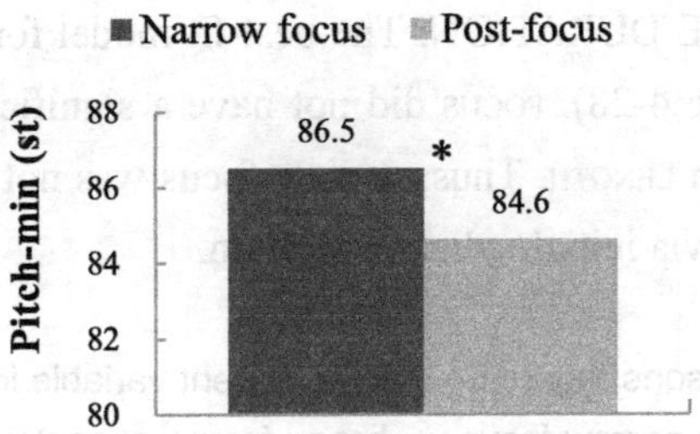

Figure 4-8 The use of pitch-min in distinguishing narrow focus from post-focus

INTERIM SUMMARY. The speakers used a longer word duration and longer initial-syllable duration, as well as a higher pitch-max and higher pitch min, that is, a higher overall pitch level, for the words in narrow focus than in post-focus.

4.4.2.2 Realisation of focus types (Narrow focus vs. broad focus vs. contrastive focus)

WORD DURATION. The best-fit model for the analysis of word duration was Model 2 (Table 4-26). The summary of this model (Table 4-27) showed that FOCUS did not have a significant main effect or have a significant interaction with LENGTH. Thus, narrow focus was not distinguished from broad focus or contrastive focus via word duration.

Table 4-26 Model comparisons regarding the dependent variable word duration in the comparison narrow focus vs. broad focus vs. contrastive focus

Model comparisons	*Pr*(>Chisq)
0 vs. 1 (adding FOCUS)	0.937
0 vs. 2 (adding LENGTH)	0.000***
2 vs. 3 (adding FOCUS : LENGTH)	0.892

Table 4-27 Model summary regarding the dependent variable word duration in the comparison narrow focus vs. broad focus vs. contrastive focus

Factor	Estimate	Std. Error	*t* value	*Pr*(>|*t*|)
Intercept (Narrow focus. Short)	0.290	0.014	20.347	0.000***
Broad focus	0.017	0.015	−1.119	0.271
Contrastive focus	0.000	0.015	0.008	0.993
Long	0.251	0.012	20.702	0.000***

INITIAL-SYLLABLE DURATION. The best-fit model for the analysis of word duration was Model 0 (Table 4-28). FOCUS did not have a significant main effect or have a significant interaction with LENGTH. Thus, narrow focus was not distinguished from broad focus or contrastive focus via initial-syllable duration.

Table 4-28 Model comparisons regarding the dependent variable initial-syllable duration in the comparison narrow focus vs. broad focus vs. contrastive focus

Model comparisons	***Pr*(>Chisq)**
0 vs. 1 (adding FOCUS)	0.302
0 vs. 2 (adding LENGTH)	0.217
0 vs. 3 (adding FOCUS : LENGTH)	0.464

PITCH SPAN. The best-fit model for the analysis of pitch span was Model 2 (Table 4-29). The summary of this model (Table 4-30) showed that FOCUS did not have a significant main effect or a significant interaction with LENGTH. Thus, narrow focus was not distinguished from broad focus or contrastive focus via pitch span.

Table 4-29 Model comparisons regarding the dependent variable pitch span in the comparison narrow focus vs. broad focus vs. contrastive focus

Model comparisons	***Pr*(>Chisq)**
0 vs. 1 (adding FOCUS)	0.346
0 vs. 2 (adding LENGTH)	0.000***
2 vs. 3 (adding FOCUS : LENGTH)	0.205

Table 4-30 Model summary regarding the dependent variable pitch span in the comparison narrow focus vs. broad focus vs. contrastive focus

Factor	**Estimate**	**Std. Error**	***t* value**	***Pr*(>|*t*|)**
Intercept (Narrow focus. Short)	2.972	0.452	6.582	0.000***
Broad focus	−1.024	0.517	−1.982	0.055
Contrastive focus	0.329	0.514	0.641	0.526
Long	3.826	0.422	9.073	0.000***

PITCH-MAX. The best-fit model for the analysis of pitch-max was Model 0 (Table 4-31). FOCUS did not have a significant main effect or have a significant interaction with

LENGTH. Thus, narrow focus was not distinguished from broad focus or contrastive focus via pitch-max.

Table 4-31 Model comparisons regarding the dependent variable pitch-max in the comparison narrow focus vs. broad focus vs. contrastive focus

Model comparisons	*Pr*(>Chisq)
0 vs. 1 (adding FOCUS)	0.482
0 vs. 2 (adding LENGTH)	0.407
2 vs. 3 (adding FOCUS : LENGTH)	0.981

PITCH-MIN. The best-fit model for the analysis of pitch-min was Model 0 (Table 4-32). The summary of this model (Table 4-33) showed that FOCUS did not have a significant main effect or a significant interaction with LENGTH. Thus, narrow focus was not distinguished from broad focus or contrastive focus via pitch-min.

Table 4-32 Model comparisons regarding the dependent variable pitch-min in the comparison narrow focus vs. broad focus vs. contrastive focus

Model comparisons	*Pr*(>Chisq)
0 vs. 1 (adding FOCUS)	0.915
0 vs. 2 (adding LENGTH)	0.004
2 vs. 3 (adding FOCUS : LENGTH)	0.443

Table 4-33 Model summary regarding the dependent variable pitch-min in the comparison narrow focus vs. broad focus vs. contrastive focus

Factor	Estimate	Std. Error	*t* value	*Pr*(>|*t*|)
Intercept (Narrow focus, Short)	87.872	1.698	51.747	0.000***
Broad focus	−0.095	0.846	-0.113	0.911
Contrastive focus	−0.412	0.845	-0.488	0.629
Long	−2.772	0.691	-4.011	0.000***

INTERIM SUMMARY. The speakers did not vary word duration, initial-syllable duration, pitch span, pitch-max, or pitch-min to distinguish narrow focus from broad focus or contrastive focus.

4.5 Conclusions

We have examined how Korean speakers use the phonological cue, namely, phrasing, as well as duration- and pitch-related phonetic cues, to distinguish narrow focus from non-focus and two other types of focus in semi-spontaneous speech.

As for the use of phrasing, we found that AP boundaries were predominant before the target words across focus conditions (> 72% in each condition), and were also frequent after the target words in certain focus conditions. Nonetheless, focus conditions are still distinguished via the IP and PW boundaries before and after the target words. With regard to the effect of narrow focus, Korean speakers use IP boundaries more frequently and PW boundaries less frequently before the target words. They use PW boundaries more frequently and IP boundaries less frequently after the target words in narrow focus as compared to pre-focus, and they use PW boundaries less frequently before the target words in narrow focus as compared to post-focus. Our findings on phrasal boundaries support previous descriptions of phrasing: a word in narrow focus initiates an Accentual Phrase (AP) or an Intonation Phrase (IP); the pre-focal words can form one or more APs, but are almost never included in the same AP as the focused word; the post-focal words frequently lose their status as separate APs and are either included in the same AP as the focused word (i.e., dephrasing) or form an AP but are not included in the same AP as the focused word (i.e., partial dephrasing) (Jun, 1993, 2011; Oh, 1999). Additionally, it is worth noting that partial dephrasing occurred much more frequently than dephrasing when the sentence-initial subject-noun is in narrow focus (NF-i). A potential account is that the boundary before the object-verb syntactic phrase might be prosodically salient and is thus not deleted though showing up post-focally, similar to Jun's (2011) finding that the boundary before a post-focal verb clause is kept and the words within this clause form one AP. Concerning the distinction of focus types differing in focal constituent size, Korean speakers more frequently use IP boundaries before and after the target words, and less frequently use PW boundaries after the target words in broad focus than in narrow focus. In other words, the subject-noun, object-noun and verb in broad focus usually form separate APs or IPs, similar to the phrasing of a "neutral" sentence (H. S. Kim, et al., 2006) and the phrasing of words in a focused VP (H. S. Kim, et al., 2006) or short NP (Jun, 2011). Regarding the distinction of focus types differing in contrastivity, Korean speakers more frequently use

PW boundaries after the target words in contrastive focus than in narrow focus, indicating that, whereas contrastive focus has a similar effect to narrow focus on phrasing in terms of manner, it more frequently induces post-focus dephrasing.

Regarding the use of phonetic cues, although the boundaries before the target words are predominantly AP boundaries across focus conditions, duration and pitch in the AP-initial words are varied to distinguish focus from non-focus. More specifically, the AP-initial words have a longer word duration and initial-syllable duration in narrow focus than in pre-focus and post-focus; they have a higher pitch-max in narrow focus than in pre-focus, and the four-syllable "long" words have a wider pitch span in narrow focus than in pre-focus; the AP-initial words were also with a higher pitch-max and pitch-min, i.e., a higher pitch register, in narrow focus than in post-focus. In addition, the phonetic differences between narrow focus and post-focus tend to be larger than between narrow focus and pre-focus, which may be caused by the so called "post-focus compression" (Y. C. Lee & Xu, 2010). The results indicate that, when focus and non-focus are not distinguished by the phrasal boundaries before the target words, duration- and pitch-related cues are still varied for such purpose. From a slightly different perspective, the phonetic differences between the focal and post-focal AP-initial words support Jun and Lee's (1998) early claim that when the post-focal words are not phonologically dephrased, they are still phonetically less prominent than focal words. As for the distinction of focus types, analysis of the AP-initial words show that narrow focus is not distinguished from broad focus or contrastive focus via phonetic cues, despite an earlier observation on read speech that narrow focus induced a higher pitch-max and a longer word duration than broad focus (referred to as "neutral focus") (Y. C. Lee & Xu, 2010).

From a cross-linguistic perspective, in Korean, phonetic cues are used when the prosodic boundary before a word is not varied to distinguish the focus condition of that word, similar to the observation on Dutch that phonetic cues are varied when focus and non-focus are not distinguished via accent type (A. Chen, 2009). In Korean, narrow focus and contrastive focus are distinguished, though only in how frequently they induce dephrasing, in contrast to Swedish (Romøren, 2016) and Mandarin (Chapter 2 of this disertation), in which no prosodic differences between these two types of focus are found in semi-spontaneous speech.

CHAPTER 5

Prosodic focus marking in Seoul Korean-speaking children: the use of prosodic phrasing[1]

Abstract

This study investigates how children acquire the use of prosodic phrasing for focus-marking purposes in Seoul Korean. Using a picture-matching game, we elicited semi-spontaneous production of sentences in various focus conditions from children aged four to eleven. We found that Seoul Korean-speaking children use prosodic phrasing to distinguish narrow focus from non-focus (i.e., pre-focus and post-focus) and two other types of focus (i.e., broad focus and contrastive focus) in an adult-like manner at the age of four to five, indicating that this phonological focus-marking cue is used early in life in Seoul Korean, similar to the early acquisition of language-specific phonological focus-marking cues in many other languages. We also found that Seoul Korean-speaking children's use of prosodic phrasing is less frequent than Seoul Korean-speaking adults, especially at younger ages. The less frequent use of this cue in children may be related to their slower speaking rate as compared to adults'.

Keywords

Acquisition, focus, prosodic phrasing, Seoul Korean

---

① A version of Chapter 5 is aimed to be submitted in article form to an appropriate journal.

5.1 Introduction

Previous studies on the acquisition of prosodic focus marking in Germanic languages have revealed that children show largely adult-like use of the language-specific phonological focus-marking cues by the age of five (A. Chen, 2011a, 2011b; Hornby & Hass, 1970; MacWhinney & Bates, 1978; Romøren, 2016; Wells, Peppé & Goulandris, 2004). Secondary phonetic use of prosody for focus-marking purposes is found to be acquired later than primary phonological focus marking (A. Chen, 2009). However, it is not clear whether phonological focus marking is also acquired early in life in languages which typologically differ from Germanic languages. The current study examines the acquisition of phonological focus marking in Seoul Korean (hereafter, Korean), which differs from the previously studied languages in prosodic systems and prosodic focus marking.

In the following, we will first briefly review the prosodic encoding of focus across languages (section 5.1.1), then the acquisition of prosodic focus marking in Germanic languages and Mandarin (section 5.1.2). Next, we describe how Korean-speaking adults use phonological and phonetic cues to mark focus (section 5.1.3). Finally, we will state the purpose and the prediction of the current study (section 5.1.4).

5.1.1 Prosodic encoding of focus across languages

Focus can be prosodically encoded in many languages (Gussenhoven, 2007; Vallduví & Engdahl, 1996). Generally, in these languages, a word is realised with more prosodic prominence in narrow focus (i.e., focus on a word or words) and contrastive focus (i.e., narrow focus carrying contrast[①]) than when not focused or in broad focus (i.e., focus over a whole sentence). Contrastive focus can have additional prosodic prominence compared to non-contrastive narrow focus. In terms of the precise use of prosody in focus marking, some languages (e.g., Mandarin and Cantonese) primarily use *phonetic cues* to mark focus; namely, speakers of these languages make fine-grained gradient changes in prosodic parameters, such as duration, pitch, and intensity for focus-marking purposes, without changing the phonological category of words (Xu, 1999, on Mandarin; Wu & Xu, 2010,

① Focus can carry contrastive information, e.g., a correction to a certain piece of information introduced previously or an alternative to what has been mentioned already (Gussenhoven, 2004, 2007).

on Cantonese). In Mandarin, for example, a word is produced with a longer duration, wider pitch span and higher intensity in narrow focus than in non-focus (Xu, 1999; Shih, 1988), while its tonal category does not change to mark focus. Some other languages (e.g., English, German, Dutch, Swedish, and Korean) primarily use *phonological cues* to mark focus. In other words, speakers of these languages make coarse-grained variations in duration, pitch, and intensity to mark focus, which leads to a change in the phonological category of words. For example, in English, German, and Dutch, speakers can either accent words with certain types of pitch accents (e.g., rising vs. falling) or not accent words to mark focus (A. Chen, 2009, 2011a; Baumann, Grice & Steindamm, 2006; Gussenhoven, 2004, 2007; Hanssen, Peters & Gussenhoven, 2008); in Swedish, speakers can either assign or not assign a prominence-marking high tone to words to mark focus (Bruce, 2007; Romøren, 2016); in Korean, speakers can either group or not group words into larger prosodic phrases (e.g., Accentual Phrase and Intonation Phrase) to mark focus (Jun, 1993; Jun & Lee, 1998). In addition, languages can also make phonetic changes within a phonological category for focus-marking purposes. For example, in Dutch, when both focused and non-focused sentence-initial words are frequently realised with a H*L pitch accent (i.e., a falling accent with the fall beginning in the stressed syllable), focused words are realised with a longer duration and lower minimum pitch than non-focused words (A. Chen, 2009).

5.1.2 The acquisition of prosodic focus marking

Previous studies on children acquiring a Germanic language have shown that the use of language-specific phonological focus-marking cues are acquired early in life: children speaking English, German, and Dutch can already use accentuation to mark focus in a largely adult-like way by the age of five, though their use of this cue can still increase in frequency and their choice of accent type is still developing after the age of five (Hornby & Hass, 1970; MacWhinney & Bates, 1978; Wells, et al., 2004, on English; Grünloh, Lieven & Tomasello, 2015, on German; A. Chen, 2011a, 2011b, on Dutch). Similarly, children speaking Swedish are largely adult-like in their use of prominence-marking high tones for focus-marking purposes by the age of five (Romøren, 2016). On the other hand, phonetic focus marking within a phonological category is acquired relatively late. For example, Dutch-speaking children's phonetic use of pitch within one phonological category to distinguish sentence-initial narrow focus from non-focus is not adult-like until the age of seven to eight, and the phonetic cues of duration for such purpose is not even adult-like by the age of eight (A. Chen, 2009, 2015).

In contrast, Mandarin-speaking children acquire phonetic focus marking early in life: they have fully acquired the use of duration for focus-marking purposes by the age of four to five; they also use certain pitch-related cues in certain tones in an adult-like way at this age, though their use of pitch for such purposes is still developing after the age of five (Chapter 3 of this dissertation; Yang & Chen, 2018). The earlier use of phonetic focus-marking cues in Mandarin than in Dutch has been argued to be related to the fact that Mandarin speakers only (and thus primarily) use phonetic cues to mark focus, and hence Mandarin-speaking children have abundant exposure to phonetic use of prosody, whereas Dutch speakers primarily use phonological cues to mark focus, relying less on phonetic cues, and Dutch-speaking children thus receive relatively less exposure to phonetic use of prosody (Yang & Chen, 2018; A. Chen, 2018).

The findings on previous studies, taken together, imply that the primary prosodic focus-marking cues (e.g., phonological cues in West Germanic languages and phonetic cues in Mandarin) are acquired earlier than the secondary cues (e.g., phonetic cues in Dutch). However, it is not clear to us whether this is the case in languages that use different primary phonological cues from in West Germanic languages. Korean is well-suited for an investigation on such a question because Korean uses a different phonological cue, prosodic phrasing (hereafter, phrasing), for focus-marking purposes.

5.1.3 Prosodic focus marking in Korean adult speech

Korean has no word-level use of pitch. Pitch movement in this language is associated with prosodic phrases (Jun, 1993, 1998, 2000, 2005). Phrasing is the typical prosodic focus-marking cue in Korean. Regarding the phonological realisation of narrow focus, our study on Korean-speaking adults (Chapter 4 of this dissertation) has shown that in semi-spontaneous production of SOV sentences, Korean-speaking adults use phrasing to distinguish narrow focus from non-focus. More specifically, a word in narrow focus initiates an Accentual Phrase (AP) or an Intonation Phrase (IP); the post-focal words frequently lose their status as separate APs and are incorporated in the same AP as the focused word (i.e., dephrasing), or form one AP but are not included in the same AP as the focused word[①] (i.e., partial dephrasing); the pre-focal words can form one or more APs, but are almost never included in the same AP as the focused word (Chapter 4 of this dissertation;

① In our study, this happens when there are two post-focal words, that is, when the sentence-initial word is in narrow focus.

see similar findings on read speech in Jun, 1993, 2011; Oh, 1999). As for the phonological realisation of different types of focus, although speakers use post-focus dephrasing frequently to mark both contrastive focus and narrow focus, as reported by Jun (1993) and Jun & Lee (1998), speakers do so with more frequency in contrastive focus than in narrow focus (Chapter 4 of this dissertation). A word in broad focus tends to form an AP by itself, and less frequently dephrases its following words than a word in narrow focus.

5.1.4 The current study

In the current study we investigate how Korean-speaking children acquire the use of the phonological cue of phrasing for focus-marking purposes. We predict that Korean-speaking children should show at least a moderate degree of adult-like use of phrasing for focus-marking purpose at the age of four to five, based on two pieces of indirect evidence. First, when phonological focus-marking cues are the primary prosodic focus-marking cues in a language, they are usually acquired early in life. Children speaking Germanic languages show largely adult-like use of language-specific phonological focus-marking cues by the age of five (A. Chen, 2011a, 2011b; Romøren, 2016; Wells, et al., 2004). Second, Korean-speaking children have developed great sensitivity to prosodic phrase boundaries in perception by the age of three (Choi & Mazuka, 2001, 2003). They can also produce certain AP pitch patterns and IP-final boundary tones before two years old (Jun, 2007), and produce prosodic and segmental cues (i.e., pausing and VOT) associated with AP or IP boundaries at the age of two to four (Choi & Mazuka, 2009). Thus, an early use of phrasing for focus-marking purposes at the age of four to five in Korean is possible.

To test the prediction, we have examined how Korean-speaking children vary phrasing to distinguish (1) Narrow focus from non-focus (Effect of focus); (2) Narrow focus from broad focus (Effect of focal constituent size); and (3) Narrow focus from contrastive focus (Effect of contrastivity).

5.2 Method

5.2.1 Participants

Three groups of children participated in the experiment, including six four- to five-year-olds (average age: 5;3, range: 4;10-5;10), eight seven- to eight-year-olds (average age: 8;0, range: 7;4-8;10), and eight ten to eleven-year-olds (average age: 10;10, range: 10;3-11;11) (see Appendix C for more participant information). They were recruited in Seoul via Hanyang Phonetics and Psycholinguistics Laboratory, and came from diverse social-economic backgrounds. They all spoke Seoul Korean as their native language.

5.2.2 The picture-matching game

We adapted the picture-matching game used in A. Chen (2011a) to elicit semi-spontaneous production of sentences. In this game, the child was supposed to help the experimenter to put pictures in matched pairs. Three piles of pictures were used. The experimenter and the child each held a pile of pictures. The third pile lay on the table in a seemingly messy fashion. The experimenter's pictures always missed some information (e.g., the subject, the action, the object, or all three). The child's pictures always contained all three pieces of information. On each trial, the experimenter showed one of her pictures to the child, described the picture and asked a question about it or made a remark about the missing information (in the contrastive focus condition). The child then took a look at the corresponding picture in his/her pile and responded to the experimenter's question or remark. The experimenter then looked for the right picture in the messy pile and matched it with her own picture to form a pair.

As rules of the game, the child was asked to answer the experimenter's questions in full sentences and not to reveal his/her pictures to the experimenter. In order to make sure that the experiment was conducted in the same way for all the children, and that adequate background information was equally provided for each trial before a question was asked or a remark was made, we constructed scripts containing what the experimenter was supposed to say and how she was supposed to respond in each trial. The experimenter was instructed to follow the scripts closely but was encouraged to make spontaneous remarks that did not affect the information structure of the child's responses for the purpose of facilitating the interaction. Prior to the picture-matching game, a picture-naming task was conducted to ensure that the child would use the intended words to refer to the entities in the pictures. This procedure also rendered all the entities in the pictures referentially accessible.

5.2.3 Experimental materials

Sixty question-answer dialogues were embedded in the picture-matching game to elicit sixty SOV sentences in five focus conditions: narrow focus on the sentence-initial subject-noun (NF-i), responding to *who*-questions; narrow focus on the sentence-medial object-noun (NF-m), responding to *what*-questions; narrow focus on the sentence-final verb (NF-f), responding to *what-does*-X-*do-to*-Y questions; contrastive focus in sentence-medial position (CF-m), correcting the experimenter's remark about the object; broad focus over the whole sentence (BF), responding to *what-happens* questions, as illustrated in (1). Including narrow focus in three sentence-positions made it possible to study the effect of narrow focus on the sentence-medial object-nouns (NF-m) compared to the same words in pre-focus (or NF-f) and post focus (or NF-i). Comparing the object-nouns in NF-m, CF-m and BF allowed us to study the prosodic difference between different focus types. Examples of question-answer dialogues in the five focus conditions are given in (1), in which the referents are referred to with the definite article in the English glossary because they had been introduced in the picture-naming task.

(1) Examples of question-answer dialogues between the experimenter (E) and participant (P):

(NF-i) E: Look! The bread, and someone looks a bit puzzled. It looks like someone looks for the bread. Who looks for the bread?

P: [소가] 빵을 찾아요 .

soka p*aŋɨl tɕʰatɕajo

[The cow] the bread looks for.

(NF-m) E: Look! The dog, and it holds a painting brush. It looks like the dog draws something. What does the dog draw?

P: 개가 [빵을] 그려요 .

kεka p*aŋɨl kɨljʌjo
The dog [the bread] draws.

(NF-f) E: Look! The rat, and the bread. It looks like the rat does something to the bread. What does the rat do to the bread?
P: 쥐가 빵을 [만져요].
tɕuka p*aŋɨl mantʃʌjo
The rat the bread [touches].

(CF-m) E: Look! The bear. The bear looks a bit puzzled. It looks like the bear looks for something. I will make a guess: the bear looks for the egg.
P: 곰이 [빵을] 찾아요 .
komi p*aŋɨl tɕʰatɕajo
The bear [the bread] looks for.

(BF) E: Look! My picture is very blurry. I cannot see anything clearly. What happens in your picture?
P: [말이 빵을 그려요].
mali p*aŋɨl kɨljʌjo
[The horse the bread draws].

The sixty SOV sentences were unique combinations of five subject-nouns, twelve target object-nouns, and three verbs (Table 5-1, see the sentences in Appendix D). Each subject-noun was a monosyllabic lexical word followed by a nominative case marker, 가 (/ka/) or 이 (/i/). The target object-nouns included six two syllable (or "short") words and six four-syllable (or "long") words, because APs① with two to four syllables tend to occur frequently in Korean. Each "short" word was a monosyllabic lexical word followed by an accusative case marker, 을 (/ɨl/) or 를 (/lɨl/). As for the "long" words, except for 까마귀를 (/k*amakwilɨl/), which consisted of a three-syllable lexical word and the accusative case marker 를 (/lɨl/), each of the other words consisted of a disyllabic lexical word, a monosyllabic suffix 들 (/tɨl/) indicating the plural form of the lexical word, and the accusative case marker 을 (/ɨl/). Each target word was initiated with either a high-tone-triggering aspirated stop (i.e., /pʰ/ or /kʰ/) or fortis stop (i.e., /p*/ or /k*/) or a low-tone-triggering lenis stop

① The AP is a word-sized unit by default (vs. focused) (Schafer & Jun, 2002; Jun, 2005).

(i.e., /p/ or /k/) or a vowel (i.e., /a/), so that there would be varied AP tonal patterns in the data. Each target word appeared once in five focus conditions (twelve target words × five focus conditions), leading to sixty "sentences" but without subject-nouns and verbs. The five subject-nouns and three verbs were then nearly evenly distributed to the "sentences", forming sixty SOV sentences. Each sentence was completed with the particle 요 (/jo/), a common politeness marker in informal Korean.

Table 5-1 Words that occurred in the SOV sentences

Subjects	개가 /kɛka/ "dog"	쥐가 /tɕuka/ "rat"	곰이 /komi/ "bear"	말이 /mali/ "horse"	소가 /soka/ "cow"	
Short objects	발을 /palɨl/ "foot"	비를 /pilɨl/ "rain"	불을 /pulɨl/ "fire"	팔을 /pʰalɨl/ "arm"	빵을 /p*aŋɨl/ "bread"	알을 /alɨl/ "egg"
Long objects	가방들을 /kapaŋtɨlɨl/ "bags"	기둥들을 /kituŋtɨlɨl/ "pillars"	구두들을 /kututɨlɨl/ "shoes"	카드들을 /kʰatɨtɨlɨl/ "cards"	까마귀를 /k*amakwilɨl/ "crow"	안경들을 /ankjʌŋtɨlɨl/ "pairs of glasses"
Verbs	그려 /kɨljʌ/ "draw"	만져 /mantʃʌ/ "touch"	찾아 /tɕʰatɕa/ "look for"			

The sixty sentences were elicited in two experimental sessions: the thirty sentences with "short" target words in Session A and the other thirty sentences with "long" target words in Session B. The trials in each session were randomised in such a way that trials from the same focus condition did not appear next to each other and the focused constituent of a trial was not mentioned on its preceding trial.

5.2.4 Experimental procedure

The children were tested individually in Hanyang Phonetics and Psycholinguistics Laboratory at Hanyang University. A female native speaker of Seoul Korean administered the experiment after having received intensive training on how to conduct the experiment. The experiment lasted about 60 minutes, including a short casual chat between the experimenter and the child before the first experimental session, and a short break between the two sessions. Audio recordings were made for each child in each session with a sampling rate of 44.1 kHz with 16 bits. Video recordings were also made for some of the children for training purposes.

5.2.5 Prosodic annotation

The audio recordings from the participants were first orthographically annotated in Praat (Boersma & Weenink, 2013). Then, usable sentences were selected (64% from the four- to five-year-olds, 70% from the seven- to eight-year-olds, and 80% from the ten- to eleven-year-olds; see the percentage for each participant in Appendix C), and unusable ones were excluded from further analysis. A target sentence was considered unusable in any of the following cases: (1) the participant produced the target sentence before the experimenter asked the question; (2) the experimenter asked a different question than the intended question in that trial; (3) the experimenter did not provide an adequate description of the picture before she asked a question; (4) the sentence was produced with strong background noise; (5) the sentence was produced with word insertion, deletion or replacement; (6) the sentence was produced with self-repair or clearly perceivable hesitation; or (7) the sentence was produced with perceivable irregular voice quality or intonation caused by cold or unstable emotion.

The usable sentences were then annotated for phrasing, following the Korean Tones and Break Indices (K-ToBI) transcription conventions (Jun, 2000, 2005). That is, the boundaries immediately before the target words (i.e., between the subject-noun and object-noun) and after the target words (i.e., between the object-noun and verb) were annotated as an AP boundary, an IP boundary, or a phrase-internal phonological word boundary (hereafter, PW boundary) by combining auditory impression and close inspection of prosodic cues to phrasing (e.g., tonal patterns, boundary tones and breaks). The AP boundary is "a minimal phrasal disjuncture, with no strong subjective sense of pause" and is associated with AP tonal patterns as described in K-ToBI (Jun, 2005). Word-final (i.e., pre-boundary) high tone and word-initial (i.e., post-boundary) low tone are taken as the typical AP boundary markers. The absence of voicing in word-initial lenis stops is also an informative indicator of an AP boundary (Jun, 1993; T. Cho, Jun, & Ladefoged, 2002). Moreover, word-initial (or post-boundary) strengthening in terms of perceptual clarity in the initial segment or syllable may also indicate an AP boundary, unless this cue contradicts another important cue such as a tonal cue. The IP boundary refers to phrasal boundaries that are demarcated by boundary tones and "a strong phrasal disjuncture, with a strong subjective sense of pause", that is, either an "objective visible pause" or a "virtual pause" cued by final lengthening, as described in K-ToBI (Jun, 2005). The PW boundary refers to word boundaries that are not demarcated by perceivable prosodic disjuncture in

K-ToBI.

The annotation for phrasing was conducted in three steps to maximise the reliability of the annotation. First, the usable sentences were annotated by the first transcriber (i.e., the author), following the above-described K-ToBI conventions, while a portion of the sentences (i.e., 81 sentences produced by two randomly selected participants①) were jointly transcribed by two expert K-ToBI transcribers and native speakers of Korean. The Cohen's Kappa test on the annotation of the first transcriber and the expert transcribers for the 81 sentences revealed a very good inter-rater agreement for the boundaries before the target words (K = 0.811, P < 0.0005), and a good inter-rater agreement after the target words (K= 0.644, P < 0.0005) (Landis & Koch, 1977). The cases of disagreements were primarily concerned with the distinction between the AP boundary and PW boundary. Second, the first transcriber and the expert transcribers discussed the cases of the disagreement, and decided that the first transcriber should give more weight to three of the cues in her decision on AP and PW boundaries; namely, the word-initial and word-final tones and word-initial strengthening. Lastly, the first transcriber re-annotated all the usable sentences without access to her previous annotation, following the expert transcribers' recommendation. The expert transcribers jointly transcribed 23% of the usable sentences (i.e., 10 sentences randomly selected from each speaker). The Cohen's Kappa test on the new annotation for 23% of the usable sentences revealed a very good inter-rater agreement between the first transcriber and the expert transcribers for the boundaries before the target words (K = 0.924, P < 0.0005), and after the target words (K= 0.897, P < 0.0005) (Landis & Koch, 1977). Our statistical analysis of children's use of phrasing was based on the second round of annotation by the first transcriber.

5.3 Statistical analyses and results

The distribution of each boundary type before and after the sentence-medial target words in each focus condition is summarized in Table 5-2 and Table 5-3 for each age group. Descriptively, we found that AP boundaries were predominant before the target words across focus conditions and age groups and were also very frequent after the target words in certain focus conditions and age groups, indicating that the children most frequently produced the three words in a sentence as three separate APs. In addition, PW

① The two participants were ka8p01 and ka8p02.

boundaries were also relatively frequent after the target words in the narrow focus (NF-m), post-focus (NF-i) and contrastive focus (CF-m) conditions (Table 5-3), suggesting the occurrence of post-focus dephrasing in these conditions.

Table 5-2 Boundaries before the target words in each focus condition each age group

Age		Focus condition				
		NF-m	NF-f	NF-i	BF	CF-m
Age 4-5	AP	45	34	46	34	43
		91.8%	94.4%	88.5%	81.0%	84.3%
	IP	4	1	4	7	8
		8.2%	2.8%	7.7%	16.7%	15.7%
	PW	0	1	2	1	0
		0.0%	2.8%	3.8%	2.4%	0.0%
Age 7-8	AP	76	67	63	52	56
		91.6%	97.1%	94.0%	92.9%	93.3%
	IP	7	0	2	4	4
		8.4%	0.0%	3.0%	7.1%	6.7%
	PW	0	2	2	0	0
		0.0%	2.9%	3.0%	0.0%	0.0%
Age 10-11	AP	78	65	78	58	68
		96.3%	91.5%	95.1%	81.7%	86.1%
	IP	3	1	2	12	11
		3.7%	1.4%	2.4%	16.9%	13.9%
	PW	0	5	2	1	0
		0.0%	7.0%	2.4%	1.4%	0.0%
Adults	AP	118	110	97	93	110
		88.7%	84.6%	75.8%	72.7%	82.1%
	IP	15	3	21	33	24
		11.3%	2.3%	16.4%	25.8%	17.9%
	PW	0	17	10	2	0
		0.0%	13.1%	7.8%	1.6%	0.0%

Table 5-3 Boundaries after the target words in each focus condition each age group

Age		Focus condition				
		NF-m	NF-f	NF-i	BF	CF-m
Age 4-5	AP	41	34	46	38	34
		83.7%	94.4%	88.5%	90.5%	66.7%
	IP	0	2	2	3	0
		0.0%	5.6%	3.8%	7.1%	0.0%
	PW	8	0	4	1	17
		16.3%	0.0%	7.7%	2.4%	33.3%
Age 7-8	AP	59	67	59	53	42
		71.1%	97.1%	88.1%	94.6%	70.0%
	IP	0	1	0	1	0
		0.0%	1.4%	0.0%	1.8%	0.0%
	PW	24	1	8	2	18
		28.9%	1.4%	11.9%	3.6%	30.0%
Age 10-11	AP	53	65	61	63	52
		65.4%	91.4%	74.4%	88.7%	65.8%
	IP	1	6	2	2	0
		1.2%	8.6%	2.4%	2.8%	0.0%
	PW	27	0	19	6	27
		33.3%	0.0%	23.2%	8.5%	34.2%
Adults	AP	56	115	55	97	36
		42.1%	88.5%	43.0%	75.8%	26.9%
	IP	6	14	6	9	3
		4.5%	10.8%	4.7%	7.0%	2.2%
	PW	71	1	67	22	95
		53.4%	0.8%	52.3%	17.2%	70.9%

To statistically examine whether and how the children's use of phrasal boundaries before and after the target words may differ across focus conditions and age groups, we conducted multinomial logistic regression (MLR) analyses in SPSS (IBM SPSS Statistics 22). The dependent variable (or the outcome variable) was BOUNDARY with three categories: AP boundary, IP boundary, and PW boundary. AP boundary and PW boundary were set, in turn, as the reference category in order to get the comparisons between each two categories.

The independent variables (or the predictor variables) were FOCUS, AGE, and LENGTH. FOCUS referred to the focus conditions. For each analysis, we compared narrow focus to another focus condition to address a specific question, so FOCUS always had two categories. AGE referred to the age groups. In addition to the three groups of children, we included a group of adults (see Chapter 4 of this dissertation), in the current analyses for comparison reasons. AGE thus had four categories (i.e., four- to five-year-olds, seven- to eight-year-olds, ten- to eleven-year-olds and adults), and the adult group were set as the reference category. length referred to the "short" and "long" contrast in the target words, and thus had two categories. The main effects of FOCUS, AGE, and LENGTH, the two-way interactions between each two of them, and the three-way interaction between them were entered into the model in a stepwise fashion using a forward entry, meaning that only significant items showed up in the final model and were provided with parameter estimates. The boundaries before and after the target words were analysed separately. The significance level was set at 0.05.

In the data, the IP and PW boundaries were sometimes absent in a certain focus condition in a certain "length" category for a certain age group, which made it impossible to obtain interpretable parameter estimates in the MLR analysis. We therefore introduced one fictive instance to each absent category, by changing one instance of the predominant boundary (i.e., the AP boundary), to the absent category (i.e., either the IP boundary or PW boundary). This operation only caused a subtle change to the Wald statistics but generated interpretable results. This method was adopted from Braun and Chen (2010) in which a similar situation was dealt with in this way.

In the analyses based on the three above-mentioned independent variables, LENGTH never had any significant interaction with either FOCUS or AGE, indicating that FOCUS or AGE had a similar effect on the use of boundaries in short and long target words. We thus decided to leave out the variable LENGTH, so that fewer fictive instances were needed in the analyses. In what follows, we report the analyses with only the independent variables FOCUS and AGE. We concentrate on the main effect of focus and the interaction of FOCUS and AGE because they are directly relevant to our research questions.

5.3.1 Narrow focus vs. pre-focus (NF-m vs. NF-f)

Analysing the boundaries before the target words, we found that only FOCUS significantly improved the model fitting ($\chi^2 = 33.39$, df = 2, $P < 0.05$), indicating that FOCUS had a similar effect on the boundaries before the target words across age groups. The parameter estimates (Table 5-4) showed that whether a target word was in the narrow focus condition

(NF-m) or in the pre-focus condition (NF-f) significantly predicted whether the boundary before the target word was an IP boundary or an AP boundary ($P < 0.05$), whether it was a PW boundary or an AP boundary ($P < 0.05$), and whether it was an IP boundary or a PW boundary ($P < 0.05$). The odds ratio (i.e., Exp (B)) indicated that the odds of the boundary before the target word being an IP boundary compared to the odds of it being an AP boundary in the NF-m condition were 4.17 (1/0.24) times as high as in the NF-f condition. The odds of the boundary before the target word being a PW boundary compared to the odds of it being an AP boundary in the NF-m condition were 0.14 (1/7.11) times as high as in the NF-f condition. The odds of the boundary before the target word being an IP boundary compared to the odds of it being a PW boundary in the NF-m condition were 33.33 (1/0.03) times as high as in the NF-f condition. In other words, the speakers were more likely to produce an IP boundary but less likely to produce a PW boundary before the target word in narrow focus (NF-m) than in pre-focus (NF-f).

Table 5-4 Narrow focus vs. pre-focus (NF-m vs. NF-f) for the boundary before the target

Boundary before the target		***B***	**Std. Error**	**Wald**	**df**	**Sig.**	**Exp (*B*)**
IP (vs. AP)	Intercept	−2.38	0.19	150.20	1	0.00**	
	NF-f	−1.45	0.46	10.05	1	0.00**	0.24
	NF-m	0			0		
PW (vs. AP)	Intercept	−4.36	0.50	75.08	1	0.00**	
	NF-f	1.96	0.54	12.97	1	0.00**	7.11
	NF-m	0			0		
IP (vs. PW)	Intercept	1.98	0.53	13.79	1	0.00**	
	NF-f	−3.41	0.70	23.65	1	0.00**	0.03
	NF-m	0			0		

Analysing the boundaries after the target words, we found that both FOCUS (χ^2 = 164.38, df = 2, $P < 0.05$) and AGE (χ^2 = 35.69, df = 6, $P < 0.05$) significantly improved the model fitting, but the interaction of FOCUS and AGE did not, indicating that FOCUS had a similar effect on the boundaries after the target words across age groups, and that AGE had a similar effect on the boundaries after the target words across focus conditions. The parameter estimates related to FOCUS (Table 5-5) showed that whether a target word was in the narrow focus condition (NF-m) or in the pre-focus condition (NF-f) did not significantly predict whether the boundary after the target word was an IP boundary or an AP boundary

($P > 0.05$), but did significantly predict whether it was a PW boundary or an AP boundary ($P < 0.05$), and whether it was an IP boundary or a PW boundary ($P < 0.05$). The odds ratio indicated that the odds of the boundary after the target word being a PW boundary compared to the odds of it being an AP boundary in the NF-m condition were 50 (1/0.02) times as high as in the NF-f condition. The odds of the boundary after the target word being an IP boundary compared to the odds of it being a PW boundary in the NF-m condition were 0.01 (1/83.75) times as high as in the NF-f condition. In other words, the speakers were more likely to produce a PW boundary but less likely to produce an IP boundary after the target word in narrow focus (NF-m) than in pre-focus (NF-f).

Moreover, the parameter estimates related to AGE showed that whether a target word was produced by a child or an adult significantly predicted whether the boundary after the target word was a PW boundary or an AP boundary ($P < 0.05$ for each group of children). The odds ratio indicated that the odds of the boundary after the target word being a PW boundary compared to the odds of it being an AP boundary in the NF-m and NF-f conditions in the adults were 5.26 (1/0.19) times as high as in the four- to five-year-olds, 2.78 (1/0.36) times as high as in the seven- to eight-year-olds, and 2.22 (1/0.45) times as high as in the ten- to eleven-year-olds. In other words, the children were less likely to produce a PW boundary after the target word than the adults when the target word was in narrow focus (NF-m) and pre-focus (NF-f), and this tendency increased as the age of children decreased.

Table 5-5 Narrow focus vs. pre-focus (NF-m vs. NF-f) for the boundary after the target

Boundary after the target		*B*	Std. Error	Wald	df	Sig.	Exp (*B*)
IP (vs. AP)	Intercept	−2.50	0.39	41.45	1	0.00**	
	NF-f	0.50	0.41	1.48	1	0.22	1.65
	NF-m	0			0		
	Age 4-5	−0.96	0.64	2.24	1	0.13	0.38
	Age 7-8	−1.93	0.75	6.60	1	0.01*	0.14
	Age 10-11	−0.63	0.46	1.87	1	0.17	0.53
	Adults	0			0		
PW (vs. AP)	Intercept	0.17	0.17	0.91	1	0.34	
	NF-f	−3.93	0.52	57.08	1	0.00**	0.02
	NF-m	0			0		
	Age 4-5	−1.65	0.41	16.48	1	0.00**	0.19
	Age 7-8	−1.03	0.29	12.38	1	0.00**	0.36

Continued

Boundary after the target		*B*	Std. Error	Wald	df	Sig.	Exp (*B*)
PW (vs. AP)	Age 10-11	−0.80	0.29	7.75	1	0.01*	0.45
	Adults	0			0		
IP (vs. PW)	Intercept	−2.67	0.40	44.89	1	0.00**	
	NF-f	4.43	0.64	47.14	1	0.00**	83.75
	NF-m	0			0		
	Age 4-5	0.69	0.74	0.88	1	0.35	2.00
	Age 7-8	−0.91	0.79	1.30	1	0.25	0.40
	Age 10-11	0.17	0.52	0.11	1	0.74	1.19
	Adults	0			0		

INTERIM SUMMARY. The raw means showed that the children produced the boundaries before and after the target words predominantly as AP boundaries in both narrow focus (NF-m) and pre-focus (NF-f) conditions. However, the statistical analyses revealed that they still varied the phrasal boundaries to distinguish narrow focus from pre-focus in an adult-like manner: they produced an IP boundary more frequently before the target word, and produced a PW boundary more frequently after the target word in narrow focus than in pre-focus, similar to the adults. However, they used a PW boundary after the target word less frequently than the adults in the dataset (i.e., narrow focus and pre-focus conditions combined). Given that the use of PW boundaries after the target words was mainly in the narrow focus condition but was minimal in the pre-focus condition across age groups, we interpret the result to suggest that the children dephrased the post-focal word in narrow focus less frequently than the adults, and this tendency increased as the age of children decreased.

5.3.2 Narrow focus vs. post-focus (NF-m vs. NF-i)

Analysing the boundaries before the target words, we found that FOCUS ($\chi^2 = 8.65$, df = 2, $P < 0.05$) and AGE ($\chi^2 = 20.79$, df = 6, $P < 0.05$) significantly improved the model fitting, but the interaction of FOCUS and AGE did not, indicating that FOCUS had a similar effect on the boundaries before the target words across age groups, and that AGE had a similar effect on the boundaries before the target words across focus conditions. The parameter estimates related to FOCUS (Table 5-6) showed that whether a target word was in the narrow focus condition (NF-m) or in the post-focus condition (NF-i) did not significantly predict whether the boundary before the target word was an IP boundary or an AP boundary ($P > 0.05$), but did significantly predict whether it was a PW boundary or an AP boundary ($P < 0.05$), and whether it was an IP boundary or a PW boundary ($P < 0.05$). The odds ratio indicated that the odds of the boundary before the target word being a PW boundary compared to the odds of it being an AP boundary in the NF-m condition were 0.23 (1/4.41) times as high as in the NF-i condition. The odds of the boundary before the target word being an IP boundary compared to the odds of it being a PW boundary in the NF-m condition were 4 (1/0.25) times as high as in the NF-i condition. In other words, the speakers were more likely to produce an IP boundary but less likely to produce a PW boundary before the target word in narrow focus (NF-m) than in post-focus (NF-i).

Table 5-6 Narrow focus vs. post-focus (NF-m vs. NF-i) for the boundary before the target

Boundary after the target		*B*	Std. Error	Wald	df	Sig.	Exp (*B*)
IP (vs. AP)	Intercept	1.83	0.23	65.17	1	0.00**	
	NF-i	0.10	0.28	0.14	1	0.71	1.11
	NF-m	0			0		
	Age 4-5	−0.64	0.41	2.44	1	0.12	0.53
	Age 7-8	−0.94	0.39	5.90	1	0.02*	0.39
	Age 10-11	−1.65	0.49	11.45	1	0.00**	0.19
	Adults	0			0		
PW (vs. AP)	Intercept	−3.93	0.54	52.04	1	0.00**	
	NF-i	1.48	0.57	6.87	1	0.01*	4.41
	NF-m	0			0		
	Age 4-5	−0.47	0.67	0.50	1	0.48	0.62
	Age 7-8	−0.81	0.66	1.50	1	0.22	0.44
	Age 10-11	−1.01	0.66	2.30	1	0.13	0.37
	Adults	0			0		
IP (vs. PW)	Intercept	2.10	0.58	13.07	1	0.00**	
	NF-i	−1.38	0.62	4.99	1	0.03*	0.25
	NF-m	0			0		
	Age 4-5	−0.17	0.76	0.05	1	0.82	0.84
	Age 7-8	−0.13	0.75	0.03	1	0.86	0.88
	Age 10-11	−0.65	0.81	0.64	1	0.42	0.52
	Adults	0			0		

Analysing the boundaries after the target words, we found that neither FOCUS nor the interaction of FOCUS and AGE was significant, indicating that whether the target word was in the narrow focus condition (NF-m) or in the post-focus condition (NF-i) did not influence the use of boundary after the target, regardless of age.

INTERIM SUMMARY. The raw means showed that the children produced a large proportion of the boundaries before and after the target words as AP boundaries in both narrow focus (NF-m) and post-focus (NF-i) conditions. However, the statistical analyses revealed that they still varied the phrasal boundaries to distinguish narrow focus from post-focus in an adult-like manner: they produced an IP boundary more frequently but produced a PW boundary less frequently before the target word in narrow focus than in post-focus, similar to the adults. The children and adults' use of phrasal boundaries after the target word was not distinguished between narrow focus and post-focus, suggesting that the use of PW boundary after the target word in both conditions was similar in frequency. That is to say the sentence-final word was dephrased with a similar frequency in both focus conditions, when the sentence-medial word (NF-m) was in narrow focus and when the sentence-initial word (NF-i) was in narrow focus. In the latter case (NF-i condition), the frequent occurrence of AP and IP boundaries before the target word suggested that although the post-focal words (i.e., the sentence-medial and sentence-final words) were very often dephrased together as one larger AP (i.e., partial dephrasing) but were rarely fully dephrased into the same AP as the focused sentence-initial word.

5.3.3 Narrow focus vs. broad focus (NF-m vs. BF)

Analysing the boundaries before the target words, we found that only FOCUS significantly improved the model fitting ($\chi^2 = 15.94$, df = 2, $P < 0.05$), indicating that FOCUS had a similar effect on the boundaries before the target words across age groups. The parameter estimates (Table 5-7) showed that whether a target word was in the narrow focus condition (NF-m) or in the broad focus condition (BF) significantly predicted whether the boundary before the target word was an IP boundary or an AP boundary ($P < 0.05$), but did not significantly predict whether it was a PW boundary or an AP boundary ($P > 0.05$) or whether it was an IP boundary or a PW boundary ($P > 0.05$). The odds ratio indicated that the odds of the boundary before the target word being an IP boundary compared to the odds of it being an AP boundary in the NF-m condition were 0.39 (1/2.56) times as high as in the BF condition. In other words, the speakers were more likely to produce an IP boundary before the target word in broad focus (BF) than in narrow focus (NF-m).

Table 5-7 Narrow focus vs. broad focus (NF-m vs. BF) for the boundary before the target

Boundary before the target		*B*	Std. Error	Wald	df	Sig.	Exp (*B*)
IP (vs. AP)	Intercept	−2.38	0.19	150.20	1	0.00**	
	BF	0.94	0.24	14.80	1	0.00**	2.56
	NF-m	0			0		
PW (vs. AP)	Intercept	−4.36	0.50	75.08	1	0.00**	
	BF	0.51	0.68	0.56	1	0.45	1.66
	NF-m	0			0		
IP (vs. PW)	Intercept	1.98	0.53	13.79	1	0.00**	
	BF	0.43	0.71	0.38	1	0.54	1.54
	NF-m	0			0		

Analysing the boundaries after the target words, we found that FOCUS ($\chi^2 = 75.30$, df = 2, $P < 0.05$) and AGE ($\chi^2 = 49.44$, df = 6, $P < 0.05$) significantly improved the model fitting, but the interaction of FOCUS and AGE did not, indicating that FOCUS had a similar effect on the boundaries after the target words across age groups, and that AGE had a similar effect on the boundaries after the target words across focus conditions. The parameter estimates related to FOCUS (Table 5-8) showed that whether a target word was in the narrow focus condition (NF-m) or in the broad focus condition (BF) did not significantly predict whether the boundary after the target word was an IP boundary or an AP boundary ($P > 0.05$), but did significantly predict whether it was a PW boundary or an AP boundary ($P < 0.05$), and whether it was an IP boundary or a PW boundary ($P < 0.05$). The odds ratio indicated that the odds of the boundary after the target word being a PW boundary compared to the odds of it being an AP boundary in the NF-m condition were 5.88 (1/0.17) times as high as in the BF condition. The odds of the boundary after the target being an IP boundary compared to the odds of it being a PW boundary in the NF-m condition were 0.14 (1/7.07) times as high as in the BF condition. In other words, the speakers were more likely to produce an IP boundary but less likely to produce a PW boundary after the target word in broad focus (BF) than in narrow focus (NF-m).

Moreover, the parameter estimates related to AGE showed that whether a target word was produced by a child or an adult significantly predicted whether the boundary after the target was a PW boundary or an AP boundary ($P < 0.05$ for each group of children). The odds ratio indicated that the odds of the boundary after the target word being a PW boundary compared to the odds of it being an AP boundary in the NF-m and BF conditions in the adults were 6.67 (1/0.15) times as high as in the four- to five-year-olds, 3.33 (1/0.30) times as high as in the seven- to eight-year-olds, and 2.44 (1/0.41) times as high as in the ten- to eleven-year-olds. In other words, the children were less likely to produce a PW boundary after the target word than the adults when the target word was in narrow focus (NF-m) and broad focus (BF), and this tendency increased as the age of children decreased.

Table 5-8 Narrow focus vs. broad focus (NF-m vs. BF) for the boundary after the target

Boundary after the target		*B*	Std. Error	Wald	df	Sig.	Exp (*B*)
IP (vs. AP)	Intercept	−2.43	0.40	37.04	1	0.00**	
	BF	0.16	0.44	0.14	1	0.71	1.18
	NF-m	0			0		
	Age 4-5	−0.63	0.58	1.15	1	0.28	0.54
	Age 7-8	−1.67	0.77	4.73	1	0.03*	0.19
	Age 10-11	−1.32	0.65	4.18	1	0.04*	0.27
	Adults	0			0		
PW (vs. AP)	Intercept	0.25	0.16	2.39	1	0.12	
	BF	−1.79	0.23	60.32	1	0.00**	0.17
	NF-m	0			0		
	Age 4-5	−1.88	0.39	23.30	1	0.00**	0.15
	Age 7-8	−1.21	0.27	20.06	1	0.00**	0.30
	Age 10-11	−0.90	0.25	12.57	1	0.00**	0.41
	Adults	0			0		
IP (vs. PW)	Intercept	−2.68	0.40	44.34	1	0.00**	
	BF	1.96	0.47	17.21	1	0.00**	7.07
	NF-m	0			0		
	Age 4-5	1.26	0.67	3.48	1	0.06*	3.51
	Age 7-8	−0.45	0.79	0.32	1	0.57	0.64
	Age 10-11	−0.42	0.67	0.39	1	0.53	0.66
	Adults	0			0		

INTERIM SUMMARY. The raw means showed that the children produced the boundaries before and after the target words predominantly as AP boundaries in both broad focus (BF) and narrow focus (NF-m) conditions. However, the statistical analyses revealed that they still varied the phrasal boundaries to distinguish broad focus from narrow focus in an adult-like manner: they produced an IP boundary more frequently before and after the target word in broad focus than in narrow focus, and produced a PW boundary less frequently after the target word in broad focus than in narrow focus. In other words, they produced each word in a sentence as a separate IP more frequently in broad focus, and they dephrased the word after the target word more frequently in narrow focus, similar to the adults. However, they used a PW boundary less frequently than the adults after the target word in the dataset (i.e., narrow focus and broad focus conditions combined). Given that the use of PW boundaries after the target words was mainly in the narrow focus condition but was much less in the broad focus condition across age groups, we interpret the result to suggest that the children dephrased the post-focal word in narrow focus less frequently than the adults, and this tendency increased as the age of children decreased.

5.3.4 Narrow focus vs. contrastive focus (NF-m vs. CF-m)

Analysing the boundaries before the target words, we found that only FOCUS significantly improved the model fitting ($\chi^2 = 6.31$, df = 2, $P < 0.05$), indicating that FOCUS had a similar effect on the boundaries before the target words across age groups. The parameter estimates (Table 5-9) showed that whether a target word was in the narrow focus condition (NF-m) or in the contrastive focus condition (CF-m) significantly predicted whether the boundary before the target word was an IP boundary or an AP boundary ($P < 0.05$), but did not significantly predict whether it was a PW boundary or an AP boundary ($P > 0.05$), or whether it was an IP boundary or a PW boundary ($P > 0.05$). The odds ratio indicated that the odds of the boundary before the target word being an IP boundary compared to the odds of it being an AP boundary in the NF-m condition were 0.54 (1/1.86) times as high as in the CF-m condition. In other words, the speakers were more likely to produce an IP boundary before the target word in contrastive focus (CF-m) than in narrow focus (NF-m).

Table 5-9 Narrow focus vs. contrastive focus (NF-m vs. CF-m) for the boundary before the target

Boundary before the target		*B*	Std. Error	Wald	df	Sig.	Exp (*B*)
IP (vs. AP)	Intercept	−2.38	0.19	150.20	1	0.00**	
	CF-m	0.62	0.25	6.13	1	0.01*	1.86
	NF-m	0			0		
PW (vs. AP)	Intercept	−4.36	0.50	75.08	1	0.00**	
	CF-m	0.14	0.71	0.04	1	0.85	1.15
	NF-m	0			0		

Continued

Boundary before the target		B	Std. Error	Wald	df	Sig.	Exp (B)
IP (vs. PW)	Intercept	1.98	0.53	13.79	1	0.00**	
	CF-m	0.48	0.75	0.42	1	0.52	1.62
	NF-m	0			0		

Analysing the boundaries after the target words, we found that both FOCUS ($\chi^2 = 7.68$, df = 2, $P < 0.05$) and AGE ($\chi^2 = 78.10$, df = 6, $P < 0.05$) significantly improved the model fitting, but the interaction of FOCUS and AGE did not, indicating that FOCUS had a similar effect on the boundaries after the target words across age groups, and that AGE had a similar effect on the boundaries after the target words across focus conditions. The parameter estimates related to FOCUS (Table 5-10) showed that whether a target word was in the narrow focus condition (NF-m) or in the contrastive focus condition (CF-m) did not significantly predict whether the boundary after the target word was an IP boundary or an AP boundary ($P > 0.05$), or whether it was an IP boundary or a PW boundary ($P > 0.05$), but did significantly predict whether it was a PW boundary or an AP boundary ($P < 0.05$). The odds ratio indicated that the odds of the boundary after the target word being a PW boundary compared to the odds of it being an AP boundary in the NF-m condition were 0.64 (1/1.57) times as high as in the CF-m condition. In other words, the speakers were more likely to produce a PW boundary after the target word in contrastive focus (CF-m) than in narrow focus (NF-m).

Moreover, the parameter estimates related to AGE showed that whether a target word was produced by a child or an adult significantly predicted whether the boundary after the target word was a PW boundary or an AP boundary ($P < 0.05$ for each group of children). The odds ratio indicated that the odds of the boundary after the target word being a PW boundary compared to the odds of it being an AP boundary in the CF-m and NF-m conditions in the adults were 5.26 (1/0.19) times as high as in the four- to five-year-olds, 4.17 (1/0.24) times as high as in the seven- to eight-year-olds, and 3.57 (1/0.28) times as high as in the ten- to eleven-year-olds. In other words, the children were less likely to produce a PW boundary after the target word than the adults when the target word was in contrastive focus (CF-m) and narrow focus (NF-m), and this tendency increased as the age of children decreased.

Table 5-10 Narrow focus vs. contrastive focus (NF-m vs. CF-m) for the boundary after the target

Boundary after the target		B	Std. Error	Wald	df	Sig.	Exp (B)
IP (vs. AP)	Intercept	−2.26	0.41	30.32	1	0.00**	
	CF-m	−0.15	0.54	0.08	1	0.78	0.86
	NF-m	0			0		
	Age 4-5	−1.27	0.80	2.52	1	0.11	0.28
	Age 7-8	−1.58	0.80	3.97	1	0.05	0.21
	Age 10-11	−1.62	0.79	4.17	1	0.04*	0.20
	Adults	0			0		
PW (vs. AP)	Intercept	0.37	0.15	5.84	1	0.02*	
	CF-m	0.45	0.17	7.11	1	0.01*	1.57
	NF-m	0			0		
	Age 4-5	-1.68	0.27	39.65	1	0.00**	0.19
	Age 7-8	−1.43	0.23	39.63	1	0.00**	0.24
	Age 10-11	-1.26	0.21	34.57	1	0.00**	0.28
	Adults	0			0		
IP (vs. PW)	Intercept	−2.63	0.41	41.89	1	0.00**	
	CF-m	−0.60	0.54	1.24	1	0.27	0.55
	NF-m	0			0		
	Age 4-5	0.42	0.81	0.27	1	0.61	1.52
	Age 7-8	−0.16	0.80	0.04	1	0.84	0.85
	Age 10-11	−0.37	0.80	0.21	1	0.65	0.69
	Adults	0			0		

INTERIM SUMMARY. The raw means showed that the children produced the boundaries before and after the target words most frequently as AP boundaries in both contrastive focus (CF-m) and narrow focus (NF-m) conditions. However, the statistical analyses revealed that they still varied the phrasal boundaries to distinguish contrastive focus from narrow focus in an adult-like manner: they produced an IP boundary before the target word and a PW boundary after the target word (i.e., dephrased the post-focal word) more frequently in contrastive focus than in narrow focus, similar to the adults. However, the children dephrased the post-focus word in the two conditions less frequently than the adults, and this tendency increased as the age of children decreased.

5.4 Discussion and conclusions

We have examined how Korean-speaking four- to five-year-olds, seven- to eight-year-olds and ten- to eleven-year-olds vary phrasal boundaries to distinguish narrow focus from non-focus (i.e., pre-focus and post-focus) and two other types of focus (i.e., broad focus and contrastive focus) in semi-spontaneous production of SOV sentences.

Based on the raw means, we observed that Korean-speaking children most frequently phrase the subject-noun, object-noun, and verb in a sentence as three separate APs, in each age group and for each focus condition, unlike Korean-speaking adults, who most frequently phrase the object-noun and verb as one AP in narrow focus (NF-m), post-focus (NF-i) and contrastive focus (CF-m) conditions. In other words, Korean-speaking adults dephrase the post-focal words more frequently than Korean-speaking children in each of these conditions (i.e., NF-m, NF-i and CF-m). However, statistically, children's use of IP and PW boundaries still varies with focus conditions even at the age of four to five, as found in adults' production, indicating their knowledge of the use of phrasing in marking focus. With regard to the distinction between narrow focus and non-focus, children's use of IP boundaries before focal words is more frequent than before pre-focal or post-focal words, and their use of PW boundaries after focal words is more frequent than after pre-focal words, similar to adults. The findings based on raw means and statistics together suggest that children mark narrow focus in an adult-like manner; namely, they produce an AP or IP boundary before a focal word and dephrase the post-focal word. However, children use post-focus dephrasing much less frequently than adults, especially the youngest group. With regard to the distinction of focus types, children already display adult-like patterns in the use of IP and PW boundaries at the age of four to five. To distinguish broad focus from narrow focus, they use IP boundaries more frequently before and after the target words, but use PW boundaries less frequently after the target words in broad focus. The findings based on raw means and statistics together show that they usually produce words in a broad focus sentence as separate APs or IPs, similar to adults. To distinguish contrastive focus from narrow focus, they use IP boundaries before the target words and PW boundaries after the target words more frequently in contrastive focus. The findings based on raw means and statistics together indicate that they mark contrastive focus in the same manner as marking narrow focus (i.e., using AP or IP boundaries before the focal word and dephrasing the post-focal word) but with more frequency than marking narrow focus. Still, their use of post-focus dephrasing in these two conditions is less frequent than adults'.

Together, our results show that Korean-speaking children most frequently produce each word in a SOV sentence as a separate AP, but they can use phrasing to distinguish focus from non-focus and different types of focus in an adult-like manner by the age of four to five. Their use of phrasing for focus-marking purposes is still developing in terms of frequency from the age of five to eleven.

As discussed in the introduction section of this chapter, considering that phrasing is the primary prosodic focus-marking cue in Korean and Korean-speaking children are competent in perceiving and producing prosodic cues associated with prosodic phrases early in life (Choi & Mazuka, 2001, 2003, 2009; Jun, 2007), we predicted that Korean-speaking children should show at least a moderate degree of adult-like use of phrasing for focus-marking purposes at the age of four to five. Given that we observed an early use of phrasing in distinguishing focus from non-focus and different types of focus in an adult-like manner in Korean-speaking children at the age of four to five, this prediction is supported. Nonetheless, there is ongoing development in the frequency of the use of phrasing for focus-marking purposes from the age of five onwards. As mentioned, children most frequently phrase each word in a sentence as a separate AP across focus conditions, thus using post-focus dephrasing less frequently than adults, and this tendency decreases as children grow older. This observation might be explained by children's speaking rate. Children generally have a slower speaking rate than adults, and they gradually increase their speaking rate from the age of three to twelve (Chermak & Schneiderman, 1985; Logan, et al., 2011; Walker, Archibald, Cherniak & Fish, 1992). Speaking rate has been found to have considerable influence on phrasing. Utterances tend to be chunked into more prosodic phrases in slow speech than in fast speech in Korean (Jun, 1993, 2003). Thus, Korean-speaking children's overuse of AP boundaries in our study might be related to their slower speaking rate. To test this, we would need to analyse the children's speaking rate as compared to the adults' as a next step. However, it is already clear to us that even if speaking rate may slow down Korean-speaking children's acqusiton of the use of phrasing for focus-marking purposes, it does not lead to a failure in the acquisition of the use of this cue at early ages.

Cross-linguistically, Korean-speaking children can use phrasing in an adult-like manner to distinguish focus from non-focus and different types of focus by the age of four to five, similar to the age at which children show fully or largely adult-like use of accentuation for focus-marking purposes in West Germanic languages (Hornby & Hass, 1970; MacWhinney & Bates, 1978; Wells, et al., 2004, on English; Grünloh, Lieven & Tomasello, 2015, on German; A. Chen, 2011a, 2011b, on Dutch). However, there still is a notable difference in the acquisition of phonological focus marking between Korean-speaking children and children speaking a West Germanic language such as Dutch① (A. Chen, 2011a, 2011b). More specifically, Dutch-speaking children by the age of five are already adult-like in the use of accentuation for focus-marking purposes, even in terms of frequency. A potential account for the relatively late mastery of the use of phrasing in Korean, unlike the use of accentuation in Dutch, might be that phrasing is conditioned by speaking rate, as mentioned earlier, whereas accentuation is used at word level and is thus barely influenced by speaking rate. After all, the competence of prosodic focus marking is not developed in isolation but is related to other speech competencies, such as speaking rate, as suggested by our study, and is also related to other linguistic abilities, such syntactic development, as suggested by Romøren and Chen (2014).

① We choose to use the studies on Dutch (A. Chen, 2011a, 2011b) for the comparison because these studies are most comparable to our own with regard to methodology.

CHAPTER 6

Prosodic focus marking in Seoul Korean-speaking children: the use of duration- and pitch-related phonetic cues[1]

Abstract

This study examines how Seoul Korean-speaking children acquire the use of duration- and pitch-related phonetic cues for focus-marking purposes when prosodic phrasing is not valid to mark focus. Using a picture-matching game, we elicited semi-spontaneous production of sentences with the sentence-medial target words in various focus conditions from children aged four to eleven. We analysed the target words which were realised as Accentual Phrase (AP)-initial words, in order to see whether the children can vary phonetic cues to distinguish focus conditions as adults do. We found that Seoul Korean-speaking children start to use duration to mark narrow focus at the age of seven, and become adult-like at the age of ten to eleven. However, they only start to show limited use of pitch in marking narrow focus at the age of ten to eleven. Like adults, they do not vary duration or pitch to distinguish narrow focus from broad focus or contrastive focus. These results reveal that Seoul Korean-speaking children acquire phonetic focus marking within a phonological category later than phonological focus marking, similar to Dutch-speaking children. Among the phonetic focus-marking cues, they acquire the use of duration earlier than the use of pitch, similar to Mandarin-speaking children, but different from Dutch-speaking children. This result suggests that the acquisition of the use of pitch for focus-marking purposes is not only conditioned by the lexical contrastiveness of pitch.

---

[1] Preliminary results of a portion of the data from Chapter 6 were presented at the 18th International Congress of Phonetic Sciences (ICPhS), and published in the proceedings (Yang, et al., 2015). A version of Chapter 6 is aimed to be submitted in article form to an appropriate journal.

Keywords
Acquisition, focus, prosody, phonetic cues, Seoul Korean

6.1 Introduction

In prosodic focus marking, phonological use of prosody (e.g., accentuation and accent type in West Germanic languages, or prosodic phrasing in Seoul Korean) does not always suffice to mark focus or other informational categories in languages that rely on it. For example, in Dutch, both sentence-initial focus and non-focus are frequently realised with the same falling pitch accent (A. Chen, 2009); in German, contrastive and non-contrastive information is not phonologically differentiated via distinctive accent patterns (Braun, 2004); in Seoul Korean (hereafter, Korean), both focal and post-focal words can initiate an Accentual Phrase (AP), though post-focal words are supposed to be dephrased; that is, incorporated in the same AP as the preceding focal word (Chapter 4 of this dissertation). In such cases, adult speakers use phonetic cues (i.e., gradient changes in the prosodic parameters) to distinguish focus conditions within a certain phonological category (A. Chen, 2009, on Dutch; Chapter 4 of this dissertation on Korean). In Korean, children frequently produce the medial word in an SOV sentence as an AP-initial word across focus conditions (Chapter 5 of this dissertation). This raises the question as to whether they use phonetic cues to distinguish focus conditions within one phonological category (i.e., AP-initial words) as Korean-speaking adults do (Chapter 4 of this dissertation).

In what follows, we will briefly review past work on the acquisition of phonetic focus marking in other languages (section 6.1.1), and how Korean-speaking adults use prosody phonetically to mark focus (section 6.1.2), and then state the purpose and predictions of the current study (section 6.1.3).

6.1.1 The acquisition of phonetic focus marking

Limited past work has investigated children's use of phonetic cues for focus-marking purposes within a phonological category on West Germanic languages (Wonnacott & Watson, 2008, on English, A. Chen, 2009, on Dutch). More specifically, English-speaking children at the age of three to four use a higher maximum pitch and higher intensity for words in contrastive focus than in broad focus, when the words in both conditions are produced with a high pitch accent, similar to English-speaking adults. Unlike adults, however, children do not use duration for such distinctions (Wonnacott & Watson, 2008). Dutch-speaking children at the age of four to five use neither pitch nor duration to distinguish sentence-initial focus from non-focus when both categories are realised with a falling pitch accent; on the other hand, Dutch-speaking adults use a lower minimum pitch, and longer vowel, syllable, and word durations for focal words than for pre-focal words with the same falling pitch accent (A. Chen, 2009). By the age of seven to eight, Dutch-speaking children vary pitch, but not duration, in an adult-like way for such distinction (A. Chen, 2009). Thus, in both English and Dutch, the use of pitch tends to be acquired earlier than the use of duration for focus-marking purposes. In addition, Dutch-speaking children acquire phonetic focus marking within one phonological category after the age of five, later than the age at which they show largely adult-like use of the phonological focus-marking cues of accentuation and accent type (A. Chen, 2011a, 2011b).

Our study on Mandarin has shown a different pattern of the acquisition of phonetic cues to focus marking than in English and Dutch (Chapter 3 of this dissertation). Mandarin-speaking children use duration for focus-marking purposes in a fully adult-like way at the age of four to five, and their use of pitch for such purposes also presents early in life at the same age, though it continues to develop after the age of five.

Taken together, phonetic focus marking as the primary prosodic focus marking means in Mandarin is acquired early in life by Mandarin-speaking children, whereas as a secondary prosodic focus marking means in Dutch is acquired later than phonological focus marking by Dutch-speaking children. However, it is not clear to us whether phonetic focus marking within a phonological category is acquired later than phonological focus marking in a language that uses a different phonological focus-marking cue than accentuation or accent type. In addition, the use of pitch and duration for focus-marking purposes are acquired in a reverse order in Mandarin compared to English and Dutch. The later acquisition of the use of pitch than the use of duration in Mandarin can be related to the fact that pitch has lexical function in Mandarin. However, it remains unclear whether the use of pitch is also acquired earlier than duration in other languages that do not use pitch lexically but differ from English and Dutch in other aspects of the prosodic system.

Korean can serve as a good test bed for the above mentioned questions from a typological perspective, because it uses prosodic phrasing as the phonological means to mark focus, and it has no lexical use of pitch.

6.1.2 Phonetic focus marking in Korean adult speech

Korean-speaking adults vary phrasal boundaries to distinguish narrow focus from non-focus and other types of focus in semi-spontaneous production of SOV sentences (Chapter 4 of this dissertation). However, they produce a predominant proportion of the boundaries before the sentence-medial words (objects) as AP boundaries in each focus condition. Analysing the predominant sentence-medial, AP-initial words, we found that the speakers produced the words with longer word and initial-syllable durations, and a higher maximum pitch in narrow focus than in non-focus. They did not vary the duration- and pitch-related phonetic cues to distinguish narrow focus from broad focus or contrastive focus (Chapter 4 of this dissertation). The findings suggest that Korean-speaking adults vary phonetic cues to mark narrow focus but not to distinguish focus types within one phonological category (i.e., AP-initial words).

6.1.3 The current study

Korean-speaking children are able to use prosodic phrasing in an adult-like manner to distinguish focus from non-focus and different types of focus at the age of four to five, though they prefer producing each word in a sentence as a separate AP across focus conditions (Chapter 5 of this dissertation). The current study examines how Korean-speaking children acquire phonetic focus marking within one phonological category (i.e., AP-initial words). Given that phonetic cues are secondary cues in Korean, and that the secondary cues are acquired later than the primary cues in Dutch (A. Chen, 2009), we predict that phonetic focus marking is acquired later than phonological focus marking in Korean, similar to the observation in Dutch. Given that pitch does not have lexical function in Korean, and that, in languages in which pitch does not have lexical function, the use of pitch tends to be acquired earlier than the use of duration for focus-marking purposes (A. Chen, 2009; Wonnacott & Watson, 2008), we predict that the use of pitch should be acquired earlier than the use of duration for such purposes in Korean.

To test the predictions, we have examined how Korean-speaking children vary duration- and pitch-related phonetic cues to distinguish (1) Narrow focus from non-focus (Effect of focus), (2) Narrow focus from broad focus (Effect of focal constituent size), and (3) Narrow focus from contrastive focus (Effect of contrastivity).

6.2 Method

The speech data were a subset of SOV sentences reported in Chapter 5. In these sentences, the sentence-medial target words were all AP-initial and were in varied focus conditions, and therefore were suitable for our current purposes. In the following, for the sake of completeness, we repeat the details on the elicitation and selection of the sentences reported in sections 6.2.1 to 6.2.5 of Chapter 5. We describe the phonetic annotation in section 6.2.6.

6.2.1 Participants

Three groups of children participated in the experiment, including six four- to five-year-olds (average age: 5;3, range: 4;10-5;10), eight seven- to eight-year-olds (average age: 8;0, range: 7;4-8;10), and eight ten to eleven-year-olds (average age: 10;10, range: 10;3-11;11) (see Appendix C for more participant information). They were recruited in Seoul via Hanyang Phonetics and Psycholinguistics Laboratory, and came from diverse social-economic backgrounds. They all spoke Seoul Korean as their native language.

6.2.2 The picture-matching game

We adapted the picture-matching game used in A. Chen (2011a) to elicit semi-spontaneous production of sentences. In this game, the child was supposed to help the experimenter to put pictures in matched pairs. Three piles of pictures were used. The experimenter and the child each held a pile of pictures. The third pile lay on the table in a seemingly messy fashion. The experimenter's pictures always missed some information (e.g., the subject, the action, the object, or all three). The child's pictures always contained all three pieces of information. On each trial, the experimenter showed one of her pictures to the child, described the picture and asked a question about it or made a remark about the missing information (in the contrastive focus condition). The child then took a look at the corresponding picture in his/her pile and responded to the experimenter's question or remark. The experimenter then looked for the right picture in the messy pile and matched it with her own picture to form a pair.

As rules of the game, the child was asked to answer the experimenter's questions in full sentences and not to reveal his/her pictures to the experimenter. In order to make sure that the experiment was conducted in the same way for all the children, and that adequate background information was equally provided for each trial before a question was asked or a remark was made, we constructed scripts containing what the experimenter was supposed to say and how she was supposed to respond in each trial. The experimenter was instructed to follow the scripts closely but was encouraged to make spontaneous remarks that did not affect the information structure of the child's responses for the purpose of facilitating the interaction. Prior to the picture-matching game, a picture-naming task was conducted to ensure that the child would use the intended words to refer to the entities in the pictures. This procedure also rendered all the entities in the pictures referentially accessible.

6.2.3 Experimental materials

Sixty question-answer dialogues were embedded in the picture-matching game to elicit sixty SOV sentences in five focus conditions: narrow focus on the sentence-initial subject noun (NF-i), responding to *who*-questions; narrow focus on the sentence-medial object noun (NF-m), responding to *what*-questions; narrow focus on the sentence-final verb (NF-f), responding to *what-does*-X-*do-to*-Y questions; contrastive focus in sentence-medial position (CF-m), correcting the experimenter's remark about the object; broad focus over the whole sentence (BF), responding to *what-happens* questions, as illustrated in (1). Including narrow focus in three sentence-positions made it possible to study the effect of narrow focus on the sentence-medial object nouns (NF-m) compared to the same words in pre-focus (or NF-f) and post focus (or NF-i). Comparing the object nouns in NF-m, CF-m and BF allowed us to study the prosodic difference between different focus types. Examples of question-answer dialogues in the five focus conditions are given in (1), in which the referents are referred to with the definite article in the English glossary because they had been introduced in the picture-naming task.

(1) Examples of question-answer dialogues between the experimenter (E) and participant (P):

(NF-i) E: Look! The bread, and someone looks a bit puzzled. It looks like someone looks for the bread. Who looks for the bread?

P: [소가] 빵을 찾아요.

		soka	p*aŋɨl	tɕʰatɕajo
		[The cow]	the bread	looks for.

(NF-m)	E:	Look! The dog, and it holds a painting brush. It looks like the dog draws something. What does the dog draw?		
	P:	개가	[빵을]	그려요 .
		kɛka	p*aŋɨl	kɨljʌjo
		The dog	[the bread]	draws.

(NF-f)	E:	Look! The rat, and the bread. It looks like the rat does something to the bread. What does the rat do to the bread?		
	P:	쥐가	빵을	[만져요].
		tɕuka	p*aŋɨl	mantʃʌjo
		The rat	the bread	[touches].

(CF-m)	E:	Look! The bear. The bear looks a bit puzzled. It looks like the bear looks for something. I will make a guess: the bear looks for the egg.		
	P:	곰이	[빵을]	찾아요 .
		komi	p*aŋɨl	tɕʰatɕajo
		The bear	[the bread]	looks for.

(BF)	E:	Look! My picture is very blurry. I cannot see anything clearly. What happens in your picture?		
	P:	[말이	빵을	그려요].
		mali	p*aŋɨl	kɨljʌjo
		[The horse	the bread	draws].

The sixty SOV sentences were unique combinations of five subject-nouns, twelve target object-nouns, and three verbs (Table 6-1, see the sentences in Appendix D). Each subject-noun was a monosyllabic lexical word followed by a nominative case marker, 가 (/ka/) or 이 (/i/). The target object-nouns included six two-syllable (or "short") words and six four-syllable (or "long") words, because APs① with two to four syllables tend to occur frequently in Korean. Each "short" word was a monosyllabic lexical word followed by an

① The AP is a word-sized unit by default (vs. focused) (Schafer & Jun, 2002; Jun, 2005).

accusative case marker, 을 (/ɨl/) or 를 (/lɨl/). As for the "long" words, except for 까마귀를 (/k*amakwilɨl/), which consisted of a three-syllable lexical word and the accusative case marker 를 (/lɨl/), each of the other words consisted of a disyllabic lexical word, a monosyllabic suffix 들 (/tɨl/) indicating the plural form of the lexical word, and the accusative case marker 을 (/ɨl/). Each target word was initiated with either a high-tone-triggering aspirated stop (i.e., /pʰ/ or /kʰ/) or fortis stop (i.e., /p*/ or /k*/) or a low-tone-triggering lenis stop (i.e., /p/ or /k/) or a vowel (i.e., /a/), so that there would be varied AP tonal patterns in the data. Each target word appeared once in five focus conditions (twelve target words × five focus conditions), leading to sixty "sentences" but without subject-nouns and verbs. The five subject-nouns and three verbs were then nearly evenly distributed to the "sentences", forming sixty SOV sentences. Each sentence was completed with the particle 요 (/jo/), a common politeness marker in informal Korean.

Table 6-1 Words that occurred in the SOV sentences

Subjects	개가 /kɛka/ "dog"	쥐가 /tɕuka/ "rat"	곰이 /komi/ "bear"	말이 /mali/ "horse"	소가 /soka/ "cow"	
Short objects	발을 /palɨl/ "foot"	비를 /pilɨl/ "rain"	불을 /pulɨl/ "fire"	팔을 /pʰalɨl/ "arm"	빵을 /p*aŋɨl/ "bread"	알을 /alɨl/ "egg"
Long objects	가방들을 /kapaŋtɨlɨl/ "bags"	기둥들을 /kituŋtɨlɨl/ "pillars"	구두들을 /kututɨlɨl/ "shoes"	카드들을 /kʰatɨtɨlɨl/ "cards"	까마귀를 /k*amakwilɨl/ "crow"	안경들을 /ankjʌŋtɨlɨl/ "pairs of glasses"
Verbs	그려 /kɨljʌ/ "draw"	만져 /mantʃʌ/ "touch"	찾아 /tɕʰatɕa/ "look for"			

The sixty sentences were elicited in two experimental sessions: the thirty sentences with "short" target words in Session A and the other thirty sentences with "long" target words in Session B. The trials in each session were randomised in such a way that trials from the same focus condition did not appear next to each other and the focused constituent of a trial was not mentioned on its preceding trial.

6.2.4 Experimental procedure

The children were tested individually in Hanyang Phonetics and Psycholinguistics Laboratory at Hanyang University. A female native speaker of Seoul Korean administered the experiment after having received intensive training on how to conduct the experiment. The experiment lasted about 60 minutes, including a short casual chat between the experimenter and the child before the first experimental session, and a short break between the two sessions. Audio recordings were made for each child in each session with a sampling rate of 44.1 kHz with 16 bits. Video recordings were also made for some of the children for training purposes.

6.2.5 Sentence selection

The audio recording from each participant was first orthographically annotated in Praat (Boersma & Weenink, 2013) by a trained native speaker. Then, usable sentences were selected (64% from the 4- to 5-year-olds; 70% from the 7- to 8-year-olds; 80% from the 10- to 11-year-olds; see the percentage for each participant in Appendix C) and unusable ones were excluded from further analysis. A target sentence was considered unusable only in one of the following cases: (1) the participant produced the target sentence before the experimenter asked the question; (2) the experimenter asked a different question than the intended question in that trial; (3) the experimenter did not provide an adequate description of the picture before she asked a question; (4) the sentence was produced with strong background noise; (5) the sentence was produced with word insertion, deletion or replacement; (6) the sentence was produced with self-repair or clearly perceivable hesitation; or (7) the sentence was produced with perceivable irregular voice quality or intonation caused by cold or unstable emotion.

In the prosodic phrasing analysis (Chapter 5 of this dissertation), we annotated the two boundaries immediately preceding and following the sentence-medial target word as AP boundaries, IP boundaries, or phrase-internal phonological word (PW) boundaries following K-ToBI (Jun, 2000, 2005). Among the three boundary types, AP boundaries were predominant before the target words, across age groups and focus conditions (Table 6-2). We selected the AP-initial target words for the current analysis.

Table 6-2 Percentages of target words preceded by an AP boundary

	Narrow focus (NF-m)	Pre-focus (NF-f)	Post-focus (NF-i)	Broad focus (BF)	Contrastive focus (CF-m)
Age 4-5	91.8%	94.4%	88.5%	81.0%	84.3%
Age 7-8	91.6%	97.1%	94.0%	92.9%	93.3%
Age 10-11	96.3%	91.5%	95.1%	81.7%	86.1%

Continued

	Narrow focus (NF-m)	Pre-focus (NF-f)	Post-focus (NF-i)	Broad focus (BF)	Contrastive focus (CF-m)
Adults	88.7%	84.6%	75.8%	72.7%	82.1%

6.2.6 Phonetic annotation

The selected target words were phonetically annotated by the author in Praat (Boersma & Weenink, 2013). We were especially interested in whether and how pitch- and duration-related cues were varied for focus-marking purposes, and thus examined a selection of these cues, including word duration, word initial syllable duration (hereafter initial-syllable duration), maximum pitch (hereafter pitch-max), minimum pitch (hereafter pitch-min), and pitch span (i.e., pitch-max minus pitch-min). Segmentation of words and syllables was done on the basis of formant intensity, formant contours, waveforms, and auditory perception (Machač & Skarnitzl, 2009; Turk, Nakai & Sugahara, 2006). In the annotation of pitch-max and pitch-min, care was taken to avoid voiced lenis stops and not to confuse local pitch fluctuations with linguistically relevant variation in pitch. A small number of trials that were affected by background noise and non-model voice quality were excluded from pitch annotation.

6.3 Statistical analysis and results

As mentioned earlier, the target words were the sentence-medial object nouns in our analysis. They were focal in the NF-m, CF-m and BF conditions, post-focal in the NF-i condition, and pre-focal in the NF-f condition. To investigate the effect of narrow focus in contrast to non-focus, the target words in narrow focus (NF-m) were compared to those in post-focus (NF-i) and pre-focus (NF-f). To examine the effect of focal constituent size, the target words in narrow focus (NF-m) were compared to those in broad focus (BF). To observe the effect of contrastivity, the target words in narrow focus (NF-m) were compared to those in contrastive focus (CF-m).

Mixed-effects modelling in the program R with the lme4 package (Bates, et al., 2014) was used to assess the data. The dependent variables were word duration, initial-syllable duration, pitch span, pitch-max, and pitch-min of the target words. The fixed factors were FOCUS, AGE, and LENGTH. FOCUS referred to the focus conditions. For each analysis, two conditions were compared to each other in order to address a specific question. FOCUS thus always had two levels (narrow focus vs. pre-focus/post-focus/broad focus/contrastive focus) in our models. AGE referred to the age groups. In addition to the three groups of children, we included an adult control group (reported in Chapter 4 of this dissertation). AGE ths had four levels. LENGTH referred to the length of the target words. Since we have two-syllable "short" words and four-syllable "long" words, LENGTH had two levels. In addition, two random factors, SPEAKER, referring to the participants, and SENTENCE, referring to the target sentences, were included in the analysis.

To find out whether a particular prosodic cue was used to distinguish two focus conditions, models were built using the aforementioned factors. Starting from an "empty" model (hereafter Model 0) containing only the random factors, we added the main effects of the fixed factors, the two-way interactions between each two fixed factors, and the three-way interaction between all of them to the model in a stepwise fashion, building seven additional models (Table 6-3). The ANOVA function in R was used to compare models in order to derive the model with the best fit. First, Model 1 was compared to Model 0, and a statistically significant difference indicated that Model 1 with the newly added parameter FOCUS could better explain the variation in the data, and thus was the "winning" model. Otherwise, Model 0 stayed as the "winning" model. Next, Model 2 was compared to its preceding "winning" model, which could be either Model 1 or Model 0. Following the same logic, each later model was compared to the preceding "winning" model. The last "winning" model was considered to be the best-fit model

Table 6-3 Model build-up procedure

Model	Factor added
Model 0	
Model 1	FOCUS
Model 2	AGE
Model 3	LENGTH
Model 4	FOCUS : AGE
Model 5	FOCUS : LENGTH
Model 6	AGE : LENGTH
Model 7	FOCUS : AGE : LENGTH

For each analysis, we report on the best-fit model, according to the model comparisons, and statistical significance of main effects and interactions, according to the summary of the best-fit model. As the model summary does not straightforwardly show the difference between two focus conditions in the use of a particular prosodic cue in each age group, we did additional analysis of each age group to obtain a clearer picture on interactions involving the factor AGE. If the best-fit model contains the three-way interaction of FOCUS, AGE and LENGTH, we discuss how the speakers in each age group distinguished the two focus conditions in words of different lengths by examining the interaction of FOCUS and LENGTH in each age group. If the best-fit model contains the two-way interaction of FOCUS and AGE, we discuss how the speakers in each age group distinguished the two focus conditions by examining the main effect of FOCUS in each age group. We do not discuss in detail the main effects of the factors when the interactions involving these factors are significant, two-way interactions when three-way interactions involving the same factors are significant, and interactions that do not involve the factors FOCUS and AGE.

6.3.1 Realisation of narrow focus

6.3.1.1 Narrow focus vs. pre-focus (NF-m vs. NF-f)

WORD DURATION. The best-fit model for the analysis of word duration was Model 6 (Table 6-4). The summary of this model (Table 6-5) showed that the main effects of FOCUS, AGE and their interaction were significant. The main effect of LENGTH and the interaction of AGE and LENGTH were also significant. Subsequent analysis of the main effect of FOCUS in each age group separately revealed that the word duration was significantly longer in narrow focus than in pre-focus in the adults (34 ms longer, $P = 0.049$) and ten- to eleven-year-olds (27 ms longer, $P < 0.05$), but not in the seven- to eight-year-olds (12 ms longer, $P > 0.05$) or in the four- to five-year-olds (8 ms shorter in narrow focus, $P > 0.05$) (Figure 6-1).

Table 6-4 Model comparisons regarding the dependent variable word duration in the comparison narrow focus vs. pre-focus

Model comparisons	Pr(>Chisq)
0 vs. 1 (adding FOCUS)	0.734
0 vs. 2 (adding AGE)	0.000***
2 vs. 3 (adding LENGTH)	0.000***

Continued

Model comparisons	Pr(>Chisq)
3 vs. 4 (adding FOCUS : AGE)	0.018
4 vs. 5 (adding FOCUS : LENGTH)	0.345
4 vs. 6 (adding AGE : LENGTH)	0.000***
6 vs. 7 (adding FOCUS : AGE : LENGTH)	0.248

Table 6-5 Model summary regarding the dependent variable word duration in the comparison narrow focus vs. pre-focus

Factor	Estimate	Std. Error	*t* value	Pr(>|*t*|)
Intercept (Adults. Narrow focus. Short)	0.290	0.019	15.004	0.000***
Pre-focus	−0.047	0.019	-2.522	0.017*
Age 4-5	0.094	0.028	3.407	0.001**
Age 7-8	0.047	0.025	1.892	0.065
Age 10-11	0.041	0.025	1.648	0.107
Long	0.254	0.018	13.739	0.000***
Pre-focus : Age 4-5	0.041	0.016	2.554	0.011*
Pre-focus : Age 7-8	0.022	0.013	1.673	0.095
Pre-focus : Age 10-11	0.005	0.013	0.410	0.682
Pre-focus : Long	0.026	0.025	1.048	0.305
Age 4-5 : Long	0.121	0.016	7.618	0.000***
Age 7-8 : Long	0.034	0.013	2.662	0.008**
Age 10-11 : Long	0.044	0.013	3.422	0.001**

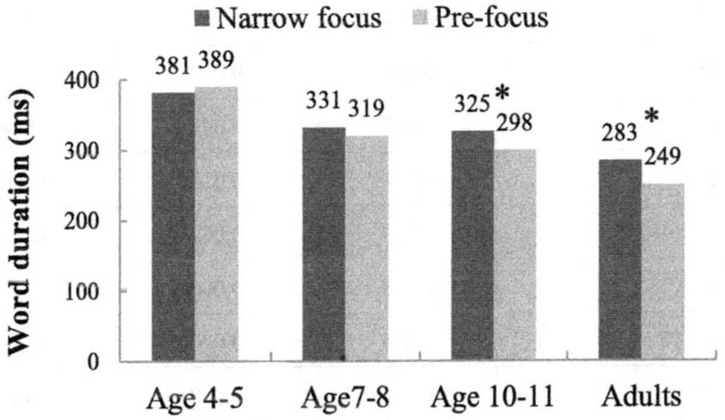

Figure 6-1 The use of word duration in distinguishing narrow focus from pre-focus

INITIAL-SYLLABLE DURATION. The best-fit model for the analysis of initial-syllable duration was Model 6 (Table 6-6). The summary of this model (Table 6-7) showed that the main effect of FOCUS was not significant, but the interaction of FOCUS and AGE was significant. The main effect of AGE and the interaction of AGE and LENGTH were also significant. Subsequent analysis of each age group revealed that the initial-syllable duration was significantly longer in narrow focus than in pre-focus in the adults (23 ms longer, $P < 0.05$) and ten- to eleven-year-olds (19 ms longer, $P < 0.05$), but not in the four- to five-year-olds or the seven- to eight-year-olds (Figure 6-2).

Table 6-6 Model comparisons regarding the dependent variable initial-syllable duration in the comparison narrow focus vs. pre-focus

Model comparisons	*Pr*(>Chisq)
0 vs. 1 (adding FOCUS)	0.133
0 vs. 2 (adding AGE)	0.001**
2 vs. 3 (adding LENGTH)	0.265
2 vs. 4 (adding FOCUS : AGE)	0.001**
4 vs. 5 (adding FOCUS : LENGTH)	0.659
4 vs. 6 (adding AGE : LENGTH)	0.010*
6 vs. 7 (adding FOCUS : AGE : LENGTH)	0.495

Table 6-7 Model summary regarding the dependent variable initial-syllable duration in the comparison narrow focus vs. pre-focus

Factor	Estimate	Std. Error	*t* value	*Pr*(>|*t*|)
Intercept (Adults. Narrow focus. Short)	0.149	0.011	14.085	0.000***
Pre-focus	−0.027	0.013	−2.032	0.052
Age 4-5	0.031	0.010	2.978	0.004**
Age 7-8	0.028	0.009	2.985	0.005**
Age 10-11	0.017	0.009	1.808	0.077
Long	−0.008	0.013	−0.611	0.546
Pre-focus : Age 4-5	0.029	0.007	4.209	0.000***
Pre-focus : Age 7-8	0.013	0.006	2.253	0.025*
Pre-focus : Age 10-11	0.004	0.006	0.734	0.463
Pre-focus : Long	0.008	0.018	0.439	0.665
Age 4-5 : Long	−0.006	0.007	−0.851	0.395

Continued

Factor	Estimate	Std. Error	*t* value	*Pr*(>|*t*|)
Age 7-8 : Long	−0.020	0.006	−3.534	0.000***
Age 10-11 : Long	−0.003	0.006	−0.622	0.534

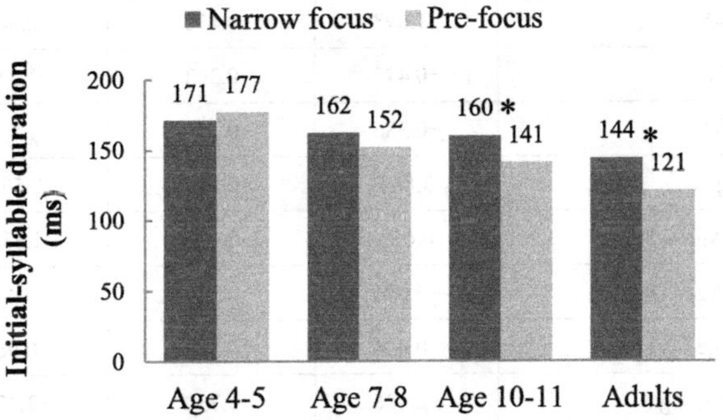

Figure 6-2 The use of initial-syllable duration in distinguishing narrow focus from pre-focus

PITCH SPAN. The best fit model for the analysis of pitch span was Model 7 (Table 6-8). The summary of this model (Table 6-9) showed that the main effect of FOCUS was not significant, but the two-way interaction of FOCUS and LENGTH and the three way interaction of FOCUS, AGE and LENGTH were significant. The main effects of AGE and LENGTH and their interaction were also significant. Subsequent analysis of each age group showed no significant main effect of FOCUS or significant interaction of FOCUS and LENGTH in any group of children, indicating that they did not vary pitch span to distinguish narrow focus from pre-focus, different from the adults who used a wider pitch span in narrow focus than in pre-focus for the four-syllable long words (2.5 st wider, $P < 0.001$).

Table 6-8 Model comparisons regarding the dependent variable pitch span in the comparison narrow focus vs. pre-focus

Model comparisons	*Pr*(>Chisq)
0 vs. 1 (adding FOCUS)	0.201
0 vs. 2 (adding AGE)	0.000***
2 vs. 3 (adding LENGTH)	0.000***
3 vs. 4 (adding FOCUS : AGE)	0.001**
4 vs. 5 (adding FOCUS : LENGTH)	0.040*
5 vs. 6 (adding AGE : LENGTH)	0.000***
6 vs. 7 (adding FOCUS : AGE : LENGTH)	0.003**

Table 6-9 Model summary regarding the dependent variable pitch span in the comparison narrow focus vs. pre-focus

Factor	Estimate	Std. Error	*t* value	*Pr*(>|*t*|)
Intercept (Adults. Narrow focus. Short)	2.927	0.397	7.369	0.000***
Pre-focus	−0.035	0.516	−0.069	0.946
Age 4-5	−1.098	0.432	−2.544	0.012*
Age 7-8	−0.477	0.363	−1.314	0.193
Age 10-11	−0.386	0.360	−1.070	0.288
Long	3.864	0.515	7.503	0.000***
Pre-focus : Age 4-5	0.659	0.493	1.336	0.182
Pre-focus : Age 7-8	−0.094	0.375	−0.250	0.803
Pre-focus : Age 10-11	−0.024	0.374	−0.065	0.948
Pre-focus : Long	−2.426	0.730	−3.323	0.002**
Age 4-5 : Long	−2.352	0.465	−5.063	0.000***
Age 7-8 : Long	−1.973	0.365	−5.402	0.000***
Age 10-11 : Long	−1.448	0.366	−3.954	0.000***
Pre-focus : Age 4-5 : Long	1.550	0.680	2.280	0.023*
Pre-focus : Age 7-8 : Long	1.843	0.532	3.466	0.001**
Pre-focus : Age 10-11 : Long	1.232	0.532	2.315	0.021*

PITCH-MAX. The best-fit model for the analysis of pitch-max was Model 6 (Table 6-10). The summary of this model (Table 6-11) showed that the main effect of FOCUS was not significant, but the interaction of FOCUS and AGE was significant. The main effect of AGE and the interaction of AGE and LENGTH were also significant. Subsequent analysis of each age group showed no significant main effect of FOCUS in any group of children, indicating that they did not vary the pitch-max to distinguish narrow focus from pre-focus, different from the adults who used a higher pitch-max in narrow focus than in pre-focus (2.0 st higher, $P < 0.05$).

Table 6-10 Model comparisons regarding the dependent variable pitch-max in the comparison narrow focus vs. pre-focus

Model comparisons	*Pr*(>Chisq)
0 vs. 1 (adding FOCUS)	0.094
0 vs. 2 (adding AGE)	0.000***
2 vs. 3 (adding LENGTH)	0.470

Continued

Model comparisons	*Pr*(>Chisq)
2 vs. 4 (adding FOCUS : AGE)	0.000***
4 vs. 5 (adding FOCUS : LENGTH)	0.906
4 vs. 6 (adding AGE : LENGTH)	0.044*
6 vs. 7 (adding FOCUS : AGE : LENGTH)	0.440

Table 6-11 Model summary regarding the dependent variable pitch-max in the comparison narrow focus vs. pre-focus

Factor	Estimate	Std. Error	*t* value	*Pr*(>|*t*|)
Intercept (Adults. Narrow focus. Short)	91.050	1.231	73.949	0.000***
Pre-focus	−1.840	1.013	−1.817	0.082
Age 4-5	6.531	1.758	3.715	0.001**
Age 7-8	6.367	1.600	3.978	0.000***
Age 10-11	3.759	1.600	2.349	0.025*
Long	0.739	1.012	0.730	0.472
Pre-focus : Age 4-5	2.038	0.364	5.598	0.000***
Pre-focus : Age 7-8	1.026	0.289	3.554	0.000***
Pre-focus : Age 10-11	0.786	0.286	2.746	0.006**
Pre-focus : Long	−0.181	1.418	−0.128	0.899
Age 4-5 : Long	−1.047	0.359	−2.915	0.004**
Age 7-8 : Long	0.038	0.288	0.132	0.895
Age 10-11 : Long	−0.051	0.284	−0.181	0.857

PITCH-MIN. The best-fit model for the analysis of pitch-min was Model 6 (Table 6-12). The summary of this model (Table 6-13) showed that the main effect of FOCUS was not significant, and it was not involved in any significant interaction, indicating that the children did not vary the pitch-min to distinguish narrow focus from pre-focus, similar to the adults.

Table 6-12 Model comparisons regarding the dependent variable pitch-min in the comparison narrow focus vs. pre-focus

Model comparisons	*Pr*(>Chisq)
0 vs. 1 (adding FOCUS)	0.454

Continued

Model comparisons	*Pr*(>Chisq)
0 vs. 2 (adding AGE)	0.000***
2 vs. 3 (adding LENGTH)	0.017*
3 vs. 4 (adding FOCUS : AGE)	0.324
3 vs. 5 (adding FOCUS : LENGTH)	0.310
3 vs. 6 (adding AGE : LENGTH)	0.001
6 vs. 7 (adding FOCUS : AGE : LENGTH)	0.154

Table 6-13 Model summary regarding the dependent variable pitch-min in the comparison narrow focus vs. pre-focus

Factor	Estimate	Std. Error	*t* value	*Pr*(>|*t*|)
Intercept (Adults. Narrow focus. Short)	87.866	1.141	77.042	0.000***
Pre-focus	−1.299	0.802	−1.619	0.118
Age 4-5	8.076	1.736	4.652	0.000***
Age 7-8	7.316	1.579	4.634	0.000***
Age 10-11	4.493	1.578	2.847	0.007**
Long	−2.672	0.802	−3.332	0.003**
Pre-focus : Age 4-5	0.628	0.349	1.801	0.072
Pre-focus : Age 7-8	0.160	0.271	0.590	0.556
Pre-focus : Age 10-11	0.129	0.271	0.476	0.634
Pre-focus : Long	1.339	1.119	1.196	0.244
Age 4-5 : Long	0.480	0.346	1.388	0.166
Age 7-8 : Long	1.126	0.270	4.170	0.000***
Age 10-11 : Long	0.809	0.269	3.001	0.003**

INTERIM SUMMARY. The four- to five-year-olds and seven- to eight-year-olds did not use any of the phonetic cues to distinguish narrow focus from pre-focus, different from the adults, who used a longer word duration, longer initial-syllable duration and higher pitch-max in narrow focus than in pre-focus and used a wider pitch span for the four-syllable "long" words in narrow focus than in pre focus. The ten- to eleven-year-olds varied word duration and initial-syllable duration in an adult-like way to distinguish narrow focus from pre-focus, but did not vary the pitch-related cues for the same purpose, different from the adults.

6.3.1.2 Narrow focus vs. post-focus (NF-m vs. NF-i)

WORD DURATION. The best-fit model for the analysis of word duration was Model 7 (Table 6-14). The summary of this model (Table 6-15) showed that the main effect of FOCUS was significant, and the interaction of FOCUS, AGE and LENGTH was also significant. The main effects of AGE and LENGTH and their interaction were also significant. Subsequent analysis of each age group showed that the main effect of FOCUS was significant but the interaction of FOCUS and LENGTH was not significant in the seven- to eight-year-olds and ten- to eleven-year-olds, indicating that these two groups of children used a longer word duration in narrow focus than in post-focus, regardless of word length (33 ms longer, $P < 0.05$ in the seven- to eight year-olds; 47 ms longer, $P < 0.001$ in the ten- to eleven-year-olds), similar to the adults (55 ms longer, $P < 0.001$). In the four- to five-year-olds, the main effect of FOCUS and the interaction of FOCUS and LENGTH were not significant, indicating that they did not vary the word duration to distinguish narrow focus from post-focus, different from the adults (Figure 6-3).

Table 6-14 Model comparisons regarding the dependent variable word duration in the comparison narrow focus vs. post-focus

Model comparisons	*Pr*(>Chisq)
0 vs. 1 (adding FOCUS)	0.521
0 vs. 2 (adding AGE)	0.000***
2 vs. 3 (adding LENGTH)	0.000***
3 vs. 4 (adding FOCUS : AGE)	0.002**
4 vs. 5 (adding FOCUS : LENGTH)	0.604
4 vs. 6 (adding AGE : LENGTH)	0.000***
6 vs. 7 (adding FOCUS : AGE : LENGTH)	0.022*

Table 6-15 Model summary regarding the dependent variable word duration in the comparison narrow focus vs. post-focus

Factor	Estimate	Std. Error	*t* value	*Pr*(>|*t*|)
Intercept (Adults. Narrow focus. Short)	0.289	0.019	15.444	0.000***
Post-focus	−0.054	0.019	−2.824	0.008**
Age 4-5	0.103	0.026	4.049	0.000***
Age 7-8	0.046	0.023	2.015	0.050

Continued

Factor	Estimate	Std. Error	*t* value	*Pr*(>|*t*|)
Age 10-11	0.039	0.023	1.702	0.096
Long	0.253	0.019	13.209	0.000***
Post-focus : Age 4-5	0.027	0.016	1.667	0.096
Post-focus : Age 7-8	0.009	0.015	0.609	0.543
Post-focus : Age 10-11	0.012	0.014	0.842	0.400
Post-focus : Long	−0.003	0.027	−0.117	0.908
Age 4-5 : Long	0.102	0.017	5.911	0.000***
Age 7-8 : Long	0.039	0.014	2.693	0.007**
Age 10-11 : Long	0.052	0.014	3.653	0.000***
Post-focus : Age 4-5 : Long	0.066	0.025	2.666	0.008**
Post-focus : Age 7-8 : Long	0.023	0.021	1.064	0.288
Post-focus : Age 10-11 : Long	−0.009	0.021	−0.414	0.679

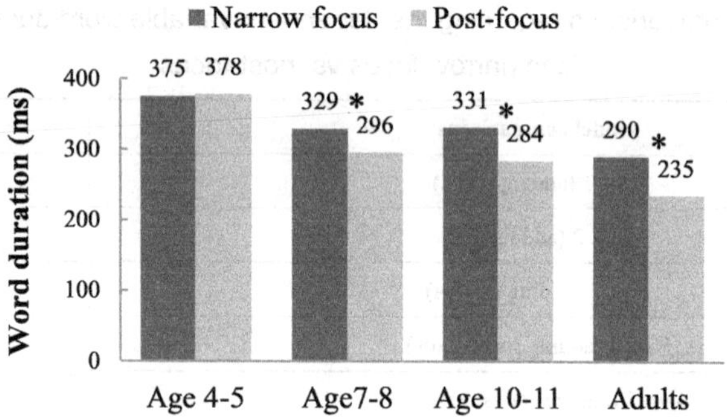

Figure 6-3 The use of word duration in distinguishing narrow focus from post-focus

INITIAL-SYLLABLE DURATION. The best-fit model for the analysis of initial-syllable duration was Model 4 (Table 6-16). The summary of this model (Table 6-17) showed that the main effects of FOCUS and AGE and the interaction of FOCUS and AGE were significant. Subsequent analysis of each age group showed that the main effect of FOCUS was significant in the seven- to eight-year-olds and ten- to eleven-year-olds, but not in the four- to five-year-olds, indicating that the two groups of older children used a longer initial-syllable duration in narrow focus than in post-focus (20 ms longer, $P < 0.05$ in the seven- to eight-year-olds; 21 ms longer, $P < 0.05$ in the ten- to eleven-year-olds), similar to the adults (28 ms longer, $P < 0.05$), but the four- to five-year-olds did not vary the initial-syllable duration to distinguish narrow focus from post-focus, different from the adults.

Table 6-16 Model comparisons regarding the dependent variable initial-syllable duration in the comparison narrow focus vs. post-focus

Model comparisons	*Pr*(>Chisq)
0 vs. 1 (adding FOCUS)	0.020*
1 vs. 2 (adding AGE)	0.001**
2 vs. 3 (adding LENGTH)	0.152
2 vs. 4 (adding FOCUS : AGE)	0.002**
4 vs. 5 (adding FOCUS : LENGTH)	0.707
4 vs. 6 (adding AGE : LENGTH)	0.746
4 vs. 7 (adding FOCUS : AGE : LENGTH)	0.623

Table 6-17 Model summary regarding the dependent variable initial-syllable duration in the comparison narrow focus vs. post-focus

Factor	Estimate	Std. Error	*t* value	*Pr*(>|*t*|)
Intercept (Adults, Narrow focus, Short)	0.150	0.009	17.343	0.000***
Post-focus	−0.028	0.008	−3.314	0.002**
Age 4-5	0.029	0.010	2.956	0.005**
Age 7-8	0.019	0.009	2.137	0.039*
Age 10-11	0.015	0.009	1.787	0.082
Long	−0.012	0.008	−1.479	0.152
Post-focus : Age 4-5	0.026	0.007	3.908	0.000***
Post-focus : Age 7-8	0.007	0.006	1.137	0.256
Post-focus : Age 10-11	0.007	0.006	1.298	0.195

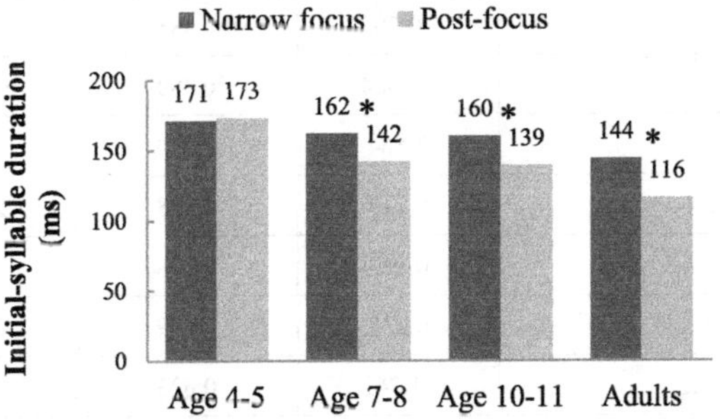

Figure 6-4 The use of initial-syllable duration in distinguishing narrow focus from post-focus

PITCH SPAN. The best-fit model for the analysis of pitch span was Model 6 (Table

6-18). The summary of this model (Table 6-19) showed that the main effect of FOCUS was not significant, but the interaction of FOCUS and AGE was significant. The main effects of AGE and LENGTH and their interaction were also significant. Subsequent analysis of each age group revealed no significant main effect of FOCUS in any age group, indicating that the children did not vary the pitch span to distinguish narrow focus from post-focus, similar to the adults.

Table 6-18 Model comparisons regarding the dependent variable pitch span in the comparison narrow focus vs. post-focus

Model comparisons	***Pr*(>Chisq)**
0 vs. 1 (adding FOCUS)	0.380
0 vs. 2 (adding AGE)	0.001**
2 vs. 3 (adding LENGTH)	0.000***
3 vs. 4 (adding FOCUS : AGE)	0.046*
4 vs. 5 (adding FOCUS : LENGTH)	0.039*
5 vs. 6 (adding AGE : LENGTH)	0.000***
6 vs. 7 (adding FOCUS : AGE : LENGTH)	0.239

Table 6-19 Model summary regarding the dependent variable pitch span in the comparison narrow focus vs. post-focus

Factor	**Estimate**	**Std. Error**	***t* value**	***Pr*(>|*t*|)**
Intercept (Adults. Narrow focus. Short)	3.035	0.382	7.945	0.000***
Post-focus	-0.075	0.458	-0.164	0.871
Age 4-5	-1.305	0.441	-2.960	0.004**
Age 7-8	-0.709	0.383	-1.853	0.069
Age 10-11	-0.484	0.380	-1.273	0.209
Long	3.664	0.460	7.959	0.000***
Post-focus : Age 4-5	0.717	0.328	2.186	0.029*
Post-focus : Age 7-8	0.413	0.278	1.487	0.138
Post-focus : Age 10-11	0.237	0.269	0.882	0.378
Post-focus : Long	-1.262	0.623	-2.027	0.054
Age 4-5 : Long	-1.899	0.333	-5.700	0.000***
Age 7-8 : Long	-1.526	0.278	-5.481	0.000***
Age 10-11 : Long	-1.297	0.272	-4.770	0.000***

PITCH-MAX. The best-fit model for the analysis of pitch-max was Model 4 (Table 6-20). The summary of this model (Table 6-21) showed that the main effects of FOCUS and AGE and their interaction were significant. Subsequent analysis of each age group showed that the main effect of focus was significant in the ten- to eleven-year-olds, but not in the four- to five-year-olds or in the seven- to eight-year-olds, indicating that the ten- to eleven-year-olds used a higher pitch-max in narrow focus than in post-focus (1.7 st higher, $P < 0.05$), similar to the adults (2.7 st higher, $P < 0.05$), but the other two groups of younger children did not vary the pitch-max to distinguish narrow focus from post-focus, different from the adults (Figure 6-5).

Table 6-20 Model comparisons regarding the dependent variable pitch-max in the comparison narrow focus vs. post-focus

Model comparisons	***Pr*(>Chisq)**
0 vs. 1 (adding FOCUS)	0.030*
1 vs. 2 (adding AGE)	0.000***
2 vs. 3 (adding LENGTH)	0.325
2 vs. 4 (adding FOCUS : AGE)	0.000***
4 vs. 5 (adding FOCUS : LENGTH)	0.917
4 vs. 6 (adding AGE : LENGTH)	0.156
4 vs. 7 (adding FOCUS : AGE : LENGTH)	0.272

Table 6-21 Model summary regarding the dependent variable pitch-max in the comparison narrow focus vs. post-focus

Factor	**Estimate**	**Std. Error**	***t* value**	***Pr*(>|*t*|)**
Intercept (Adults. Narrow focus. Short)	91.070	1.163	78.336	0.000***
Post-focus	-2.716	0.711	-3.818	0.001**
Age 4-5	6.020	1.739	3.463	0.001**
Age 7-8	6.404	1.583	4.045	0.000***
Age 10-11	3.754	1.583	2.371	0.023*
Long	0.665	0.691	0.962	0.346
Post-focus : Age 4-5	2.848	0.381	7.480	0.000***
Post-focus : Age 7-8	1.685	0.331	5.096	0.000***
Post-focus : Age 10-11	1.047	0.318	3.288	0.001**

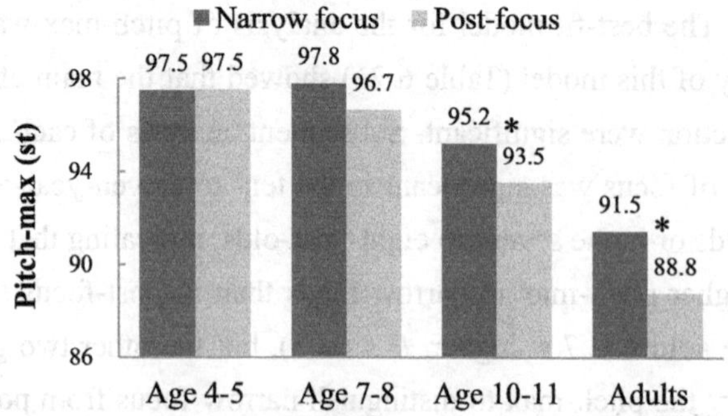

Figure 6-5 The use of pitch-max in distinguishing narrow focus from post-focus

PITCH-MIN. The best-fit model for the analysis of pitch-min was Model 6 (Table 6-22). The summary of this model (Table 6-23) showed that the main effect of FOCUS and the interaction of FOCUS and AGE were significant. The main effects of AGE and LENGTH and their interaction were also significant. Subsequent analysis of each age group showed that the main effect of focus was not significant in any group of children, indicating that the children did not vary the pitch-min to distinguish narrow focus from post-focus, different from the adults, who used a higher pitch-min in narrow focus than in post-focus (1.9 st higher, $P < 0.05$).

Table 6-22 Model comparisons regarding the dependent variable pitch-min in the comparison narrow focus vs. post-focus

Model comparisons	*Pr*(>Chisq)
0 vs. 1 (adding FOCUS)	0.087
0 vs. 2 (adding AGE)	0.000***
2 vs. 3 (adding LENGTH)	0.028*
3 vs. 4 (adding FOCUS : AGE)	0.000***
4 vs. 5 (adding FOCUS : LENGTH)	0.186
4 vs. 6 (adding AGE : LENGTH)	0.006**
6 vs. 7 (adding FOCUS : AGE : LENGTH)	0.152

Table 6-23 Model summary regarding the dependent variable pitch-min in the comparison narrow focus vs. post-focus

Factor	Estimate	Std. Error	*t* value	*Pr*(>|*t*|)
Intercept (Adults. Narrow focus. Short)	87.829	1.137	77.269	0.000***
Post-focus	−2.661	0.812	−3.275	0.003**

Continued

Factor	Estimate	Std. Error	*t* value	*Pr*(>|*t*|)
Age 4-5	7.837	1.724	4.545	0.000***
Age 7-8	7.386	1.568	4.711	0.000***
Age 10-11	4.641	1.567	2.962	0.005**
Long	−2.660	0.814	−3.267	0.003**
Post-focus : Age 4-5	1.945	0.362	5.370	0.000***
Post-focus : Age 7-8	1.176	0.306	3.838	0.000***
Post-focus : Age 10-11	0.700	0.296	2.360	0.019*
Post-focus : Long	1.475	1.132	1.303	0.205
Age 4-5 : Long	0.837	0.369	2.267	0.024*
Age 7-8 : Long	1.060	0.308	3.441	0.001**
Age 10-11 : Long	0.607	0.301	2.018	0.044*

INTERIM SUMMARY. The four- to five-year-olds did not use any of the phonetic cues to distinguish narrow focus from post-focus, different from the adults, who used a longer word duration, longer initial-syllable duration, higher pitch-max and higher pitch-min in narrow focus than in pre-focus. The seven- to eight-year-olds and ten- to eleven-year-olds varied word duration and initial-syllable duration in an adult-like way to distinguish narrow focus from post-focus. In addition, the ten- to eleven-year-olds also showed adult-like use of pitch-max for the same purpose. However, they did not vary the pitch-min for this purpose, different from the adults.

6.3.2 Realisation of focus types

6.3.2.1 Narrow focus vs. broad focus (NF-m vs. BF)

WORD DURATION. The best-fit model for the analysis of word duration was Model 6 (Table 6-24). The summary of this model (Table 6-25) showed that the main effect of FOCUS was not significant, but the interaction of FOCUS and AGE was significant. The main effects of AGE and LENGTH and their interaction were also significant. Subsequent analysis of each age group revealed no significant main effect of FOCUS in any age group, indicating that the children did not vary the word duration to distinguish narrow focus from broad focus, similar to the adults.

Table 6-24 Model comparisons regarding the dependent variable word duration in the comparison narrow focus vs. broad focus

Model comparisons	*Pr*(>Chisq)
0 vs. 1 (adding FOCUS)	0.968
0 vs. 2 (adding AGE)	0.000***
2 vs. 3 (adding LENGTH)	0.000***
3 vs. 4 (adding FOCUS : AGE)	0.001**
4 vs. 5 (adding FOCUS : LENGTH)	0.671
4 vs. 6 (adding AGE : LENGTH)	0.000***
6 vs. 7 (adding FOCUS : AGE : LENGTH)	0.684

Table 6-25 Model summary regarding the dependent variable word duration in the comparison narrow focus vs. broad focus

Factor	Estimate	Std. Error	*t* value	*Pr*(>|*t*|)
Intercept (Adults. Narrow focus. Short)	0.291	0.018	15.759	0.000***
Broad focus	-0.023	0.019	-1.198	0.240
Age 4-5	0.097	0.025	3.924	0.000***
Age 7-8	0.042	0.022	1.888	0.066
Age 10-11	0.039	0.022	1.778	0.082
Long	0.251	0.019	13.272	0.000***
Broad focus : Age 4-5	0.050	0.014	3.450	0.001**
Broad focus : Age 7-8	0.032	0.012	2.603	0.010*
Broad focus : Age 10-11	0.007	0.012	0.601	0.548
Broad focus : Long	0.012	0.026	0.477	0.638
Age 4-5 : Long	0.114	0.014	7.991	0.000***
Age 7-8 : Long	0.048	0.012	3.916	0.000***
Age 10-11 : Long	0.049	0.012	4.118	0.000***

INITIAL-SYLLABLE DURATION. The best-fit model for the analysis of initial-syllable duration was Model 4 (Table 6-26). The summary of this model (Table 6-27) showed that the main effect of FOCUS was not significant, but the main effect of AGE and the interaction of FOCUS and AGE were significant. Subsequent analysis of each age group revealed no significant main effect of FOCUS in any age group, indicating that the children did not vary the initial-syllable duration to distinguish narrow focus from broad focus, similar to the adults.

Table 6-26 Model comparisons regarding the dependent variable initial-syllable duration in the comparison narrow focus vs. broad focus

Model comparisons	*Pr*(>Chisq)
0 vs. 1 (adding FOCUS)	0.623
0 vs. 2 (adding AGE)	0.001**
2 vs. 3 (adding LENGTH)	0.074
2 vs. 4 (adding FOCUS : AGE)	0.000***
4 vs. 5 (adding FOCUS : LENGTH)	0.995
4 vs. 6 (adding AGE : LENGTH)	0.078
4 vs. 7 (adding FOCUS : AGE : LENGTH)	0.168

Table 6-27 Model summary regarding the dependent variable initial-syllable duration in the comparison narrow focus vs. broad focus

Factor	Estimate	Std. Error	*t* value	*Pr*(>|*t*|)
Intercept (Adults. Narrow focus. Short)	0.151	0.009	17.462	0.000***
Broad focus	−0.014	0.009	−1.689	0.101
Age 4-5	0.029	0.010	2.919	0.006**
Age 7-8	0.019	0.009	2.112	0.041*
Age 10-11	0.015	0.009	1.702	0.097
Long	0.014	0.008	−1.811	0.083
Broad focus : Age 4-5	0.030	0.008	3.986	0.000***
Broad focus : Age 7-8	0.017	0.007	2.536	0.012*
Broad focus : Age 10-11	0.009	0.006	1.448	0.148

PITCH SPAN. The best-fit model for the analysis of pitch span was Model 6 (Table 6-28). The summary of this model (Table 6-29) showed that the main effect of FOCUS was not significant, but the interaction of FOCUS and AGE was significant. The main effects of AGE and LENGTH and their interaction were also significant. Subsequent analysis of each age group revealed no significant main effect of FOCUS in any age group, indicating that the children did not vary the pitch span to distinguish narrow focus from broad focus, similar to the adults.

Table 6-28 Model comparisons regarding the dependent variable pitch span in the comparison narrow focus vs. broad focus

Model comparisons	***Pr*(>Chisq)**
0 vs. 1 (adding FOCUS)	0.361
0 vs. 2 (adding AGE)	0.001**
2 vs. 3 (adding LENGTH)	0.000***
3 vs. 4 (adding FOCUS : AGE)	0.016*
4 vs. 5 (adding FOCUS : LENGTH)	0.279
4 vs. 6 (adding AGE : LENGTH)	0.000***
6 vs. 7 (adding FOCUS : AGE : LENGTH)	0.866

Table 6-29 Model summary regarding the dependent variable pitch span in the comparison narrow focus vs. broad focus

Factor	**Estimate**	**Std. Error**	***t* value**	***Pr*(>|*t*|)**
Intercept (Adults. Narrow focus. Short)	2.951	0.414	7.121	0.000***
Broad focus	−0.653	0.518	−1.260	0.218
Age 4-5	−1.135	0.445	−2.552	0.013*
Age 7-8	−0.490	0.381	−1.287	0.204
Age 10-11	−0.446	0.379	−1.176	0.245
Long	3.822	0.515	7.425	0.000***
Broad focus : Age 4-5	1.069	0.347	3.082	0.002**
Broad focus : Age 7-8	0.891	0.287	3.105	0.002**
Broad focus : Age 10-11	0.387	0.281	1.375	0.170
Broad focus : Long	−0.808	0.705	−1.147	0.263
Age 4-5 : Long	-2.170	0.349	−6.217	0.000***
Age 7-8 : Long	-1.946	0.283	−6.886	0.000***
Age 10-11 : Long	-1.338	0.281	-4.770	0.000***

PITCH-MAX. The best-fit model for the analysis of pitch-max was Model 4 (Table 6-30). The summary of this model (Table 6-31) showed that the main effect of FOCUS was not significant, but the main effect of AGE and the interaction of FOCUS and AGE was significant. Subsequent analysis of each age group revealed no significant main effect of FOCUS in any age group, indicating that the children did not vary the pitch-max to distinguish narrow focus from broad focus, similar to the adults.

Table 6-30 Model comparisons regarding the dependent variable pitch-max in the comparison narrow focus vs. broad focus

Model comparisons	*Pr*(>Chisq)
0 vs. 1 (adding FOCUS)	0.377
0 vs. 2 (adding AGE)	0.001**
2 vs. 3 (adding LENGTH)	0.377
2 vs. 4 (adding FOCUS : AGE)	0.023*
4 vs. 5 (adding FOCUS : LENGTH)	0.885
4 vs. 6 (adding AGE : LENGTH)	0.202
4 vs. 7 (adding FOCUS : AGE : LENGTH)	0.121

Table 6-31 Model summary regarding the dependent variable pitch-max in the comparison narrow focus vs. broad focus

Factor	Estimate	Std. Error	*t* value	*Pr*(>|*t*|)
Intercept (Adults. Narrow focus. Short)	91.055	1.210	75.263	0.000***
Broad focus	−1.123	0.780	−1.440	0.162
Age 4-5	6.123	1.762	3.474	0.001**
Age 7-8	6.402	1.606	3.988	0.000***
Age 10-11	3.707	1.605	2.309	0.027*
Long	0.700	0.766	0.914	0.370
Broad focus : Age 4-5	0.862	0.365	2.360	0.019*
Broad focus : Age 7-8	0.888	0.309	2.879	0.004**
Broad focus : Age 10-11	0.437	0.299	1.462	0.144

PITCH-MIN. The best-fit model for the analysis of pitch min was Model 6 (Table 6-32). The summary of this model (Table 6-33) showed that the main effect of FOCUS was not significant, and it was not involved in any interaction, indicating that the children did not vary the pitch-min to distinguish narrow focus from broad focus, similar to the adults.

Table 6-32 Model comparisons regarding the dependent variable pitch-min in the comparison narrow focus vs. broad focus

Model comparisons	*Pr*(>Chisq)
0 vs. 1 (adding FOCUS)	0.871
0 vs. 2 (adding AGE)	0.001**

Continued

Model comparisons	Pr(>Chisq)
2 vs. 3 (adding LENGTH)	0.014*
3 vs. 4 (adding FOCUS : AGE)	0.962
3 vs. 5 (adding FOCUS : LENGTH)	0.920
3 vs. 6 (adding AGE : LENGTH)	0.000***
6 vs. 7 (adding FOCUS : AGE : LENGTH)	0.088

Table 6-33 Model summary regarding the dependent variable pitch-min in the comparison narrow focus vs. broad focus

Factor	Estimate	Std. Error	*t* value	*Pr*(>|*t*|)
Intercept (Adults. Narrow focus. Short)	87.915	1.180	74.475	0.000***
Broad focus	−0.534	0.882	−0.606	0.550
Age 4-5	7.668	1.761	4.354	0.000***
Age 7-8	7.279	1.601	4.546	0.000***
Age 10-11	4.476	1.601	2.796	0.008**
Long	−2.864	0.880	−3.255	0.003**
Broad focus : Age 4-5	−0.230	0.350	−0.659	0.510
Broad focus : Age 7-8	−0.071	0.289	−0.247	0.805
Broad focus : Age 10-11	−0.028	0.283	−0.098	0.922
Broad focus : Long	1.023	1.230	0.831	0.414
Age 4-5 : Long	1.419	0.353	4.022	0.000***
Age 7-8 : Long	1.294	0.285	4.546	0.000***
Age 10-11 : Long	0.854	0.283	3.022	0.003**

INTERIM SUMMARY. The children did not vary any of the phonetic cues to distinguish narrow focus from broad focus, similar to the adults.

6.3.2.2 Narrow focus vs. contrastive focus (NF-m vs. CF-m)

WORD DURATION. The best-fit model for the analysis of word duration was Model 6 (Table 6-34). The summary of this model (Table 6-35) showed that the main effect of FOCUS was not significant, but the interaction of FOCUS and AGE was significant. The main effects of AGE and LENGTH and their interaction were also significant. Subsequent analysis of each age group revealed no significant main effect of FOCUS in any age group, indicating that the children did not vary the word duration to distinguish narrow focus from contrastive focus, similar to the adults.

Table 6-34 Model comparisons regarding the dependent variable word duration in the comparison narrow focus vs. contrastive focus

Model comparisons	*Pr*(>Chisq)
0 vs. 1 (adding FOCUS)	0.840
0 vs. 2 (adding AGE)	0.000***
2 vs. 3 (adding LENGTH)	0.000***
3 vs. 4 (adding FOCUS : AGE)	0.009**
4 vs. 5 (adding FOCUS : LENGTH)	0.659
4 vs. 6 (adding AGE : LENGTH)	0.000***
6 vs. 7 (adding FOCUS : AGE : LENGTH)	0.778

Table 6-35 Model summary regarding the dependent variable word duration in the comparison narrow focus vs. contrastive focus

Factor	Estimate	Std. Error	*t* value	*Pr*(>|*t*|)
Intercept (Adults. Narrow focus. Short)	0.290	0.018	16.516	0.000***
Contrastive focus	0.004	0.018	0.194	0.848
Age 4-5	0.099	0.023	4.362	0.000***
Age 7-8	0.043	0.021	2.092	0.042*
Age 10-11	0.041	0.020	2.023	0.049*
Long	0.254	0.018	13.899	0.000***
Contrastive focus : Age 4-5	0.028	0.013	2.231	0.026*
Contrastive focus : Age 7-8	0.035	0.011	3.163	0.002**
Contrastive focus : Age 10-11	0.007	0.011	0.629	0.530
Contrastive focus : Long	−0.011	0.025	−0.424	0.676
Age 4-5 : Long	0.103	0.013	8.163	0.000***
Age 7-8 : Long	0.041	0.011	3.748	0.000***
Age 10-11 : Long	0.044	0.011	4.172	0.000***

INITIAL-SYLLABLE DURATION. The best-fit model for the analysis of initial-syllable duration was Model 4 (Table 6-36). The summary of this model (Table 6-37) showed that the main effect of FOCUS was not significant, but the main effect of AGE and the interaction of FOCUS and AGE was significant. Subsequent analysis of each age group revealed no significant main effect of FOCUS in any age group, indicating that the children did not vary the initial-syllable duration to distinguish narrow focus from contrastive focus, similar to the adults.

Table 6-36 Model comparisons regarding the dependent variable initial-syllable duration in the comparison narrow focus vs. contrastive focus

Model comparisons	*Pr*(>Chisq)
0 vs. 1 (adding FOCUS)	0.494
0 vs. 2 (adding AGE)	0.004**
2 vs. 3 (adding LENGTH)	0.087
2 vs. 4 (adding FOCUS : AGE)	0.016*
4 vs. 5 (adding FOCUS : LENGTH)	0.754
4 vs. 6 (adding AGE : LENGTH)	0.261
4 vs. 7 (adding FOCUS : AGE : LENGTH)	0.588

Table 6-37 Model summary regarding the dependent variable initial-syllable duration in the comparison narrow focus vs. contrastive focus

Factor	Estimate	Std. Error	*t* value	*Pr*(>|*t*|)
Intercept (Adults. Narrow focus. Short)	0.153	0.010	15.730	0.000***
Contrastive focus	0.001	0.010	0.076	0.940
Age 4-5	0.028	0.009	2.932	0.005**
Age 7-8	0.018	0.008	2.111	0.041*
Age 10-11	0.015	0.008	1.712	0.095
Long	-0.017	0.010	-1.784	0.087
Contrastive focus : Age 4-5	0.018	0.007	2.587	0.010*
Contrastive focus : Age 7-8	0.013	0.006	2.277	0.023*
Contrastive focus : Age 10-11	0.004	0.006	0.763	0.446

PITCH SPAN. The best-fit model for the analysis of pitch span was Model 6 (Table 6-38). The summary of this model (Table 6-39) showed that the main effect of FOCUS was not significant, and it was not involved in any interaction, indicating that the children did not vary the pitch span to distinguish narrow focus from contrastive focus, similar to the adults.

Table 6-38 Model comparisons regarding the dependent variable pitch span in the comparison narrow focus vs. contrastive focus

Model comparisons	*Pr*(>Chisq)
0 vs. 1 (adding FOCUS)	0.722
0 vs. 2 (adding AGE)	0.001**
2 vs. 3 (adding LENGTH)	0.000***
3 vs. 4 (adding FOCUS : AGE)	0.641
3 vs. 5 (adding FOCUS : LENGTH)	0.762
3 vs. 6 (adding AGE : LENGTH)	0.000***
6 vs. 7 (adding FOCUS : AGE : LENGTH)	0.110

Table 6-39 Model summary regarding the dependent variable pitch span in the comparison narrow focus vs. contrastive focus

Factor	Estimate	Std. Error	*t* value	*Pr*(>|*t*|)
Intercept (Adults. Narrow focus. Short)	2.819	0.440	6.402	0.000***
Contrastive focus	0.178	0.524	0.340	0.737
Age 4-5	−0.707	0.499	−1.416	0.162
Age 7-8	−0.377	0.436	−0.866	0.391
Age 10-11	−0.265	0.434	−0.612	0.543
Long	4.126	0.525	7.853	0.000***
Contrastive focus : Age 4-5	0.183	0.351	0.522	0.602
Contrastive focus : Age 7-8	0.039	0.291	0.134	0.893
Contrastive focus : Age 10-11	−0.290	0.285	−1.017	0.310
Contrastive focus : Long	0.262	0.718	0.365	0.718
Age 4-5 : Long	−3.074	0.346	−8.875	0.000***
Age 7-8 : Long	−2.189	0.292	−7.508	0.000***
Age 10-11 : Long	−1.816	0.286	−6.358	0.000***

PITCH-MAX. The best-fit model for the analysis of pitch-max was Model 2 (Table 6-40). The summary of this model (Table 6-41) showed that the main effect of FOCUS was not significant, and it was not involved in any interaction, indicating that the children did not vary the pitch-max to distinguish narrow focus from contrastive focus, similar to the adults.

Table 6-40 Model comparisons regarding the dependent variable pitch-max in the comparison narrow focus vs. contrastive focus

Model comparisons	*Pr*(>Chisq)
0 vs. 1 (adding FOCUS)	0.982
0 vs. 2 (adding AGE)	0.003**
2 vs. 3 (adding LENGTH)	0.409
2 vs. 4 (adding FOCUS : AGE)	0.894
2 vs. 5 (adding FOCUS : LENGTH)	0.954
2 vs. 6 (adding AGE : LENGTH)	0.710
2 vs. 7 (adding FOCUS : AGE : LENGTH)	0.466

Table 6-41 Model summary regarding the dependent variable pitch-max in the comparison narrow focus vs. contrastive focus

Factor	Estimate	Std. Error	*t* value	*Pr*(>|*t*|)
Intercept (Adults. Narrow focus)	91.358	1.163	78.525	0.000***
Contrastive focus	0.019	0.790	0.025	0.981
Age 4-5	6.246	1.771	3.526	0.001**
Age 7-8	6.486	1.616	4.013	0.000***
Age 10-11	3.761	1.616	2.328	0.026*

PITCH-MIN. The best-fit model for the analysis of pitch-min was Model 7 (Table 6-42). The summary of this model (Table 6-43) showed that the main effect of FOCUS was not significant, but the two-way interaction of FOCUS and AGE and the three-way interaction of FOCUS, AGE and LENGTH were significant. The main effects of AGE and LENGTH and their interaction were also significant. Subsequent analysis of each age group showed no significant main effect of FOCUS or significant interaction of FOCUS and LENGTH in any age group, indicating that the children did not vary the pitch-min to distinguish narrow focus from contrastive focus, similar to the adults.

Table 6-42 Model comparisons regarding the dependent variable pitch-min in the comparison narrow focus vs. contrastive focus

Model comparisons	*Pr*(>Chisq)
0 vs. 1 (adding FOCUS)	0.802
0 vs. 2 (adding AGE)	0.000***

Continued

Model comparisons	*Pr*(>Chisq)
2 vs. 3 (adding LENGTH)	0.003**
3 vs. 4 (adding FOCUS : AGE)	0.709
3 vs. 5 (adding FOCUS : LENGTH)	0.842
3 vs. 6 (adding AGE : LENGTH)	0.000***
2 vs. 7 (adding FOCUS : AGE : LENGTH)	0.007**

Table 6-43 Model summary regarding the dependent variable pitch-min in the comparison narrow focus vs. contrastive focus

Factor	Estimate	Std. Error	*t* value	*Pr*(>|*t*|)
Intercept (Adults. Narrow focus. Short)	87.980	1.208	72.839	0.000***
Contrastive focus	−0.017	0.996	−0.017	0.986
Age 4-5	7.806	1.738	4.490	0.000***
Age 7-8	7.109	1.577	4.507	0.000***
Age 10-11	4.366	1.577	2.769	0.009**
Long	-2.975	0.999	-2.978	0.006**
Contrastive focus : Age 4-5	-1.053	0.521	-2.020	0.044*
Contrastive focus : Age 7-8	−0.041	0.436	−0.093	0.926
Contrastive focus : Age 10-11	0.079	0.426	0.186	0.852
Contrastive focus : Long	−0.697	1.414	−0.493	0.626
Age 4-5 : Long	1.123	0.524	2.142	0.033*
Age 7-8 : Long	1.662	0.412	4.030	0.000***
Age 10-11 : Long	1.106	0.413	2.675	0.008**
Contrastive focus : Age 4-5 : Long	2.500	0.732	3.414	0.001**
Contrastive focus : Age 7-8 : Long	0.203	0.617	0.328	0.743
Contrastive focus : Age 10-11 : Long	0.542	0.602	0.900	0.369

INTERIM SUMMARY. The children did not vary any of the phonetic cues to distinguish narrow focus from contrastive focus, similar to the adults.

6.4 Discussion and conclusions

We have asked whether Korean-speaking children are similar to adults in their use of duration- and pitch-related phonetic cues to distinguish words in different focus conditions when the words are in the same phonological category (i.e., when they are AP-initial words). To address this question, we have examined the phonetic realisation of AP-initial words in narrow focus compared to the same words in non-focus and two other types of focus in Korean-speaking four- to eleven-year-olds' and adults' semi-spontaneous production of SOV sentences.

With regard to the realisation of narrow focus, Korean-speaking children do not use any of the phonetic cues to distinguish narrow focus from pre-focus or post-focus at the age of four to five, unlike adults, who use longer word and initial-syllable durations, and a higher pitch-max for words in narrow focus than in pre-focus and post-focus. By the age of seven to eight, they only vary word duration and initial-syllable duration in an adult-like way to distinguish narrow focus from post-focus. By the age of ten to eleven, they use word duration and initial-syllable duration to distinguish narrow focus from both pre-focus and post-focus, similar to adults. However, their use of the pitch-related cues at this age is still limited; namely, they only use pitch-max in an adult-like way to distinguish narrow focus from post-focus. Additionally, children appear to vary the duration- and pitch-related cues to a smaller degree than adults do. As for the distinction of focus types, children do not vary any of the phonetic cues to distinguish narrow focus from broad focus or contrastive focus, similar to adults. Taken together, Korean-speaking children only start to use the phonetic focus-marking cues after the age of five, and become adult-like in the use of duration-related cues only by the age of ten- to eleven. At this age, their use of pitch-related cues remains limited.

As mentioned in the introduction of this chapter, given that the phonetic focus-marking cues are the secondary prosodic focus-marking cues in Korean, and secondary prosodic focus-marking cues are acquired later than the primary cues in Dutch (A. Chen, 2009), we predicted that phonetic focus marking is acquired later than phonological focus marking in Korean. We have found that Korean-speaking children start to use the phonetic cues to mark focus after the age of five, later than they acquire phonological focus marking (Chapter 3 of this dissertation). Thus, our prediction turns out to be correct. This result is in line with findings from previous work on Dutch-speaking children (A. Chen, 2009). Together, they provide solid evidence for the later acquisition of phonetic focus marking than phonological focus marking in languages that primarily use phonological cues for focus-marking purposes.

In contrast, in Mandarin, phonetic focus-marking cues are the only and thus the primary prosodic focus-marking cues, and are used or fully acquired early in life by Mandarin-speaking children by the age of five (Chapter 3 of this dissertation). The findings on different languages suggest that primary prosodic focus-marking cues (like phonological cues in Korean and Dutch, and phonetic cues in Mandarin) are acquired relatively early in life, while secondary cues (like the use of the phonetic cues within one phonological category in Korean and Dutch) are acquired relatively late.

We also predicted that Korean-speaking children should acquire the use of pitch earlier than the use of duration for focus-marking purposes, based on previous findings that, in languages in which pitch does not have lexical function, the use of pitch is acquired earlier than the use of duration (Wonnacott & Watson, 2008, on English; A. Chen, 2009, on Dutch). However, we have found that Korean-speaking children acquire the use of pitch-related cues later than duration-related cues for focus-marking purposes. Our prediction is, thus, not borne out. We suggest that an explanation of this mismatch may lie in an important area of language acquisition: the role of the input. Korean-speaking children's later acquisition of the use of pitch than the use of duration for focus marking may be related to properties of the input in the following way: Korean-speaking adults vary pitch-max but do not (systematically) vary pitch span to mark focus, and their use of pitch is limited to the distinction between narrow focus and non-focus (Chapter 4 of this dissertation). Korean-speaking children may thus have rather limited exposure to phonetic use of pitch for focus-marking purposes. Because of this, it may take them a long time to acquire the use of pitch for such purpose. It is thus possible that the acquisition of the use of a phonetic focus-marking cue is not only conditioned by the lexical contrastiveness of this cue, but is also influenced by other factors such as input. Future studies should bear out whether and how children's acquisition of prosodic focus marking is affected by input.

CHAPTER 7

General discussion and conclusions

7.1 Introduction

This dissertation investigated how Mandarin Chinese-speaking and Seoul Korean-speaking children acquire prosodic focus marking from the age of four to eleven. We chose to include Mandarin Chinese and Seoul Korean (hereafter Mandarin and Korean) in the study because these two languages typologically differ in their prosodic systems and prosodic focus marking, both from each other and from West Germanic languages, on which previous studies on the same topic were mainly done.

Regarding the prosodic systems, Mandarin and Korean differ from each other and from West Germanic languages in the lexical contrastiveness of pitch. Mandarin uses pitch to distinguish words, and the lexical use of pitch coexists with sentence-level use of pitch. In contrast, Korean does not have lexical use of pitch. In this language pitch movement is not specific to a certain syllable or word, but is associated with larger prosodic units, i.e., prosodic phrases, and changes with prosodic phrasing (hereafter, phrasing). West Germanic languages such as English, Dutch, and German have no lexical use of pitch either, similar to Korean but different from Mandarin. However, different from Korean, in these languages, pitch movement is specific to words. A word can be produced with or without a pitch accent. The type of pitch accent (e.g., rise vs. fall) assigned to a word can change to serve diverse communication purposes.

As for prosodic focus marking, Mandarin and Korean differ from each other and from West Germanic languages in the relative importance of the use of phonological means and the use of phonetic means. Mandarin only (and thus primarily) uses phonetic cues to mark focus (i.e., by increasing/reducing duration, pitch, and intensity in a gradient fashion), but Korean resembles West Germanic languages in that it has both phonological and phonetic cues, and primarily relies on the phonological cue for focus-marking purposes. However, the phonological cue used in Korean (i.e., phrasing) is different from those used in West Germanic languages (i.e., accentuation and accent type). Furthermore, as mentioned above, the phonetic focus-marking cue, pitch, is also used to distinguish words in Mandarin but not in Korean or West Germanic languages

Given the above mentioned differences in prosodic systems and prosodic focus marking between languages, the developmental path to adult-like prosodic focus marking described for West Germanic languages in previous studies may not be generalised to Mandarin and Korean. An investigation into Mandarin and Korean allows us to have a better understanding of how the above mentioned cross-linguistic differences shape the developmental paths to adult-like prosodic focus marking in different languages (Overarching research question). More specifically, it allows us to understand whether the presence of a lexically contrastive prosodic property inhibits or facilitates the acquisition of the same property used for focus-marking purposes (Research question I), and whether the relative importance of prosodic focus-marking cues in a language (i.e., whether the cues are primary or a secondary cues) influences the acquisition of this these cues (Research question II).

To address the research questions, we collected cross-sectional production data from four- to five-year-olds, seven- to eight-year-olds and ten- to eleven-year-olds in the two languages, and compared children's production to adult controls' production. In the following sections, we first summarise the main findings in each language (Section 7.2), and then discuss how the findings supported or rejected the hypotheses and predictions proposed in Chapter 1, and what the answers to the research questions are (Section 7.3). Last, we suggest directions for future studies of the development of prosodic focus marking in children (Section 7.4).

7.2 Summary of the main findings

7.2.1 The acquisition of prosodic focus marking in Mandarin

In adult Mandarin speakers' semi-spontaneous production of SVO sentences (Chapter 2), speakers produce the words in narrow focus with a longer duration and a wider pitch span than the same words in pre-focus and post-focus, similar to previous findings on Mandarin speakers' realisation of narrow focus in read speech (Y. Chen & Braun, 2006; Shih, 1988; Xu, 1999). The pitch span difference between narrow focus and pre-focus appears to stem from a combined effect of pitch-max rising and pitch-min lowering in the focused words, whereas the pitch span difference between narrow focus and post-focus appears to be only related to pitch-max rising in the focused non-Tone 1 words. Tone 1 words have a higher overall pitch register (or level) in narrow focus than in post-focus. Furthermore, Mandarin-speakers produce words in narrow focus with a longer duration and a slightly wider pitch span than those in broad focus, similar to previous findings on read speech (Shih, 1988; Xu, 1999). However, the pitch span difference in our study is much smaller than that reported in previous studies on read speech (Xu, 1999). Finally, Mandarin speakers use neither duration nor pitch span to distinguish narrow focus from contrastive focus, different from a previous finding on read speech that contrastive focus tends to be more prominent in pitch than narrow focus (Y. Chen & Braun, 2006).

The analysis of Mandarin-speaking children's production (Chapter 3) showed that children can use duration to distinguish narrow focus from pre-focus and post-focus in an adult-like way at the age of four to five, but they make no systematic use of pitch span for the same purposes at this age. Nonetheless, they can vary pitch-max and pitch-min to distinguish focus from post-focus and vary pitch-min to distinguish focus from pre-focus in an adult-like way in certain tonal categories. Regarding the distinction of focus types differing in focal constituent size, four- to five-year-olds can already vary duration in an adult-like way in distinguishing narrow focus from broad focus. However, they also use a higher pitch-max for narrow focus than for broad focus, different from adults. As for the distinction of focus types differing in contrastivity, children at this age do not use duration to distinguish narrow focus from contrastive focus but use a lower pitch-min in contrastive focus than in narrow focus, different from adults.

By the age of seven to eight, Mandarin-speaking children are more adult-like in marking narrow focus than younger children: in addition to adult-like use of duration, they can also vary pitch span in an adult-like way to distinguish narrow focus from pre-focus regardless of tone, and to distinguish narrow focus from post-focus in Tone 2 and Tone 4. At this age, they are adult-like in distinguishing focus types differing in focal constituent size and contrastivity; namely, they use a longer duration for words in narrow focus than in broad focus, and they do not prosodically distinguish narrow focus from contrastive focus.

By the age of ten to eleven, Mandarin-speaking children become even more adult-like in marking narrow focus: in addition to adult-like use of duration, they use pitch span to distinguish focus from post-focus in an adult-like fashion in all but Tone 1. At this age, they use a longer duration and a wider pitch span for words in narrow focus than in broad focus, similar to what adults do in read speech (Xu, 1999). In addition, children's use of pitch-max and pitch-min is still not fully adult-like by the age of eleven, thus un-adult-like in how they realise the difference in pitch span between different focus conditions. Further, children, regardless of age, vary the duration- and pitch-related cues to a greater degree than adults do.

Summarising the findings on the acquisition of prosodic focus marking in Mandarin, we can see that (1) Mandarin-speaking children have acquired an adult-like use of duration in distinguishing focus from non-focus and from broad focus by the age of four to five; (2) their use of pitch for focus-marking purposes has started by the age of four to five, but is still conditioned by tonal category and is not fully adult-like by the age of eleven. The acquisition of prosodic focus marking in Mandarin can thus be characterised as an early mastery of the duration-related cue at the age of four or five, and an early use but a later mastery of pitch-related cues, compared to duration.

7.2.2 The acquisition of prosodic focus marking in Korean

In adult Korean speakers' semi-spontaneous production of SOV sentences (Chapter 4), a predominant proportion of the boundaries before the sentence-medial words (objects) are produced as AP boundaries in each focus condition. Still, focus conditions are distinguished via the distribution of different types of prosodic boundaries. To realise narrow focus, Korean speakers use IP boundaries more frequently before the sentence-medial words and use PW boundaries more frequently after the sentence-medial words when the words are in narrow focus than in pre-focus. They use PW boundaries less frequently before the sentence-medial words in narrow focus than in post-focus. In other words, speakers usually start a prosodic phrase from the focal word and dephrase the post-focal word, consistent with previous descriptions about the effect of narrow focus on read speech (Jun, 1993, 2011; Oh, 1999). To distinguish broad focus from narrow focus, Korean speakers use IP boundaries more frequently before and after the sentence-medial words, and use PW boundaries less frequently after the sentence-medial words when the words are in broad focus than in narrow focus. In other words, speakers usually produce the words in a SOV sentence in broad focus as separate APs or IPs. The phrasing of words in broad focus is thus similar to the phrasing of words in a "neutral" sentence (H. S. Kim, et al., 2006) and the phrasing of words in a focused VP (H. S. Kim, et al., 2006) or short NP (Jun, 2011). To distinguish contrastive focus from narrow focus, Korean speakers use PW boundaries more frequently after the sentence-medial words in contrastive focus than in narrow focus. In other words, they dephrase the post-focal words more frequently in the contrastive focus condition than in the narrow focus condition.

We further looked into the phonetic variation in the predominant AP-initial words (objects) in different focus conditions. To realise narrow focus, Korean speakers produce the AP-initial words with a longer word duration, initial-syllable duration, and higher pitch-max in narrow focus than in pre-focus and post-focus. They produce the four-syllable "long" words with a wider pitch span in narrow focus than in pre-focus. They also produce the words with a higher pitch-min in narrow focus than in post-focus; that is, they produce the words with a higher pitch register in narrow focus than in post-focus. In addition, Korean speakers do not vary duration or pitch to distinguish narrow focus from broad focus or contrastive focus, despite an earlier observation that Korean speakers produce words with a higher pitch-max and a longer word duration in narrow focus than in broad focus in read speech (Y. C. Lee & Xu, 2010).

The analysis of Korean-speaking children (Chapter 3) showed that children use AP boundaries most frequently before and after the sentence-medial words in SOV sentences regardless of age group or focus condition. In spite of the overuse of AP boundaries across focus conditions, children can vary prosodic boundaries to distinguish narrow focus from non-focus (i.e., pre-focus and post-focus) and the other two types of focus (i.e., broad focus and contrastive focus) in an adult-like manner even at the age of four to five. The only evidence of development in terms of phrasing is that the younger the children are, the less frequently they dephrase the post-focal words, as compared to the adults. Thus we consider that Korean-speaking children are adult-like in the use of phrasing/dephrasing (or the varying of phrasal boundaries) in terms of manner for focus-marking purposes by the age of four to five, but their use of this cue is not consolidated in terms of frequency even at the age of ten to eleven.

With regard to the acquisition of phonetic focus marking, analysis of the predominant AP-initial words showed that Korean-speaking children at the age of four to five do not use any of the phonetic cues to distinguish narrow focus from pre-focus or post-focus, unlike adults. By the age of seven to eight, they only vary word duration and initial-syllable duration in an adult-like way to distinguish narrow focus from post-focus. By the age of ten to eleven, they use word duration and initial-syllable duration to distinguish narrow focus from both pre-focus and post-focus, similar to adults. Their use of the pitch-related cues at this age is still limited to the distinction of narrow focus and post-focus via the pitch-max. Additionally, Korean-speaking children tend to vary the duration- and pitch-related cues to a smaller degree than adults do, which is different from our findings on Mandarin-speaking children. As for the distinction of focus types, Korean-speaking children do not vary any of the phonetic cues to distinguish narrow focus from broad focus or contrastive focus, similar to adults.

To sum up, Korean-speaking children can use phrasing in an adult-like manner for focus-marking purposes by the age of four to five, though they use this cue with a much lower frequency compared to adults. Further, they do not use duration- or pitch-related cues to mark focus at this age. At the age of seven to eight, they use phrasing more frequently than the younger children, and they start to use duration to mark focus. At the age of ten to eleven, their use of phrasing is even more frequent, but still not as frequent as adults' use of phrasing. In addition, they start to show limited use of pitch for focus marking at this age. The acquisition of prosodic focus marking in Korean can thus be characterised as an early use of the phonological cue (i.e., phrasing) at the age of four to five, a late use of the phonetic cues (i.e., duration and pitch) after the age of five, and a later use of pitch than duration within the phonetic cues.

7.2.3 The developmental paths to adult-like prosodic focus marking

Based on the aforementioned findings, we can depict the developmental paths to adult-like prosodic focus marking for each language in Table 7-1.

Table 7-1 Developmental paths to adult-like prosodic focus marking

Language	Prosodic cues	Age		
		Age 4-5	Age 7-8	Age 10-11
Mandarin	Duration	Adult-like		
	Pitch	Limited use	Conditioned by tones	Nearly adult-like
Korean	Phrasing	Adult-like manner, but low frequency	More frequent	Even more frequent
	Duration	No use	Limited use	Adult-like
	Pitch	No use	No use	Limited use

As can be seen in Table 7-1, the primary prosodic focus-marking cues in each language, i.e., the phonetic cues in Mandarin and the phonological cue in Korean, are acquired at a similar pace; namely, the use of these cues is present by the age of four to five, and is gradually consolidated from then on. This path is quite similar to the acquisition of the primary prosodic focus-marking cues, accentuation and accent type, in English (Hornby & Hass, 1970; MacWhinney & Bates, 1978; Wells, Peppé & Goulandris, 2004) and Dutch (A. Chen, 2011a, 2011b; Romøren, 2016).

Regarding the acquisition of the secondary cues, Korean-speaking children start to use the phonetic cues to distinguish narrow focus from non-focus within one phonological category (i.e., AP-initial words) after the age of five, that is, later than they acquire phonological focus marking (i.e., phrasing). This is similar to previous findings on the acquisition of phonetic focus marking within one phonological category in Dutch (A. Chen, 2009).

In both languages, children acquire the use of duration earlier than the use of pitch for focus-marking purposes, different from children speaking English (Wonnacott & Watson, 2008) and Dutch (A. Chen, 2009), who acquire the use of duration later than the use of pitch for such purposes.

7.3 Hypotheses and predictions revisited

In Chapter 1, we have proposed four hypotheses and corresponding predictions for the acquisition of prosodic focus marking in Mandarin-speaking and Korean-speaking children. The first two hypotheses and the corresponding predictions were made based on the fact that the prosodic focus-marking cue, pitch, has lexical function in Mandarin but not in Korean, and concern the influence of the lexical function of pitch on the acquisition of the use of pitch for focus-marking purposes.

On the one hand, in Mandarin, the potential difficulty of varying pitch to mark focus within the limited acoustic space left by tonal realisation may slow down Mandarin-speaking children's acquisition of the use of pitch for focus-marking purposes. However, in Korean, pitch does not have lexical function. Moreover, in languages in which pitch does not have lexical function, the use of pitch is found to be acquired earlier than the use of duration for focus-marking purposes (Wonnacott & Watson, 2008, on English; A. Chen, 2009, on Dutch). Along this line of consideration, we have proposed Hypothesis I (a) and two predictions, which are repeated as follows:

> Hypothesis Ⅰ (a): The lexical use of pitch in a language slows down the acquisition of the use of pitch as a cue to focus.
>
> Predictions: Mandarin-speaking children should acquire the use of pitch later than the use of duration for focus-marking purposes, whereas Korean-speaking children should acquire the use of pitch earlier than the use of duration for focus-marking purposes.

On the other hand, Mandarin-speaking children are competent to control pitch to realise tones early in life (Wong, 2012; Wong, Schwartz & Jenkins, 2005; Zhu, 2002), which may facilitate their acquisition of the use of pitch for focus-marking purpose. However, Korean-speaking children's acquisition of the use of pitch for focus marking does not benefit from the acquisition of lexical tones. Thus, in opposition to Hypothesis I (a), we have proposed Hypothesis Ⅰ (b) and two predictions, which are repeated as follows:

> Hypothesis Ⅰ (b): The lexical use of pitch in a language facilitates the acquisition of the use of pitch as a cue to focus.
>
> Predictions: Both Mandarin-speaking and Korean-speaking children should acquire the use of pitch earlier than the use of duration for focus-marking purposes (Order of acquisition), but Mandarin-speaking children acquire the use of pitch earlier than Korean-speaking children for such purposes (Rate of acquisition).

We have found that Mandarin-speaking children have fully mastered the use of duration for focus-marking purposes by the age of four to five. At this age, they have also started to use pitch for focus-marking purposes for words in certain tones in an adult-like way, but they have not fully mastered the use of pitch for such purposes. Hence, Mandarin-speaking children acquire the use of duration earlier than the use of pitch for focus-marking purposes. This finding is in line with the prediction of the order of acquisition in Mandarin that stemmed from Hypothesis Ⅰ(a) but not the one that stemmed from Hypothesis Ⅰ(b). Interestingly, the acquisition of the use of pitch in Mandarin is still earlier than that in Korean, which starts after the age of eight. This observation is consistent with the prediction concerning the rate of acquisition of the use of pitch in the two languages that stemmed from Hypothesis Ⅰ(b). We thus speculate that Mandarin-speaking children's early competence in the use of pitch for lexical purpose induces an early use of pitch for focus-marking purposes, but does not lead to an early mastery of the use of pitch for such purpose. They gradually develop their ability to use pitch to mark focus over a rather long time span, which may be related to the inherent complexity of varying pitch within the limited acoustic space left by tonal realisation. Therefore, both Hypotheses Ⅰ(a) and Ⅰ(b) are supported to a moderate degree.

As for the order of acquisition in Korean, we have found that Korean-speaking children also acquire the use of duration earlier than the use of pitch for focus-marking purposes, similar to children acquiring Mandarin but different from children acquiring a West Germanic language (Wonnacott & Watson, 2008, on English; A. Chen, 2009, on Dutch). This finding contradicts our prediction about the order of acquisition in Korean, and might be explained from the perspective of input. Korean-speaking adults show rather limited use of pitch for focus-marking purposes: they only vary pitch-max but do not (systematically) vary pitch span to mark focus, and their use of pitch is limited to the distinction between narrow focus and non-focus. Children may thus have rather limited exposure to phonetic use of pitch for focus-marking purposes and thus take a long time to acquire the use of pitch for such purpose. This implies that the acquisition of prosodic focus marking is not only conditioned by the prosodic system, but is also influenced by other factors such as input.

Returning to the research question of whether the lexical use of a prosodic parameter (i.e., pitch in Mandarin) influences the acquisition of the same parameter used for focus marking (Research question Ⅰ), the answer is "yes". According to our findings, the lexical use of pitch in Mandarin influences both the rate and order of acquisition of the use of pitch for focus marking, as compared to the acquisition of the use of the same cue in Korean or to the acquisition of the use of duration in Mandarin.

The second two hypotheses and the corresponding predictions were made based on the fact that the phonetic cues are the primary prosodic focus-marking cues in Mandarin but are the secondary cues in Korean, and concern the influence of the relative importance of the phonetic cues on the acquisition of the use of these cues for focus-marking purposes.

On the one hand, Mandarin-speaking children may have abundant exposure to phonetic use of prosody, whereas Korean-speaking children receive relatively less exposure to phonetic use of prosody. In view of these, we have proposed Hypothesis Ⅱ(a) and a prediction, which are repeated as follows:

> Hypothesis Ⅱ(a): Phonetic focus marking is acquired early when it is the primary means of prosodic focus marking, but is acquired late when it is a secondary means of prosodic focus marking in languages.
>
> Prediction: Mandarin-speaking children should acquire phonetic focus marking at an earlier age than Korean-speaking children.

On the other hand, children may need a similar amount of time to establish the form-function mapping between prosodic variation and focus in the input, and to develop sufficient control of prosodic parameters in production, regardless of their native language. Thus, opposing Hypothesis Ⅱ(a), we have proposed Hypothesis Ⅱ(b) and a prediction, which are repeated as follows:

> Hypothesis Ⅱ(b): Phonetic use of prosody is equally demanding for children speaking different languages.
>
> Prediction: Mandarin-speaking and Korean-speaking children should acquire phonetic focus marking at a similar age.

We have found that Mandarin-speaking children have fully mastered the use of duration and have started to use pitch to mark focus by the age of five. However, Korean-speaking children start to use both duration- and pitch-related phonetic focus-marking cues after the age of five, similar to Dutch-speaking children (A. Chen, 2009), but different from Mandarin-speaking children. The findings are consistent with the prediction that stemmed from Hypothesis Ⅱ (a), but contradict the prediction that stemmed from Hypothesis Ⅱ (b). Thus, Hypothesis Ⅱ (a) is supported.

Returning to the research question of whether the relative importance of prosodic focus-marking cues in a language influences the acquisition of these cues (Research question Ⅱ), the answer is also positive. According to our findings on Mandarin and Korean and previous findings on Dutch, the relative importance of the phonetic focus-marking cues in a language influences the rate of acquisition of these cues in this language.

This dissertation was carried out to determine how cross-linguistic differences in prosodic systems and prosodic focus marking shape the developmental paths to adult-like prosodic focus marking. First of all, we have seen that which prosodic focus marking means is acquired first in a language depends on what is the primary prosodic focus marking means in the language (i.e., the phonological means in Korean and the phonetic means in Mandarin). Furthermore, we have seen evidence showing that the presence of lexical use of a prosodic property in a language influences the rate and route of the acquisition of prosodic focus marking in the language. Our findings indicated that the effort involved in acquiring different prosodic cues in one language (e.g., pitch and duration in Mandarin) or the same prosodic cue in different languages (e.g., pitch in Mandarin and Korean) may differ. Last, our findings also suggested that the developmental path to adult-like prosodic focus marking is not only shaped by the prosodic system and prosodic focus-marking system, but can also be influenced by other factors, such as input (as suggested in Chapter 3 and Chapter 6 of this dissertation), or children's other speech competencies, like speaking rate (as suggested in Chapter 5 of this dissertation).

7.4 Limitations and directions for future studies

One critical note on this study is that only a relatively small number of speakers per age group were tested and analysed due to practical constraints. The numbers of speakers conform to the standard in published studies of prosodic development and adults' prosodic focus marking. Furthermore, our data had large case to condition ratios (43:1-46:1 in Chapter 2, 26:1-46:1 in Chapter 3, 54:1-67:1 in Chapter 4, 43:1-134:1 in Chapter 5, and 20:1-57:1 in Chapter 6), which contributes to the validity of our analyses. However, the use of a small number of speakers can increase the risk of Type I errors (i.e., false positives). It can thus be very meaningful to conduct replication studies with larger sample sizes to check the generalisability of the current results.

There are also limitations in the way in which our analyses were done. First, the fixed factors were not included as random slopes in the mixed-effects modelling. The models without random slopes assume that the effect found for a fixed factor would be the same for each speaker. This is, however, unlikely to be the case, especially in the youngest group. Second, the factor focus condition was defined for each research question separately. Consequently, two of the five focus conditions were compared in each model, which involved the repeated use of parts of the data. This violates the principle of "ne bis in idem" (i.e., not using the same data more than once). Such a violation can lead to over-estimated effects, and thus cast doubt on the generalisability of the results. Finally, the outcome variables (i.e. pitch- and duration-related measurements and type of phrasal boundary) can be correlated to some degree. For example, if a speaker uses pitch span to distinguish narrow focus from post-focus, he or she may also vary pitch minimum and maximum for the same purpose. Additional analysis is needed to study how the uses of the different cues are related and change over time in children.

Regarding directions for future studies, we found that some of the prosodic cues, such as duration and pitch in Mandarin and phrasing in Korean, are present in the four-year-olds' production, indicating that the acquisition of these cues have started before the age of four. Future studies are thus needed to shed light on the development in younger children. A major challenge of investigating younger children is that they can differ substantially in their ability to produce full sentences in conversations. Thus, suitable elicitation methods need to be developed, taking into account young children's tendency to give shortened answers and their limited short-term memory span.

We also found that children's use of prosody in focus marking in production varies between age groups. However, do children at a certain age use the same cues to perceive focus as the cues they use in their production? To have a comprehensive understanding on the acquisition of prosodic focus, future studies can investigate the perception of prosodic focus in children. Such an investigation may also provide evidence for the speculations we have on children's production. For example, we found that certain prosodic focus-marking cues are used later in life than others in production (e.g., the later use of phonetic cues than the phonological cue in Korean). As mentioned, we speculated that the later acquisition might be at least partly related to input: children take a longer time to grasp the cues that are less frequent and less salient to them in the input. However, are discrete phonological cues more salient than gradient phonetic cues in perception? Do children speaking different languages differ in their sensitivity to a certain prosodic cue in perception? Past work on children's sensitivity to prosodic variation in perception has been mainly concerned with infants acquiring a Germanic language (Frota, Butler, & Vigário, 2014; L. Liu & Kager, 2014), and thus cannot answer our questions. A study on older children's perception of prosodic focus may provide us insight into such questions.

REFERENCES

[1] ASTRUC L, PAYNE E, POST B, et al. Tonal targets in early child English, Spanish, and Catalan[J]. Language and Speech, 2013, 56(2):229-253.

[2] BARD E G, AYLETT M. The dissociation of deaccenting, givenness, and syntactic role in spontaneous speech[C]//OHALA J J, HASEGAWA Y, OHALA M, et al (Eds.). Proceedings of the International Congress of Phonetic Sciences. San Francisco: University of California, 1999, 14:1753-1756.

[3] BATES D M, MAECHLER M, BOLKER B, et al. Lme4: linear mixed-effects models using Eigen and S4. R package (version 3.1.2) [computer programme][EB/OL]. [2016-6-21]. http://cran.r-project.org/package¼lme4.

[4] BAUMANN S, GRICE M, STEINDAMM S. Prosodic marking of focus domains-categorical or gradient[C]//Proceedings of the International Conference on Speech Prosody. Germany: Dresden, 2006, 3:301-304.

[5] BAUMANN S, BECKER J, GRICE M, et al. Tonal and articulatory marking of focus in German[C]//Proceedings of the International Congress of Phonetic Sciences. Pirrot GmbH: Dudweiler, 2007, 16:1029-1032.

[6] BIRCH S, CLIFTON C Jr. Focus, accent, and argument structure: effects on language comprehension[J]. Language and Speech, 1995, 38(4):365-391.

[7] BOERSMA P, WEENINK D. Praat: doing phonetics by computer (version 5.3) [computer software][EB/OL]. [2013-7-2]. http://www.praat.org.

[8] BRAUN B. Phonetics and phonology of contrast marking in German: issues for the prosody-semantics interface[J]. Proceedings of Konvens, 2004, 7:29-36.

[9] BRAUN B, CHEN A. Intonation of "now" in resolving scope ambiguity in English and Dutch[J]. Journal of Phonetics, 2010, 38:431-444.

[10] BREEN M, FEDORENKO, E, WAGNER M, et al. Acoustic correlates of information structure[J]. Language and Cognitive Processes, 2010, 25(7-9):1044-1098.

[11] BRUCE G. Components of a prosodic typology of Swedish intonation[C]//RIAD T, GUSSENHOVEN C (Eds.). Tones and tunes. Typological and comparative studies in word and sentence prosody. Berlin: Mouton de Gruyter, 2007, 1:113-146.

[12] CHAFE W L. Givenness, contrastiveness, definiteness, subjects, topics, and point of view[C]//LI C N (Eds.). Subject and topic. New York: Academic Press, 1976:25-55.

[13] CHAFE W L. Cognitive constraints on information flow[C]//TOMLIN R S (Eds.).

Coherence and grounding in discourse. Amsterdam: John Benjamins, 1987:21-51.

[14] CHAO Y R. A grammar of spoken Chinese[M]. Berkeley: University of California Press, 1965.

[15] CHEN A. The phonetics of sentence-initial topic and focus in adult and child Dutch[C]// VIGÁRIO M, FROTA S, FREITAS M J (Eds.). Phonetics and phonology: interactions and interrelations. Amsterdam: Benjamins, 2009:91-106.

[16] CHEN A. Tuning information packaging: intonational realization of topic and focus in child Dutch.[J]. Journal of child language, 2011, 38(5):1055-1083.

[17] CHEN A. The developmental path to phonological focus marking in Dutch[C]// FROTA S, ELORDIETA G, PRIETO P (Eds.). Prosodic categories: production, perception and comprehension. Dordrecht: Springer, 2011:93-109.

[18] CHEN A. Prosodic investigation on information structure[C]//KRIFKA M, MUSAN R (Eds.). The expression of information structure. Berlin: Mouton de Gruyter, 2012:251-286.

[19] CHEN A. Production-comprehension (A)Symmetry: individual differences in the acquisition of prosody focus marking[C]//Proceedings of the International Conference on Speech Prosody, 2014, 7:423-427.

[20] CHEN A. Children's use of intonation in reference and the role of input[C]//SERRATRICE L, ALLEN S (Eds.). The acquisition of reference. Amsterdam: John Benjamins, 2015:83-104.

[21] CHEN A. Different children different prosody: individual differences in prosodic development[C]//Keynote lecture at International Conference on Speech Prosody. Boston: Boston University, 2016, 8.

[22] CHEN A. Get the focus right across languages: acquisition of prosodic focus marking in production[G]//PRIETO P, ESTEVE-GIBERT N (Eds.). Prosodic development. Amsterdam: Benjamins, 2018:295-314.

[23] CHEN A. A phonetics-phonology interface-based approach to intonational realisation of topic and focus in Dutch[C]. Laboratory Phonology.[under revision].

[24] CHEN S W, WANG B, XU Y. Closely related languages, different ways of realizing focus[C]//Interspeech, 2009:1007-1010.

[25] CHEN Y, BRAUN B. Prosodic realization of information structure categories in standard Chinese[C]//Proceedings of the International Conference on Speech Prosody. Germany: Dresden, 2006, 3.

[26] CHEN Y, GUSSENHOVEN C. Emphasis and tonal implementation in Standard Chinese[J]. Journal of Phonetics, 2008, 36(4):724-746.

[27] CHERMAK G, SCHNEIDERMAN C. Speech timing variability of children and adults[J]. Journal of Phonetics, 1986, 13(4):477-480.

[28] CHO S B. A phonological study of Korean: with a historical analysis[M]. Uppsala: Universitetet, 1967.

[29] CHO T, SUN S A, LADEFOGED P. Acoustic and aerodynamic correlates of Korean stops and fricatives[J]. Journal of Phonetics, 2002, 30(2):193-228.

[30] CHOI Y O, MAZUKA R. Are prosodic units universally important to children in their early language acquisition? Korean children's detection and use of language-specific prosodic units[J]. Journal of Cognitive Science, 2001, 2(2):171-193.

[31] CHOI Y O, MAZUKA R. Young children's use of prosody in sentence parsing-[J]. Journal of Psycholinguistic Research, 2003, 32(2):197-217.

[32] CHOI Y O, MAZUKA R. Acquisition of prosody in Korean[G]// LEE C, KIM Y, SIMPSON G (Eds.). Handbook of East Asian psycholinguistics, part Ⅲ: Korean psycholinguistics. London: Cambridge University Press, 2009.

[33] CLUMECK H V. Studies in the acquisition of Mandarin phonology[D]. Berkeley: University of California, 1977.

[34] CUTLER A, DAHAN D, VAN DONSELAAR W. Prosody in the comprehension of spoken language: a literature review[J]. Language and Speech, 1997, 40(2):141-201.

[35] DE RUITER L. Studies on intonation and information structure in child and adult German[D]. Nijmegen: Max Planck Institute for Psycholinguistics, 2010.

[36] EADY S J, COOPER W E. Speech intonation and focus location in matched statements and questions[J]. Journal of the Acoustical Society of America, 1986, 80(2):402-415.

[37] FÉRY C. German intonational patterns[M]. Tübingen: Niemeyer, 1993.

[38] FROTA S, BUTLER J, VIGÁRIO M. Infants' perception of intonation: Is it a statement or a question?[J]. Infancy, 2014, 19(2):194-213.

[39] FU Q J, ZENG F G. Identification of temporal envelope cues in Chinese tone recognition[J]. Asia Pacific Journal of Speech, Language and Hearing, 2000, 5:45-57.

[40] GREIF M. Contrastive focus in mandarin Chinese[C]//Proceedings of Speech Prosody. Chicago: UAS, 2010, 5.

[41] GRÜNLOH T, LIEVEN E, TOMASELLO M. Young children's intonational marking of new, given and contrastive referents[J]. Language Learning and Development, 2015, 11(2):95-127.

[42] GUNDEL J K, FRETHEIM T. Topic and focus[G]//HORN L R, WARD G (Eds.). The handbook of pragmatics. Oxford: Blackwell, 2004:175-196.

[43] GUSSENHOVEN C. On the grammar and semantics of sentence accents[M]. Dordrecht: Foris, 1984.

[44] GUSSENHOVEN C. The phonology of tone and intonation[M]. Cambridge: Cambridge University Press, 2004.

[45] GUSSENHOVEN C. Types of Focus in English[C]//LEE C, GORDON M, BÜRING D (Eds.). Topic and focus: cross-linguistic perspectives on meaning and intonation. London: Springer, 2007:83-100.

[46] GUSSENHOVEN C, RIETVELD T. The behavior of H* and L* under variations in pitch range in Dutch rising contours[J]. Language and Speech, 2000, 43(2):183-203.

[47] HANSSEN J, PETERS J, GUSSENHOVEN C. Prosodic effects of focus in Dutch declaratives[C]//Proceedings of the International Conference on Speech Prosody, 2008, 4:609-612.

[48] HORNBY P A, HASS W A. Use of contrastive stress by preschool children[J]. Journal of Speech and Hearing Research, 1970, 13:359-399.

[49] JEON H S, NOLAN F. Prosodic marking of narrow focus in Seoul Korean[J]. Laboratory Phonology: Journal of the Association for Laboratory Phonology, 2017, 8(1):1-30.

[50] JUN S A. The phonetics and phonology of Korean prosody[D]. Columbus: Ohio State University, 1993.

[51] JUN S A. The accentual phrase in the Korean prosodic hierarchy[J]. Phonology, 1998, 15(2):189-226.

[52] JUN S A. K-ToBI (Korean ToBI) Labeling Conventions[J]. UCLA Working Papers in Phonetics, 2000, 99:149-173.

[53] JUN S A. The effect of phrase length and speech rate on prosodic phrasing[C]// Proceedings of the International Congress of Phonetic Sciences, 2003, 15:483-486.

[54] JUN S A. Korean intonational phonology and prosodic transcription[C]//JUN S A (Eds.). Prosodic Typology: The phonology of intonation and phrasing. Oxford: Oxford University Press, 2005:201-229.

[55] JUN S A. Intonational Phonology of Seoul Korean Revisited[C]//VANCE T J, JONES K (Eds.). Japanese-Korean linguistics. Stanford: Center for the Study of Language and Information, 2006, 14:15–26.

[56] JUN S A. Phonological development of Korean: a case study[C]//UCLA Working Papers in Phonetics, 2007, 105:51–65.

[57] JUN S A. Prosodic markings of complex NP focus, syntax, and the pre-/post-focus string[C]//Proceedings of the West Coast Conference on Formal Linguistics. Somerville,

MA: Cascadilla Press, 2011, 28:214-230.

[58] JUN S A, KIM H S, LEE H J, et al. An experimental study on the effect of argument structure on VP focus[J]. Korean Linguistics, 2006, 13:89-112.

[59] JUN S A, KIM H S. VP focus and narrow focus in Korean[C]//Proceedings of the International Congress of Phonetic Sciences. Germany: Saarbruecken, 2007, 16: 1277-1280.

[60] JUN S A, LEE H J. Phonetic and phonological markers of contrastive focus in Korean[C]//Proceedings of the International Conference on Spoken Language Processing. Australia: Sydney, 1998, 4:1295-1298.

[61] KIM H S, JUN S A, LEE H J, et al. Argument structure and focus projection in Korean[C]//HOFFMANN R, MIXDORFF H (Eds.). Procccdings of spcech prosody. Dresden, 2006, 3.

[62] KIM S Y. The role of prosodic phrasing in Korean word segmentation[D]. Los Angeles: University of California, 2004.

[63] KOO II S. An cxpcrimcntal acoustic study of thc phonetics of intonation in standard Korean[M]. Seoul: Hanshin Publishing Co, 1986.

[64] KRIFKA M, MUSAN R. Information structure: overview and linguistic issues [G]// KRIFKA M, MUSAN R (Eds.). The expression of information structure. Berlin: Walter de Gruyter, 2012:1-44.

[65] LADD D R. Intonational phonology[M]. Cambridge: Cambridge University Press, 1996.

[66] LAMBRECHT K. Information structure and sentence form: topic, focus, and the mental representations of discourse referents[M]. Cambridge: Cambridge University Press, 1994.

[67] LANDIS J R, KOCH G G. The measurement of observer agreement for categorical data[J]. Biometrics, 1997, 33:159-174.

[68] LEE Y C, XU Y. Phonetic realization of contrastive focus in Korean[C]//Proceedings of Speech Prosody. Chicago, 2010, 5:1-4.

[69] LEE H B. A study of Korean (Seoul) intonation[D]. London: University of London, 1964

[70] LI C N, Thompson S A. The acquisition of tone in Mandarin-speaking children[J]. Journal of Child Language, 1997, 4(2):185-199.

[71] LIN Y H. The sounds of Chinese[M]. Cambridge: Cambridge University Press, 2007.

[72] LIU F, XU Y. Parallel encoding of focus and interrogative meaning in Mandarin

intonation[J]. Phonetica, 2005, 62(2-4):70-87.

[73] LIU L, KAGER R. Perception of tones by infants learning a non-tone language[J]. Cognition, 2014, 133(2):385-394.

[74] LIU S, SAMUEL A G. Perception of Mandarin lexical tones when f0 information is neutralized[J]. Language and Speech, 2004, 47:109–138.

[75] LIU Y, SHU H, LI P. Word naming and psycholinguistic norms: Chinese[J]. Behavior Research Methods, 2007, 39:192-198.

[76] LOGAN K J, BYRD C T, MAZZOCCHI E M, et al. Speaking rate characteristics of elementary-school-aged children who do and do not stutter[J]. Journal of Communication Disorders, 2011, 44(1):130-147.

[77] MACHAČ P, SKARNITZL R. Principles of phonetic segmentation[M]. Praha: Epocha, 2009.

[78] MACWHINNEY B, BATES E. Sentential devices for conveying givenness and newness: a cross- cultural developmental study[J]. Journal of Verbal Learning and Verbal Behavior, 1978, 17:539-558.

[79] MARTIN S E. Korean morphophonemics[M]. Linguistic Society of America, 1954.

[80] MÜLLER A, HÖHLE B, SCHMITZ M, et al. Focus-to-stress alignment in 4-to 5-year-old German-learning children[C]//BELLETTI A, BENNATI E, CHESI C, et al (Eds.). Proceedings of GALA. Newcastle: Cambridge Scholars Press, 2005:393-407.

[81] NAGAHARA H. Phonological phrasing in Japanese[D]. Los Angeles: University of California, 1994.

[82] OH M. Korean prosodic structure and focus[C]//Proceedings of the International Conference of Phonetic Sciences 14. 1999:1517-1520.

[83] OUYANG I C, KAISER E. Prosody and information structure in a tone language: an investigation of Mandarin Chinese[J]. Language, Cognition and Neuroscience, 2015, 30(1-2):57-72.

[84] PARK M J. The meaning of Korean prosodic boundary tones[M]. Leiden: Brill, 2012.

[85] PENG S H. Lexical versus "phonological" representations of Mandarin Sandhi tones[G]// BROE M B, PIERREHUMBERT J B (Eds.). Laboratory phonology V: acquisition and the lexicon. Cambridge: Cambridge University Press, 2000:152-167.

[86] PIERREHUMBERT J B. The phonology and phonetics of English intonation[D]. Cambridge, MA: Massachusetts Institute of Technology, 1980.

[87] PIERREHUMBERT J B, BECKMAN M. Japanese tone structure[J]. Linguistic

Inquiry Monographs, 1988, 15:1-282.

[88] ROBERTS C. Information structure in discourse: towards an integrated formal theory of pragmatics[J]. Semantics and Pragmatics, 2012, 5(6):1-69.

[89] ROMØREN A S H. Hunting highs and lows: the acquisition of prosodic focus marking in Swedish and Dutch[D]. Utrecht: LOT, 2016.

[90] ROMØREN A S H, Chen A. The acquisition of prosodic focus marking in Central Swedish: sorting out lexical and post-lexical tones[C]//WOLTERS M, LIVINGSTONE J, BEATTIE B, et al (Eds.). Proceedings of the International Congress of Phonetic Sciences. Glasgow: the University of Glasgow, 2015, 18, 0628:1-5.

[91] SCHAFER A J, JUN S A. Effects of accentual phrasing on adjective interpretation[G]// NAKAYAMA M (Eds.). East Asian language processing. Stanford: CSLI, 2002:223-255.

[92] SHIH C. Tone and intonation in mandarin[J]. Working Papers of the Cornell Phonetics Laboratory, 1988, 3: 83-109.

[93] SHIH C. Declination in Mandarin[C]//BOTINIS A, KOUROUPETROGLOU G, CARAYANNIS G (Eds.). Intonation: theory, models and applications: proceedings of an ESCA workshop. Athens, 1997: 293-296.

[94] SHIH C. Tonal effects on intonation[C]//Proceedings of the International Symposium on Tonal Aspects of Languages. 2004, 1:163-168.

[95] TURK A, NAKAI S, SUGAHARA M. Acoustic segment durations in prosodic research: a practical guide[J]. Methods in Empirical Prosody Research, 2006, 3:1-28.

[96] VALLDUVÍ E, ENGDAHL E. The linguistic realization of information packaging[J]. Linguistics, 1996, 34(3):459-520.

[97] WALKER J F, ARCHIBALD L M, CHERNIAK S R, et al. Articulation rate in 3-and 5-year-old children[J]. Journal of Speech, Language, and Hearing Research, 1992, 35(1):4-13.

[98] WANG B, XU Y. Differential prosodic encoding of topic and focus in sentence-initial position in Mandarin Chinese[J]. Journal of Phonetics, 2011, 39(4):595-611.

[99] WATSON D, ARNOLD J E, TANENHAUS M K. Not just given and new: the effects of discourse and task based constraints on acoustic prominence[C]//The 2005 CUNY Human Sentence Processing Conference. Tucson, AZ, 2005.

[100] WELLS B, PEPPÉ S, GOULANDRIS N. Intonation development from five to thirteen[J]. Journal of Child Language, 2004, 31(4):749-778.

[101] WHALEN D H, XU Y. Information for Mandarin tones in the amplitude contour and in brief segments[J]. Phonetica, 1992, 49: 25-47.

[102] WONG P. Acoustic characteristics of three-year-olds' correct and incorrect monosyllabic Mandarin lexical tone productions[J]. Journal of Phonetics, 2012, 40(1):141-151.

[103] WONG P, SCHWARTZ R G, JENKINS J J. Perception and production of lexical tones by 3-year-old, Mandarin-speaking children[J]. Journal of Speech, Language, and Hearing Research, 2005, 48(5):1065-1079.

[104] WONNACOTT E, WATSON D G. Acoustic emphasis in four year olds. Cognition, 2008, 107(3):1093-1101.

[105] WU W L, XU Y. Prosodic focus in Hong Kong Cantonese without post-focus compression[C]// Proceedings of Speech Prosody. Chicago, 2010, 5, 100040:1-4.

[106] XU Y. Production and perception of coarticulated tones[J]. Journal of the Acoustical Society of America, 1994, 95:2240-2253.

[107] XU Y. Contextual tonal variations in Mandarin[J]. Journal of Phonetics, 1997, 25 (1):61-83.

[108] XU Y. Effects of tone and focus on the formation and alignment of f0 contours[J]. Journal of Phonetics, 1999, 27(1), 55-105.

[109] XU Y. Understanding tone from the perspective of production and perception[J]. Language and Linguistics, 2004, 5: 757-797.

[110] XU Y. Post-focus compression: Cross-linguistic distribution and historical origin[C]//Proceedings of the International Congress of Phonetic Sciences. Hong Kong: City University of Hong Kong, 2011, 17:152-155.

[111] XU Y, CHEN S W, WANG B. Prosodic focus with and without post-focus compression (PFC): a typological divide within the same language family?[J]. The Linguistic Review, 2012, 29: 131-147.

[112] XU Y, WANG Q E. Pitch targets and their realization: evidence from Mandarin Chinese[J]. Speech Communication, 2001, 33(4):319-337.

[113] XU Y, XU C X. Phonetic realization of focus in English declarative intonation[J]. Journal of Phonetics, 2005, 33(2), 159-197.

[114] YANG A, CHEN A. Prosodic focus marking in child and adult Mandarin Chinese[G]//GUSSENHOVEN C, CHEN Y, DEDIU D (Eds.). Proceedings of the International Symposium on Tonal Aspects of Languages. Nijmegen, 2014a, 4:54-58.

[115] YANG A, CHEN A. Prosodic focus marking in Chinese four- and eight-year-olds[C]//CAMPBELL N, GIBBON D, HIRST D. Proceedings of the Speech Prosody. Dublin, 2014b, 7:713-717.

[116] YANG A, CHEN A. The developmental path to adult-like prosodic focus marking in Mandarin Chinese-speaking children[J]. First Language, 2018, 38(1): 26-46.

[117] YANG A, CHO T, KIM S, et al. Phonetic focus marking in Korean-speaking 7- to 8-year-olds and adults[C]//WOLTERS M, LIVINGSTONE J, BEATTIE B, et al (Eds.). Proceedings of the International Congress of Phonetic Sciences. Glasgow: the University of Glasgow, 2015, 18, 0673:1-5.

[118] ZHU H. Phonological development in specific contexts: studies of Chinese-speaking children[M]. Clevedon: Multilingual Matters Ltd, 2002.

APPENDICES

Appendix A: Mandarin speakers

Speaker	Age group	Age of testing	Gender	List	Usable sentences
cha4p01	4- to 5-year-old	4;10	F	List 1	47(59%)
cha4p02	4- to 5-year-old	4;10	F	List 1	38(48%)
cha4p04	4- to 5-year-old	4;11	M	List 2	28(35%)
cha4p05	4- to 5-year-old	4;9	M	List 2	38(48%)
cha4p06	4- to 5-year-old	4;11	F	List 2	53(66%)
cha4p09	4- to 5-year-old	4;6	M	List 1	58(73%)
cha5p02	4- to 5-year-old	5;6	M	List 2	46(58%)
cha5p04	4- to 5-year-old	5;10	F	List 2	38(48%)
cha5p06	4- to 5-year-old	5;7	M	List 2	64(80%)
cha5p08	4- to 5-year-old	5;4	F	List 1	49(61%)
cha5p09	4- to 5-year-old	5;6	F	List 1	68(85%)
cha5p13	4- to 5-year-old	5;6	M	List 1	43(54%)
cha7p01	7- to 8-year-old	7;6	F	List 2	52(65%)
cha7p02	7- to 8-year-old	7;5	F	List 2	57(71%)
cha7p04	7- to 8-year-old	7;2	M	List 2	49(61%)
cha7p05	7- to 8-year-old	7;9	F	List 1	77(96%)
cha7p06	7- to 8-year-old	7;11	F	List 1	74(93%)
cha8p01	7- to 8-year-old	8;2	F	List 1	70(88%)
cha8p03	7- to 8-year-old	8;3	F	List 1	76(95%)
cha8p04	7- to 8-year-old	8;2	M	List 2	56(70%)
cha8p05	7- to 8-year-old	8;3	F	List 2	67(84%)
cha8p06	7- to 8-year-old	8;3	M	List 2	78(98%)
cha10p01	10- to 11-year-old	10;4	F	List 1	68(85%)
cha10p02	10- to 11-year-old	10;5	F	List 1	69(86%)

Continued

Speaker	Age group	Age of testing	Gender	List	Usable sentences
cha10p03	10- to 11-year-old	10;1	F	List 1	67(84%)
cha10p04	10- to 11-year-old	10;10	M	List 2	63(79%)
cha10p05	10- to 11-year-old	10;1	F	List 2	72(90%)
cha10p06	10- to 11-year-old	10;4	F	List 2	75(94%)
cha11p01	10- to 11-year-old	11;4	M	List 2	80(100%)
cha11p02	10- to 11-year-old	11;0	F	List 2	79(99%)
cha11p03	10- to 11-year-old	11;3	M	List 1	74(93%)
cha11p04	10- to 11-year-old	11;0	F	List 1	77(96%)
cha11p05	10- to 11-year-old	11;5	M	List 1	68(85%)
cha11p06	10- to 11-year-old	11;4	M	List 2	73(91%)
chaap01	adult	18	F	List 2	78(98%)
chaap02	adult	18	M	List 2	78(98%)
chaap03	adult	19	M	List 1	79(99%)
chaap04	adult	18	M	List 2	75(94%)
chaap05	adult	18	M	List 2	73(91%)
chaap06	adult	18	F	List 2	64(80%)
chaap07	adult	20	M	List 1	65(81%)
chaap08	adult	20	M	List 1	74(93%)
chaap09	adult	19	F	List 1	75(94%)
chaap10	adult	19	F	List 1	73(91%)
chaap11	adult	19	F	List 2	75(94%)
chaap12	adult	20	F	List 1	72(90%)

Appendix B: Mandarin sentences

Table 1 Sentences for practice trials

Session	Order	Focus condition	Subject	Verb	Object	Sentence	Word for word gloss
A	P1	NF-i	xiao3 xiong2	reng1	shu1	[小熊]扔书	[Little bear] throw book
A	P2	NF-m	xiao3 gou3	mai2	qiu2	小狗[埋]球	Little dog [bury] ball
A	P3	NF-f	xiao3 mao1	jian3	bi3	小猫剪[笔]	Little cat cut [pen]
A	P4	CF-m	xiao3 tu4	yun4	cai4	小兔[运]菜	Little rabbit [transport] vegetable
A	P5	BF	xiao3 mao1	reng1	qiu2	[小猫扔球]	[Little cat throw ball]
B	P1	NF-i	xiao3 xiong2	jiao1	hua1	[小熊]浇花	[Little bear] water flower
B	P2	NF-m	xiao3 gou3	wen2	li2	小狗[闻]梨	Little dog [smell] pear
B	P3	NF-f	xiao3 mao1	tian3	cao3	小猫舔[草]	Little cat lick [grass]
B	P4	CF-m	xiao3 tu4	mai4	shu4	小兔[卖]树	Little rabbit [sell] tree
B	P5	BF	xiao3 mao1	wen2	hua1	[小猫闻花]	[Little cat smell flower]

Table 2 List 1 Session A sentences

Sentence ID	Randomised order	Focus condition	Subject	Verb	Object	Sentence	Word for word gloss
1	32	NF-i	xiao3 mao1	reng1	shu1	[小猫]扔书	[Little cat] throw book
2	7	NF-i	xiao3 xiong2	reng1	qiu2	[小熊]扔球	[Little bear] throw ball
5	37	NF-i	xiao3 tu4	mai2	shu1	[小兔]埋书	[Little rabbit] bury book
6	2	NF-i	xiao3 mao1	mai2	qiu2	[小猫]埋球	[Little cat] bury ball
11	12	NF-i	xiao3 mao1	jian3	bi3	[小猫]剪笔	[Little cat] cut pen
12	22	NF-i	xiao3 xiong2	jian3	cai4	[小熊]剪菜	[Little bear] cut vegetable
15	27	NF-i	xiao3 tu4	yun4	bi3	[小兔]运笔	[Little rabbit] transport pen
16	17	NF-i	xiao3 mao1	yun4	cai4	[小猫]运菜	[Little cat] transport vegetable
17	35	NF-m	xiao3 tu4	reng1	shu1	小兔[扔]书	Little rabbit [throw] book
18	40	NF-m	xiao3 gou3	reng1	qiu2	小狗[扔]球	Little dog [throw] ball

Continued

Sentence ID	Randomised order	Focus condition	Subject	Verb	Object	Sentence	Word for word gloss
21	25	NF-m	xiao3 mao1	mai2	shu1	小猫[埋]书	Little cat [bury] book
22	10	NF-m	xiao3 tu4	mai2	qiu2	小兔[埋]球	Little rabbit [bury] ball
27	5	NF-m	xiao3 tu4	jian3	bi3	小兔[剪]笔	Little rabbit [cut] pen
28	20	NF-m	xiao3 gou3	jian3	cai4	小狗[剪]菜	Little dog [cut] vegetable
31	30	NF-m	xiao3 mao1	yun4	bi3	小猫[运]笔	Little cat [transport] pen
32	15	NF-m	xiao3 tu4	yun4	cai4	小兔[运]菜	Little rabbit [transport] vegetable
33	1	NF-f	xiao3 xiong2	reng1	shu1	小熊扔[书]	Little bear throw [book]
34	21	NF-f	xiao3 tu4	reng1	qiu2	小兔扔[球]	Little rabbit throw [ball]
37	6	NF-f	xiao3 gou3	mai2	shu1	小狗埋[书]	Little dog bury [book]
38	16	NF-f	xiao3 xiong2	mai2	qiu2	小熊埋[球]	Little bear bury [ball]
43	26	NF-f	xiao3 xiong2	jian3	bi3	小熊剪[笔]	Little bear cut [pen]
44	31	NF-f	xiao3 tu4	jian3	cai4	小兔剪[菜]	Little rabbit cut [vegetable]
47	36	NF-f	xiao3 gou3	yun4	bi3	小狗运[笔]	Little dog transport [pen]
48	11	NF-f	xiao3 xiong2	yun4	cai4	小熊运[菜]	Little bear transport [vegetable]
49	13	CF-m	xiao3 gou3	reng1	shu1	小狗[扔]书	Little dog [throw] book
50	38	CF-m	xiao3 mao1	reng1	qiu2	小猫[扔]球	Little cat [throw] ball
53	23	CF-m	xiao3 xiong2	mai2	shu1	小熊[埋]书	Little bear [bury] book
54	18	CF-m	xiao3 gou3	mai2	qiu2	小狗[埋]球	Little dog [bury] ball
59	3	CF-m	xiao3 gou3	jian3	bi3	小狗[剪]笔	Little dog [cut] pen
60	28	CF-m	xiao3 mao1	jian3	cai4	小猫[剪]菜	Little cat [cut] vegetable
63	33	CF-m	xiao3 xiong2	yun4	bi3	小熊[运]笔	Little bear [transport] pen
64	8	CF-m	xiao3 gou3	yun4	cai4	小狗[运]菜	Little dog [transport] vegetable
65	19	BF	xiao3 mao1	reng1	shu1	[小猫扔书]	[Little cat throw book]
66	29	BF	xiao3 xiong2	reng1	qiu2	[小熊扔球]	[Little bear throw ball]
69	34	BF	xiao3 gou3	mai2	shu1	[小狗埋书]	[Little dog bury book]
70	14	BF	xiao3 mao1	mai2	qiu2	[小猫埋球]	[Little cat bury ball]

Continued

Sentence ID	Randomised order	Focus condition	Subject	Verb	Object	Sentence	Word for word gloss
75	9	BF	xiao3 mao1	jian3	bi3	[小猫剪笔]	[Little cat cut pen]
76	39	BF	xiao3 xiong2	jian3	cai4	[小熊剪菜]	[Little bear cut vegetable]
79	24	BF	xiao3 gou3	yun4	bi3	[小狗运笔]	[Little dog transport pen]
80	4	BF	xiao3 mao1	yun4	cai4	[小猫运菜]	[Little cat transport vegetable]

Table 3 List 1 Session B sentences

Sentence ID	Randomised order	Focus condition	Subject	Verb	Object	Sentence	Word for word gloss
83	52	NF-i	xiao3 gou3	jiao1	cao3	[小狗]浇草	[Little dog] water grass
84	72	NF-i	xiao3 tu4	jiao1	shu4	[小兔]浇树	[Little rabbit] water tree
87	57	NF-i	xiao3 xiong2	wen2	cao3	[小熊]闻草	[Little bear] smell grass
88	42	NF-i	xiao3 gou3	wen2	shu4	[小狗]闻树	[Little dog] smell tree
89	47	NF-i	xiao3 gou3	tian3	hua1	[小狗]舔花	[Little dog] lick flower
90	67	NF-i	xiao3 tu4	tian3	li2	[小兔]舔梨	[Little rabbit] lick pear
93	77	NF-i	xiao3 xiong2	mai4	hua1	[小熊]卖花	[Little bear] sell flower
94	62	NF-i	xiao3 gou3	mai4	li2	[小狗]卖梨	[Little dog] sell pear
99	60	NF-m	xiao3 xiong2	jiao1	cao3	小熊[浇]草	Little bear [water] grass
100	75	NF-m	xiao3 mao1	jiao1	shu4	小猫[浇]树	Little cat [water] tree
103	55	NF-m	xiao3 gou3	wen2	cao3	小狗[闻]草	Little dog [smell] grass
104	50	NF-m	xiao3 xiong2	wen2	shu4	小熊[闻]树	Little bear [smell] tree
105	70	NF-m	xiao3 xiong2	tian3	hua1	小熊[舔]花	Little bear [lick] flower
106	65	NF-m	xiao3 mao1	tian3	li2	小猫[舔]梨	Little cat [lick] pear
109	80	NF-m	xiao3 gou3	mai4	hua1	小狗[卖]花	Little dog [sell] flower
110	45	NF-m	xiao3 xiong2	mai4	li2	小熊[卖]梨	Little bear [sell] pear
115	41	NF-f	xiao3 mao1	jiao1	cao3	小猫浇[草]	Little cat water [grass]
116	66	NF-f	xiao3 gou3	jiao1	shu4	小狗浇[树]	Little dog water [tree]
119	46	NF-f	xiao3 tu4	wen2	cao3	小兔闻[草]	Little rabbit smell [grass]
120	61	NF-f	xiao3 mao1	wen2	shu4	小猫闻[树]	Little cat smell [tree]
121	51	NF-f	xiao3 mao1	tian3	hua1	小猫舔[花]	Little cat lick [flower]
122	76	NF-f	xiao3 gou3	tian3	li2	小狗舔[梨]	Little dog lick [pear]
125	56	NF-f	xiao3 tu4	mai4	hua1	小兔卖[花]	Little rabbit sell [flower]

Continued

Sentence ID	Randomised order	Focus condition	Subject	Verb	Object	Sentence	Word for word gloss
126	71	NF-f	xiao3 mao1	mai4	li2	小猫卖[梨]	Little cat sell [pear]
131	58	CF-m	xiao3 tu4	jiao1	cao3	小兔[浇]草	Little rabbit [water] grass
132	48	CF-m	xiao3 xiong2	jiao1	shu4	小熊[浇]树	Little bear [water] tree
135	73	CF-m	xiao3 mao1	wen2	cao3	小猫[闻]草	Little cat [smell] grass
136	53	CF-m	xiao3 tu4	wen2	shu4	小兔[闻]树	Little rabbit [smell] tree
137	63	CF-m	xiao3 tu4	tian3	hua1	小兔[舔]花	Little rabbit [lick] flower
138	78	CF-m	xiao3 xiong2	tian3	li2	小熊[舔]梨	Little bear [lick] pear
141	68	CF-m	xiao3 mao1	mai4	hua1	小猫[卖]花	Little cat [sell] flower
142	43	CF-m	xiao3 tu4	mai4	li2	小兔[卖]梨	Little rabbit [sell] pear
147	69	BF	xiao3 tu4	jiao1	cao3	[小兔浇草]	[Little rabbit water grass]
148	44	BF	xiao3 gou3	jiao1	shu4	[小狗浇树]	[Little dog water tree]
151	64	BF	xiao3 xiong2	wen2	cao3	[小熊闻草]	[Little bear smell grass]
152	79	BF	xiao3 tu4	wen2	shu4	[小兔闻树]	[Little rabbit smell tree]
153	74	BF	xiao3 tu4	tian3	hua1	[小兔舔花]	[Little rabbit lick flower]
154	59	BF	xiao3 gou3	tian3	li2	[小狗舔梨]	[Little dog lick pear]
157	54	BF	xiao3 xiong2	mai4	hua1	[小熊卖花]	[Little bear sell flower]
158	49	BF	xiao3 tu4	mai4	li2	[小兔卖梨]	[Little rabbit sell pear]

Table 4 List 2 Session A sentences

Sentence ID	Randomised order	Focus condition	Subject	Verb	Object	Sentence	Word for word gloss
3	112	NF-i	xiao3 gou3	reng1	bi3	[小狗]扔笔	[Little dog] throw pen
4	92	NF-i	xiao3 tu4	reng1	cai4	[小兔]扔菜	[Little rabbit] throw vegetable
7	102	NF-i	xiao3 xiong2	mai2	bi3	[小熊]埋笔	[Little bear] bury pen
8	82	NF-i	xiao3 gou3	mai2	cai4	[小狗]埋菜	[Little dog] bury vegetable
9	87	NF-i	xiao3 gou3	jian3	shu1	[小狗]剪书	[Little dog] cut book
10	107	NF-i	xiao3 tu4	jian3	qiu2	[小兔]剪球	[Little rabbit] cut ball
13	97	NF-i	xiao3 xiong2	yun4	shu1	[小熊]运书	[Little bear] transport book
14	117	NF-i	xiao3 gou3	yun4	qiu2	[小狗]运球	[Little dog] transport ball
19	115	NF-m	xiao3 xiong2	reng1	bi3	小熊[扔]笔	Little bear [throw] pen
20	90	NF-m	xiao3 mao1	reng1	cai4	小猫[扔]菜	Little cat [throw] vegetable

Continued

Sentence ID	Randomised order	Focus condition	Subject	Verb	Object	Sentence	Word for word gloss
23	120	NF-m	xiao3 gou3	mai2	bi3	小狗[埋]笔	Little dog [bury] pen
24	95	NF-m	xiao3 xiong2	mai2	cai4	小熊[埋]菜	Little bear [bury] vegetable
25	110	NF-m	xiao3 xiong2	jian3	shu1	小熊[剪]书	Little bear [cut] book
26	100	NF-m	xiao3 mao1	jian3	qiu2	小猫[剪]球	Little cat [cut] ball
29	105	NF-m	xiao3 gou3	yun4	shu1	小狗[运]书	Little dog [transport] book
30	85	NF-m	xiao3 xiong2	yun4	qiu2	小熊[运]球	Little bear [transport] ball
35	96	NF-f	xiao3 mao1	reng1	bi3	小猫扔[笔]	Little cat throw [pen]
36	101	NF-f	xiao3 gou3	reng1	cai4	小狗扔[菜]	Little dog throw [vegetable]
39	86	NF-f	xiao3 tu4	mai2	bi3	小兔埋[笔]	Little rabbit bury [pen]
40	106	NF-f	xiao3 mao1	mai2	cai4	小猫埋[菜]	Little cat bury [vegetable]
41	116	NF-f	xiao3 mao1	jian3	shu1	小猫剪[书]	Little cat cut [book]
42	91	NF-f	xiao3 gou3	jian3	qiu2	小狗剪[球]	Little dog cut [ball]
45	81	NF-f	xiao3 tu4	yun4	shu1	小兔运[书]	Little rabbit transport [book]
46	111	NF-f	xiao3 mao1	yun4	qiu2	小猫运[球]	Little cat transport [ball]
51	98	CF-m	xiao3 tu4	reng1	bi3	小兔[扔]笔	Little rabbit [throw] pen
52	88	CF-m	xiao3 xiong2	reng1	cai4	小熊[扔]菜	Little bear [throw] vegetable
55	93	CF-m	xiao3 mao1	mai2	bi3	小猫[埋]笔	Little cat [bury] pen
56	118	CF-m	xiao3 tu4	mai2	cai4	小兔[埋]菜	Little rabbit [bury] vegetable
57	83	CF-m	xiao3 tu4	jian3	shu1	小兔[剪]书	Little rabbit [cut] book
58	113	CF-m	xiao3 xiong2	jian3	qiu2	小熊[剪]球	Little bear [cut] ball
61	108	CF-m	xiao3 mao1	yun4	shu1	小猫[运]书	Little cat [transport] book
62	103	CF-m	xiao3 tu4	yun4	qiu2	小兔[运]球	Little rabbit [transport] ball
67	109	BF	xiao3 tu4	reng1	bi3	[小兔扔笔]	[Little rabbit throw pen]
68	84	BF	xiao3 gou3	reng1	cai4	[小狗扔菜]	[Little dog throw vegetable]
71	104	BF	xiao3 xiong2	mai2	bi3	[小熊埋笔]	[Little bear bury pen]
72	114	BF	xiao3 tu4	mai2	cai4	[小兔埋菜]	[Little rabbit bury vegetable]
73	94	BF	xiao3 tu4	jian3	shu1	[小兔剪书]	[Little rabbit cut book]
74	119	BF	xiao3 gou3	jian3	qiu2	[小狗剪球]	[Little dog cut ball]
77	99	BF	xiao3 xiong2	yun4	shu1	[小熊运书]	[Little bear transport book]
78	89	BF	xiao3 tu4	yun4	qiu2	[小兔运球]	[Little rabbit transport ball]

Table 5 List 2 Session B sentences

Sentence ID	Randomised order	Focus condition	Subject	Verb	Object	Sentence	Word for word gloss
81	152	NF-i	xiao3 mao1	jiao1	hua1	[小猫]浇花	[Little cat] water flower
82	127	NF-i	xiao3 xiong2	jiao1	li2	[小熊]浇梨	[Little bear] water pear
85	157	NF-i	xiao3 tu4	wen2	hua1	[小兔]闻花	[Little rabbit] smell flower
86	122	NF-i	xiao3 mao1	wen2	li2	[小猫]闻梨	[Little cat] smell pear
91	137	NF-i	xiao3 mao1	tian3	cao3	[小猫]舔草	[Little cat] lick grass
92	147	NF-i	xiao3 xiong2	tian3	shu4	[小熊]舔树	[Little bear] lick tree
95	142	NF-i	xiao3 tu4	mai4	cao3	[小兔]卖草	[Little rabbit] sell grass
96	132	NF-i	xiao3 mao1	mai4	shu4	[小猫]卖树	[Little cat] sell tree
97	135	NF-m	xiao3 tu4	jiao1	hua1	小兔[浇]花	Little rabbit [water] flower
98	130	NF-m	xiao3 gou3	jiao1	li2	小狗[浇]梨	Little dog [water] pear
101	150	NF-m	xiao3 mao1	wen2	hua1	小猫[闻]花	Little cat [smell] flower
102	155	NF-m	xiao3 tu4	wen2	li2	小兔[闻]梨	Little rabbit [smell] pear
107	125	NF-m	xiao3 tu4	tian3	cao3	小兔[舔]草	Little rabbit [lick] grass
108	145	NF-m	xiao3 gou3	tian3	shu4	小狗[舔]树	Little dog [lick] tree
111	160	NF-m	xiao3 mao1	mai4	cao3	小猫[卖]草	Little cat [sell] grass
112	140	NF-m	xiao3 tu4	mai4	shu4	小兔[卖]树	Little rabbit [sell] tree
113	121	NF-f	xiao3 xiong2	jiao1	hua1	小熊浇[花]	Little bear water [flower]
114	146	NF-f	xiao3 tu4	jiao1	li2	小兔浇[梨]	Little rabbit water [pear]
117	126	NF-f	xiao3 gou3	wen2	hua1	小狗闻[花]	Little dog smell [flower]
118	141	NF-f	xiao3 xiong2	wen2	li2	小熊闻[梨]	Little bear smell [pear]
123	131	NF-f	xiao3 xiong2	tian3	cao3	小熊舔[草]	Little bear lick [grass]
124	151	NF-f	xiao3 tu4	tian3	shu4	小兔舔[树]	Little rabbit lick [tree]
127	156	NF-f	xiao3 gou3	mai4	cao3	小狗卖[草]	Little dog sell [grass]
128	136	NF-f	xiao3 xiong2	mai4	shu4	小熊卖[树]	Little bear sell [tree]
129	133	CF-m	xiao3 gou3	jiao1	hua1	小狗[浇]花	Little dog [water] flower
130	148	CF-m	xiao3 mao1	jiao1	li2	小猫[浇]梨	Little cat [water] pear
133	153	CF-m	xiao3 xiong2	wen2	hua1	小熊[闻]花	Little bear [smell] flower
134	138	CF-m	xiao3 gou3	wen2	li2	小狗[闻]梨	Little dog [smell] pear
139	123	CF-m	xiao3 gou3	tian3	cao3	小狗[舔]草	Little dog [lick] grass
140	143	CF-m	xiao3 mao1	tian3	shu4	小猫[舔]树	Little cat [lick] tree
143	158	CF-m	xiao3 xiong2	mai4	cao3	小熊[卖]草	Little bear [sell] grass

Continued

Sentence ID	Randomised order	Focus condition	Subject	Verb	Object	Sentence	Word for word gloss
144	128	CF-m	xiao3 gou3	mai4	shu4	小狗[卖]树	Little dog [sell] tree
145	139	BF	xiao3 mao1	jiao1	hua1	[小猫浇花]	[Little cat water flower]
146	144	BF	xiao3 xiong2	jiao1	li2	[小熊浇梨]	[Little bear water pear]
149	159	BF	xiao3 gou3	wen2	hua1	[小狗闻花]	[Little dog smell flower]
150	134	BF	xiao3 mao1	wen2	li2	[小猫闻梨]	[Little cat smell pear]
155	129	BF	xiao3 mao1	tian3	cao3	[小猫舔草]	[Little cat lick grass]
156	149	BF	xiao3 xiong2	tian3	shu4	[小熊舔树]	[Little bear lick tree]
159	154	BF	xiao3 gou3	mai4	cao3	[小狗卖草]	[Little dog sell grass]
160	124	BF	xiao3 mao1	mai4	shu4	[小猫卖树]	[Little cat sell tree]

Appendix C: Korean speakers

Speaker	Age group	Age of testing	Gender	Usable sentences
ka4p03	4- to 5-year-old	4;10	M	39(65%)
ka4p07	4- to 5-year-old	4;11	M	34(57%)
ka5p04	4- to 5-year-old	5;10	F	34(57%)
ka5p05	4- to 5-year-old	5,9	M	48(80%)
ka5p06	4- to 5-year-old	5;0	F	37(62%)
ka5p08	4- to 5-year-old	5;5	M	38(63%)
ka7p01	7- to 8-year-old	7;10	F	55(92%)
ka7p02	7- to 8-year-old	7;9	F	42(70%)
ka7p03	7- to 8-year-old	7;7	F	35(58%)
ka7p04	7- to 8-year-old	7;1	F	40(67%)
ka8p01	7- to 8-year-old	8;0	F	41(68%)
ka8p02	7- to 8-year-old	8;0	M	40(67%)
ka8p03	7- to 8-year-old	8;10	F	47(78%)
ka8p04	7- to 8-year-old	8;10	M	35(58%)
ka10p01	10- to 11-year-old	10;9	F	50(83%)
ka10p02	10- to 11-year-old	10;9	M	55(92%)
ka10p03	10- to 11-year-old	10;3	M	42(70%)
ka10p05	10- to 11-year-old	10;11	F	39(65%)
ka10p06	10- to 11-year-old	10;9	F	55(92%)
ka10p07	10- to 11-year-old	10;6	M	49(82%)
ka11p03	10- to 11-year-old	11;11	M	45(75%)
ka11p04	10- to 11-year-old	11;1	F	49(82%)
kaap05	adult	25	F	56(93%)
kaap08	adult	19	F	53(88%)
kaap13	adult	23	M	53(88%)
kaap14	adult	25	F	48(80%)
kaap15	adult	23	F	55(92%)

Continued

Speaker	Age group	Age of testing	Gender	Usable sentences
kaap16	adult	22	F	53(88%)
kaap18	adult	27	F	56(93%)
kaap19	adult	28	M	58(97%)
kaap20	adult	25	M	50(83%)
kaap21	adult	25	M	54(90%)
kaap22	adult	23	M	60(100%)
kaap23	adult	26	M	57(95%)

Appendix D: Korean sentences

Table 1 Sentences for practice trials

Session	Order	Focus condition	Subject IPA	Object IPA	Verb IPA	Sentence	Word for word gloss
A	P1	NF-i	komi	pʰalɨl	kiljʌ	[곰이] 팔을 그려요	[Bear] arm draw
A	P2	NF-m	kɛka	p*aŋil	mantʃʌ	개가 [빵을] 만져요	Dog [bread] touch
A	P3	NF-f	soka	alɨl	tɕʰatɕa	소가 알을 [찾아] 요	Cow egg [look for]
A	P4	CF-m	tɕuka	palɨl	mantʃʌ	쥐가 [발을] 만져요	Rat [foot] touch
A	P5	BF	mali	pulɨl	kiljʌ	[말이 불을 그려요]	[Horse fire draw]
B	P1	NF-i	komi	kututɨlɨl	kiljʌ	[곰이] 구두들을 그려요	[Bear] shoes draw
B	P2	NF-m	mali	k*amakwilɨl	mantʃʌ	말이 [까마귀를] 만져요	Horse [crow] touch
B	P3	NF-f	tɕuka	kapaŋtɨlɨl	tɕʰatɕa	쥐가 가방들을 [찾아] 요	Rat bags [look for]
B	P4	CF-m	soka	kituŋtɨlɨl	mantʃʌ	소가 [기둥들을] 만져요	Cow [pillars] touch
B	P5	BF	kɛka	ankjʌŋtɨlɨl	kiljʌ	[개가 안경들을 그려요]	[Dog glasses draw]

Table 2 Session A sentences (with two-syllable target words)

Original ID	Randomised order	Focus condition	Subject IPA	Object IPA	Verb IPA	Sentence	Word for word gloss
1	2	NF-i	kɛka	palɨl	kiljʌ	[개가] 발을 그려요	[Dog] foot draw
2	6	NF-i	tɕuka	pilɨl	kiljʌ	[쥐가] 비를 그려요	[Rat] rain draw
3	11	NF-i	komi	pulil	mantʃʌ	[곰이] 불을 만져요	[Bear] fire touch
4	26	NF-i	mali	pʰalɨl	mantʃʌ	[말이] 팔을 만져요	[Horse] arm touch
5	16	NF-i	soka	p*aŋɨl	tɕʰatɕa	[소가] 빵을 찾아요	[Cow] bread look for
6	21	NF-i	kɛka	alɨl	tɕʰatɕa	[개가] 알을 찾아요	[Dog] egg look for
7	19	NF-m	tɕuka	palɨl	mantʃʌ	쥐가 [발을] 만져요	Rat [foot] touch

Continued

Original ID	Randomised order	Focus condition	Subject IPA	Object IPA	Verb IPA	Sentence	Word for word gloss
8	14	NF-m	komi	pilɨl	mantʃʌ	곰이 [비를] 만져요	Bear [rain] touch
9	29	NF-m	mali	pulɨl	tɕʰatɕa	말이 [불을] 찾아요	Horse [fire] look for
10	24	NF-m	soka	pʰalɨl	tɕʰatɕa	소가 [팔을] 찾아요	Cow [arm] look for
11	4	NF-m	kɛka	p*aŋɨl	kɨljʌ	개가 [빵을] 그려요	Dog [bread] draw
12	9	NF-m	tɕuka	alɨl	kɨljʌ	쥐가 [알을] 그려요	Rat [egg] draw
13	5	NF-f	komi	palɨl	tɕʰatɕa	곰이 발을 [찾아] 요	Bear foot [look for]
14	10	NF-f	mali	pilɨl	tɕʰatɕa	말이 비를 [찾아] 요	Horse rain [look for]
15	20	NF-f	soka	pulɨl	kɨljʌ	소가 불을 [그려] 요	Cow fire [draw]
16	15	NF-f	kɛka	pʰalɨl	kɨljʌ	개가 팔을 [그려] 요	Dog arm [draw]
17	1	NF-f	tɕuka	p*aŋɨl	mantʃʌ	쥐가 빵을 [만져] 요	Rat bread [touch]
18	25	NF-f	komi	alɨl	mantʃʌ	곰이 알을 [만져] 요	Bear egg [touch]
19	22	CF-m	mali	palɨl	kɨljʌ	말이 [발을] 그려요	Horse [foot] draw
20	12	CF-m	soka	pilɨl	kɨljʌ	소가 [비를] 그려요	Cow [rain] draw
21	7	CF-m	kɛka	pulɨl	mantʃʌ	개가 [불을] 만져요	Dog [fire] touch
22	17	CF-m	tɕuka	pʰalɨl	mantʃʌ	쥐가 [팔을] 만져요	Rat [arm] touch
23	27	CF-m	komi	p*aŋɨl	tɕʰatɕa	곰이 [빵을] 찾아요	Bear [bread] look for
24	3	CF-m	mali	alɨl	tɕʰatɕa	말이 [알을] 찾아요	Horse [egg] look for
25	30	BF	soka	palɨl	mantʃʌ	[소가 발을 만져요]	[Cow foot touch]
26	23	BF	kɛka	pilɨl	mantʃʌ	[개가 비를 만져요]	[Dog rain touch]
27	13	BF	tɕuka	pulɨl	tɕʰatɕa	[쥐가 불을 찾아요]	[Rat fire look for]
28	8	BF	komi	pʰalɨl	tɕʰatɕa	[곰이 팔을 찾아요]	[Bear arm look for]
29	18	BF	mali	p*aŋɨl	kɨljʌ	[말이 빵을 그려요]	[Horse bread draw]
30	28	BF	soka	alɨl	kɨljʌ	[소가 알을 그려요]	[Cow egg draw]

Table 3 Session B sentences (with four-syllable target words)

Original ID	Randomised order	Focus condition	Subject IPA	Object IPA	Verb IPA	Sentence	Word for word gloss
31	37	NF-i	kɛka	kapaŋtɨlɨl	kɨljʌ	[개가] 가방들을 그려요	[Dog] bags draw
32	32	NF-i	tɕuka	kituŋtɨlɨl	kɨljʌ	[쥐가] 기둥들을 그려요	[Rat] pillars draw

Continued

Original ID	Randomised order	Focus condition	Subject IPA	Object IPA	Verb IPA	Sentence	Word for word gloss
33	42	NF-i	komi	kututɨlɨl	mantʃʌ	[곰이] 구두들을 만져요	[Bear] shoes touch
34	47	NF-i	mali	kʰatɨtɨlɨl	mantʃʌ	[말이] 카드들을 만져요	[Horse] cards touch
35	57	NF-i	soka	k*amak-wilɨl	tɕʰatɕa	[소가] 까마귀를 찾아요	[Cow] crow look for
36	52	NF-i	kɛka	ankjʌŋtɨli	tɕʰatɕa	[개가] 안경들을 찾아요	[Dog] glasses look for
37	45	NF-m	tɕuka	kapaŋtɨlɨl	mantʃʌ	쥐가 [가방들을] 만져요	Rat [bags] touch
38	55	NF-m	komi	kituŋtɨlɨl	mantʃʌ	곰이 [기둥들을] 만져요	Bear [pillars] touch
39	50	NF-m	mali	kututɨlɨl	tɕʰatɕa	말이 [구두들을] 찾이요	Horse [shoes] look for
40	35	NF-m	soka	kʰatɨtɨlɨl	tɕʰatɕa	소가 [카드들을] 찾아요	Cow [cards] look for
41	60	NF-m	kɛka	k*amak-wilɨl	kɨljʌ	개가 [까마귀를] 그려요	Dog [crow] draw
42	40	NF-m	tɕuka	ankjʌŋtɨli	kɨljʌ	쥐가 [안경들을] 그려요	Rat [glasses] draw
43	31	NF-f	komi	kapaŋtɨlɨl	tɕʰatɕa	곰이 가방들을 [찾아] 요	Bear bags [look for]
44	41	NF-f	mali	kituŋtɨlɨl	tɕʰatɕa	말이 기둥들을 [찾이] 요	Horse pillars [look for]
45	46	NF-f	soka	kututɨlɨl	kɨljʌ	소가 구두들을 [그려] 요	Cow shoes [draw]
46	56	NF-f	kɛka	kʰatɨtɨlɨl	kɨljʌ	게가 카드들을 [그려] 요	Dog cards [draw]
47	51	NF-f	tɕuka	k*amak-wilɨl	mantʃʌ	쥐가 까마귀를 [만져] 요	Rat crow [touch]
48	36	NF-f	komi	ankjʌŋtili	mantʃʌ	곰이 안경들을 [만져] 요	Bear glasses [touch]
49	43	CF-m	mali	kapaŋtɨlɨl	kɨljʌ	말이 [가방들을] 그려요	Horse [bags] draw
50	53	CF-m	soka	kituŋtɨlɨl	kɨljʌ	소가 [기둥들을] 그려요	Cow [pillars] draw

Continued

Original ID	Randomised order	Focus condition	Subject IPA	Object IPA	Verb IPA	Sentence	Word for word gloss
51	33	CF-m	kɛka	kututɨlɨl	mantʃʌ	개가 [구두들을] 만져요	Dog [shoes] touch
52	58	CF-m	tɕuka	kʰatɨtɨlɨl	mantʃʌ	쥐가 [카드들을] 만져요	Rat [cards] touch
53	48	CF-m	komi	k*amak-wilɨl	tɕʰatɕa	곰이 [까마귀를] 찾아요	Bear [crow] look for
54	38	CF-m	mali	ankjʌŋtɨlɨ	tɕʰatɕa	말이 [안경들을] 찾아요	Horse [glasses] look for
55	59	BF	soka	kapaŋtɨlɨl	mantʃʌ	[소가 가방들을 만져요]	[Cow bags touch]
56	39	BF	kɛka	kituŋtɨlɨl	mantʃʌ	[개가 기둥들을 만져요]	[Dog pillars touch]
57	54	BF	tɕuka	kututɨlɨl	tɕʰatɕa	[쥐가 구두들을 찾아요]	[Rat shoes look for]
58	44	BF	komi	kʰatɨtɨlɨl	tɕʰatɕa	[곰이 카드들을 찾아요]	[Bear cards look for]
59	34	BF	mali	k*amak-wilɨl	kiljʌ	[말이 까마귀를 그려요]	[Horse crow draw]
60	49	BF	soka	ankjʌŋtɨlɨ	kiljʌ	[소가 안경들을 그려요]	[Cow glasses draw]

SAMENVATTING

In gesproken communicatie maken sprekers nieuwe informatie doorgaans prominenter dan informatie die al bij de toehoorder bekend is. De nieuwe informatie staat bekend als de "focus" van de zin. Het accuraat markeren van focus door sprekers kan toehoorders ondersteunen bij een efficiënte verwerking van de gecommuniceerde informatie en is dus nuttig bij het begrijpen van gesproken taal. Focusmarkering is daarmee een belangrijke vaardigheid die kinderen moeten verwerven in de context van taalontwikkeling. Deze dissertatie is een cross-linguïstisch onderzoek naar hoe Mandarijnsprekende en Seoul-Koreaanssprekende kinderen de capaciteit ontwikkelen voor focusmarkering in hun spraakproductie.

We hebben gekozen voor Mandarijn en Koreaans in dit onderzoek omdat deze twee talen typologisch verschillen in hun prosodische systemen en prosodische focusmarkering. Wat betreft de prosodische systemen verschillen Mandarijn en Koreaans in de lexicale contrastiviteit van toonhoogte. Het Mandarijn gebruikt toonhoogte om woorden van elkaar te onderscheiden, en het lexicale gebruik van toonhoogte gaat samen met het gebruik van toonhoogte op zinsniveau. Het Koreaans maakt daarentegen geen lexicaal onderscheid in toonhoogte. Wat betreft prosodische focusmarkering is er een verschil in primaire prosodische kenmerken tussen de twee talen. Het Mandarijn gebruikt enkel fonetische kenmerken om focus te markeren. Preciezer gezegd: eigenschappen van de prosodie zoals duur, toonhoogte en intensiteit worden enkel gradueel verhoogd of verlaagd, zonder dat dit leidt tot een verandering van de fonologische categorie. Anderzijds gebruikt het Koreaans zowel fonologische middelen (i.e. prosodische frasering) als fonetische middelen (i.e. graduele variatie in duur, toonhoogte en intensiteit binnen één fonologische categorie) om focus te markeren, waarbij de fonologische middelen het meest gebruikt worden. Gegeven de genoemde verschillen tussen het Mandarijn en Koreaans qua prosodische systemen en prosodische focusmarkering, was onze overkoepelende onderzoeksvraag hoe die verschillen invloed hebben op de ontwikkeling tot een met volwassenen overeenkomstige manier van focusmarkering bij Mandarijnsprekende en Koreaanssprekende kinderen. Om op deze vraag in te gaan hebben we parallele studies verricht naar de verwerving van prosodische focusmarkering bij Mandarijn en Koreaanssprekende kinderen.

In hoofdstuk 1 beschrijven we de onderzoeksmotivatie, stellen we onderzoeksvragen (sectie 2), geven we een overzicht van achtergrondliteratuur (secties 3, 4 en 5), en opperen we hypotheses en voorspellingen (sectie 6).

De studies naar prosodische focusaanduiding bij Mandarijn- en Koreaanssprekende kinderen en controlegroepen van volwassenen worden gerapporteerd in hoofdstuk 2 tot en met hoofdstuk 6 in de vorm van een reeks op zichzelf staande artikelen.

Hoofdstuk 2 betreft het gebruik van prosodie voor focusmarkering door Mandarijnsprekende volwassenen in semi-spontane spraak. Het doel van dit hoofdstuk is om de doelvorm van prosodische focusaanduiding weer te geven die Mandarijnsprekende kinderen worden geacht te verwerven. We hebben een plaatjes-matching-taak gebruikt om semi-spontane spraakproducties van korte zinnen in verschillende focusomstandigheden op te wekken bij de participanten (Dezelfde methode van spraakelicitatie is ook in de andere hoofdstukken gebruikt). We vonden in deze studie dat nauwe focus gerealiseerd wordt met een langere duur en een grotere spreidingsbreedte van de toonhoogte dan non-focus, zoals dat ook is bevonden voor voorgelezen spraak in het Mandarijn. Nauwe focus wordt niet onderscheiden van contrastieve focus, wat afwijkt van de bevindingen voor voorgelezen spraak. In het Mandarijn zijn nauwe focus en non-focus dus duidelijk prosodisch verschillend van elkaar, en zijn de onderlinge verschillen tussen de verscheidene focustypes groter bij voorgelezen spraak dan bij semi-spontane spraak.

Hoofdstuk 3 onderzoekt hoe kinderen prosodische focusmarkering verwerven in het Mandarijn. Met behulp van het plaatjes-matching-spel wekten we de semi-spontane productie op van zinnen met diverse focusomstandigheden bij kinderen in de leeftijd van vier tot elf. We vonden dat Mandarijnsprekende kinderen in de leeftijd van vier tot vijf sommige toonhoogte-gerelateerde kenmerken gebruiken voor sommige tonen, en duur voor alle tonen, op een aan volwassenen gelijkende manier. Hun gebruik van toonhoogte-gerelateerde kenmerken is op elfjarige leeftijd nog niet hetzelfde als bij volwassenen. Daarnaast zijn ze gelijkend aan volwassen in het gebruik van duur om nauwe en wijde focus van elkaar te onderscheiden op vier- tot vijfjarige leeftijd, maar pas gelijkend aan volwassenen in het niet gebruiken van het toonhoogte-gerelateerde kenmerk pitch-max voor dit doel op zeven- tot achtjarige leeftijd. De latere verwerving van toonhoogte-gerelateerde kenmerken kan te maken hebben met het gebruik van toonhoogte voor lexicale doeleinden, en de verschillen in het gebruik van toonhoogte voor de verschillende tonen kan worden verklaard door verschillen in hoe makkelijk het is om te variëren in toonhoogte-gerelateerde parameters zonder de tonale identiteit te veranderen.

Hoofdstuk 4 bespreekt het gebruik van het fonologische focusmarkeringskenmerk van frasering door Koreaanssprekende volwassenen, en daarnaast hun gebruik van duur- en toonhoogte-gerelateerde fonetische kenmerken voor focusmarkering. Het streven van dit hoofdstuk is om de doelvorm van prosodische focusmarkering weer te geven die Koreaanssprekende kinderen worden geacht te verwerven. We hebben de semi-spontane spraakproductie opgewekt van zinnen in het Koreaans onder diverse focusomstandigheden. Wat betreft fonologische focusmarkering gebruiken volwassen sprekers van het Koreaans prosodische frasering om nauwe focus te onderscheiden van non-focus (i.e. pre-focus en post-focus) en van twee andere typen focus (namelijk wijde focus en contrastieve focus). Wat betreft fonetische focusmarkering gebruikten de sprekers bij Accentual Phrase-initiële woorden voor nauwe focus ten opzichte van non-focus een langere woordduur, langere duur van de woord-initiële syllabe en een hogere maximale toonhoogte. Ze maakten in hun gebruik van fonetische kenmerken geen onderscheid tussen nauwe focus tegenover wijde focus of contrastieve focus.

Hoofdstuk 5 onderzoekt hoe kinderen het gebruik van prosodische frasering voor focusmarkering verwerven in het Seoul Koreaans. We hebben semi-spontane spraakproductie onder diverse focusomstandigheden opgewekt bij kinderen in de leeftijd van vier tot elf. We vonden in deze studie dat Seoul Koreaanssprekende kinderen prosodische frasering gebruiken om nauwe focus te onderscheiden van non-focus (i.e. pre-focus en post-focus) en van twee andere typen focus (namelijk wijde focus en contrastieve focus) vanaf vier- of vijfjarige leeftijd, wat aangeeft dat dit fonologische focusmarkeringskenmerk al op vroege leeftijd wordt gebruikt in het Seoul Koreaans, vergelijkbaar met de vroege verwerving van taalspecifieke fonologische focusmarkeringscues in veel andere talen. We vonden verder dat het gebruik van prosodische frasering bij Seoul Koreaanssprekende kinderen minder frequent is dan bij Seoul Koreaanssprekende volwassenen, vooral op jonge leeftijd. Het minder frequente gebruik van dit kenmerk door kinderen kan samenhangen met hun lagere spreeksnelheid, vergeleken met volwassenen.

Hoofdstuk 6 bekijkt hoe Seoul Koreaanssprekende kinderen het gebruik van duur- en toonhoogte-gerelateerde fonetische kenmerken voor focusmarkering verwerven wanneer prosodische frasering geen rol speelt bij de focusmarkering. We hebben een subset van de zinnen gebruikt die waren opgewekt bij Koreaanssprekende kinderen en volwassenen in hoofdstuk 4 en hoofdstuk 5. We hebben de doelwoorden geanalyseerd die werden gerealiseerd als Accentual Phrase-initiële woorden, om te zien of kinderen op dezelfde manier als volwassenen fonetische kenmerken kunnen variëren om verschillende focustypen van elkaar te onderscheiden. We vonden dat Koreaanssprekende kinderen duur beginnen te gebruiken om nauwe focus te markeren vanaf zevenjarige leeftijd, en dat ze dit op een aan volwassenen gelijkende manier doen op tien- of elfjarige leeftijd. Anderzijds beginnen ze pas op tien- tot elfjarige leeftijd in beperkte mate toonhoogte te gebruiken bij het markeren van nauwe focus. Net als volwassenen variëren ze duur en toonhoogte niet om nauwe focus te onderscheiden van wijde focus of contrastieve focus. Deze resultaten laten zien dat Seoul Koreaanssprekende kinderen fonetische focusmarkeringen binnen een fonologische categorie later verwerven dan fonologische focusmarkering, net als Nederlandssprekende kinderen. Van de fonetische focusmarkeringskenmerken verwerven Koreaanssprekende kinderen het gebruik van duur sneller dan het gebruik van toonhoogte, net als Mandarijnsprekende kinderen, maar anders dan Nederlandssprekende kinderen. Dit resultaat suggereert dat de verwerving van het gebruik van toonhoogte voor focusmarkeringsdoeleinden niet alleen afhangt van de lexicale contrastiviteit van toonhoogte.

Ten slotte geven we in hoofdstuk 7 een overzicht van de hoofdbevindingen, en grijpen we terug op de hypotheses, voorspellingen en onderzoeksvragen uit hoofdstuk 1 door te bespreken hoe cross-linguïstische verschillen in prosodische systemen en prosodische focusmarkeringen invloed hebben op de verwerving van focusmarkering in het Mandarijn en Koreaans, en suggereren we richtingen voor vervolgonderzoek.

ACKNOWLEDGEMENTS

I started my PhD study in Utrecht in the spring of 2012. Ever since then (and even before that) I have received so much kindness and help from many people, which gave me courage to go this far. As this period of life is coming to an end, I would like to say thank you to these people, though the simple words I typed cannot completely express my gratitude to them.

First of all, I would like to thank my supervisors, Dr. Aoju Chen, Prof. René Kager, and Prof. Wim Zonneveld, for their full support and guidance throughout this project. Aoju has taught me so many things in the past five and half years, from the knowledge of language acquisition to how to match colours for a poster. The devotion to work and attention to detail I saw in her has impressed me and will have a long-lasting influence on me. René has generously made time to give me comments at his busiest time. Without his difficult but important questions, my dissertation would not take shape. I was touched by his story of taking the adventurous field trip to the rain forest in Peru, and encouraged by his enthusiasm to scientific research. Wim has given me constructive and practical advice using his special red-and-blue commenting system, which I liked a lot. I was encouraged when he said that I was close to finishing my dissertation, before which I felt as if I was walking along an endless road.

I would like to thank Prof. Taehong Cho and Dr. Sahyang Kim for their expert advice and crucial input on the design of the Korean experiment and the analysis of the Korean data. They were wonderfully supportive when I collected data at the Hanyang Phonetics and Psycholinguistics Lab in Seoul. The Korean barbecue dinners they brought me to were the best I've ever had.

I would also like to thank my reading committee for their careful reading and insightful comments: Prof. Taehong Cho, Prof. Petra Hendriks, Prof. Hugo Quené, Dr. Judith Rispens, and Prof. Yi Xu.

I am grateful to Dr. Sam Hellmuth and Dr. Traci Walker, who introduced me to phonology and acquisition when I did my MA study at the University of York. Without their help and encouragement, I would never have started my PhD study.

My special thanks go to a group of amazing people, who worked in the "get the focus right" programme: Anna Sara Romøren, Frank Bijlsma, Joe Rodd, Martine Veenendaal, Mengru Han, Saskia Verstegen, Xiaoli Dong, Zenghui Liu, and the sadly missed Paula

Cox. Thank you for being so helpful, efficient and warm. Anna Sara and Zenghui, thank you for always being there when I needed help, and thank you for all the jokes, but in two different styles.

I would like to thank the people who helped me with the experiments for this dissertation: Daejin Kim and Miroo Lee at Hanyang University, Seoul; Min Zhu, Jun Bian, and Yian Liang at Beijing 21st Century Kindergarten; Shushuang Yu at Beijing 21st Century International School; Mei Ou laoshi, Mengting Huang, Xingzhi Yao, and Yun Li at Beijing Forestry University. My sincere gratitude goes to the participants of the experiments and the parents of the child participants.

I thank Mattis van den Bergh, Prof. Huub van den Bergh and Kirsten Schutter for teaching me statistics. I bothered Huub many times with my very amateurish questions, and he always helped me with great patience. I also thank Prof. Sun-Ah Jun for teaching me prosodic typology and discussing my study in the master class of the LOT summer school, and providing practical suggestions at conferences.

I thank Jeroen Breteler for translating the summary of my dissertation to Dutch, and Rachel Gargiulo and Aelish Hart for proofreading my manuscript.

I thank our research coordinator, Maaike Schoorlemmer, who was one of the first persons I knew in Utrecht. She showed me around in Trans, Janskerkhof, and Drift in my first week here, and she has given me practical advice on various things ever since then. My heartfelt thanks also go to the secretary of LOT, Martine Paulissen and the secretaries of UiL OTS, Mariëtte Bonenkamp, Martien Camphuis, and Yvonne van Adrichem. They made the paperwork easy for me.

I thank my colleagues and friends at UiL OTS: Dominique Blok, Erin Pretorius, Franca Wesseling, Maartje Schulpen, Martijn van der Klis, Mengru Han, and Misha Knyazev — they were my officemates. Maartje, thank you for delivering the letters from Sinterklaas, and for the walks to the woods in Zuilen. Franca, thank you for being around and introducing your beautiful children to me. Mengru, thank you for all the lunches and chats, and for sharing the growing up stories of Dabao Ye. I thank the people who nested in the neighbouring offices on the top floor of Trans 8, for your steady supply of smiles and laughter: Alexia Guerra Rivera, Andrea Santana Covarrubias, Anja Goldschmidt, Anna Volkova, Björn't Hart, Heidi Klockmann, Jingwei Zhang, Jolien Scholten, Jorik van Engeland, Kiki Kushartanti, Luying Hou, Marjolein van Egmond, Marta Castella, Myrthe Bergstra, Sandrien van Ommen, Shuangshuang Hu, and Zenghui Liu. And, of course, I thank many others who worked and are working in the institute: Ana Auilar Guevara, Anna Sara Romøren, Anne-France Pinget, Anne van Leeuwen, Ao Chen, Assaf Toledo,

Bei Peng, Brigitta Keij, Chou Mo, Eva Poortman, Fang Li, Ileana Grama, Jeroen Breteler, Jun Zhang, Liquan Liu, Liv Persson, Marko Hladnik, Marko Simonovic, Mike Olson, Shanshan Fan, Stavroula Alexandropoulou, Tom Lentz, Xin Li, Yipu Wei, Yuan Xie, Yunning Sun, and Yunmin Zou. I would also like to thank Ting Zou and Qian Li from Leiden University. We were together at conferences and summer schools. Dear people, thank you for your company.

I also thank the people who lived and are living in Plesmanlaan: Xiaoli Dong, Simon Le Bruyn, Bert Le Bruyn, Mengru Han, Yuning Sun, Shuangshuang Hu, Qiulan Zhang. You are like my family in the Netherlands.

Last, I would like to express my deepest gratitude to my family in China for their unconditional love and support.

感谢大家！

CURRICULUM VITAE

Anqi Yang was born in 1986 in Hebei, China. She studied English language and literature as an undergraduate at Zhejiang Agriculture and Forestry University from 2005 to 2009. She did her MA study in Linguistics from 2010 to 2011 at the University of York, where her interests in phonology and language acquisition started to grow. After completing her MA study, she was offered a PhD position at the Utrecht Institute of Linguistics OTS, Utrecht University. This dissertation is the result of work that Anqi carried out between 2012 and 2017 as a PhD candidate at Utrecht University.